# WALES

Alice Thomas Ellis was born in Liverpool and educated at Bangor Grammar School and Liverpool School of Art. She is the author of eight widely praised novels, *The Sin Eater, The Birds of the Air, The 27th Kingdom, The Other Side of the Fire, Unexplained Laughter, The Skeleton in the Cupboard, The Clothes in the Wardrobe* and *The Fly in the Ointment,* and two studies of juvenile delinquency, *Secrets of Strangers* and *The Loss of the Good Authority,* written with a psychiatrist, Tom Pitt-Aikens. She lives in London and Wales with her husband and five children.

# WALES

*An Anthology*

SELECTED BY
ALICE THOMAS ELLIS

WITH ILLUSTRATIONS BY
KYFFIN WILLIAMS

Fontana
*An Imprint of* HarperCollins*Publishers*

First published in Great Britain by
William Collins Sons & Co. Ltd 1989

First issued by Fontana Paperbacks in 1991

Printed in Great Britain by
T.J. Press (Padstow) Ltd, Padstow, Cornwall

*To Gladys Mary Coles*

I should like to thank Eiluned Rees of the
National Library of Wales for her advice, Gladys
Mary Coles for doing so much work, Kyffin
Williams for the illustrations, Janet Boud for her
patience and Eifion, Mair and Elinor for their
encouragement.

# CONTENTS

*The Land of My Fathers*

O Land of my fathers, so dear unto me!
Fam'd land of the minstrel, fair home of the free!
Thy warriors who wielded, undaunted, thy sword,
For Freedom their life-blood have poured.

Thy rocks and thy crags o'er thy valleys keep guard,
Thy mountains still shelter the haunts of the bard;
Thy rills and thy brooks sing their way to the sea
In music so moving to me.

Though foemen have trampled in triumph thy vales,
Yet failed they to silence the old tongue of Wales.
Thy harp-strings, unbroken by traitor's fell hand,
Still sing to me songs of my land.

> *Chorus:*
> *Home, home, true am I to home,*
> *While seas secure the land so pure,*
> *Oh may the old language endure.*

# INTRODUCTION

I have learned one great lesson in the course of working on this anthology and that is never, *never* to attempt such an exercise again. Already people have said to me, 'But you haven't put in John Jones of Llanfyllin,' or 'You've left out Dafydd Davies of Merthyr Tydfil.' Of course I have. At the time of writing, I've just realized I've left out Merlin and Arthur. Does one include the tale of the Red and White Dragon because it's well known, or leave it out because it's well known?

I had always assumed that I had a fairly good – if only a schoolchild's – grasp of the history of Wales, but now I find I was mistaken. I no longer believe that anybody has a good grasp of the history of Wales. It is too rich, too vivid and too confusing. I have just read three versions of the death of Llywelyn, some learned (and opposing) views on the identity of Myrddyr Wyllt, a proposition that our local saint was not (as I had supposed) one of the myriad Irish saints, but a descendant of Macsen Wledig, and a suggestion that Helig-ap-Glannawg escaped with his people from the inundation of Morfa Rhianedd. This is a story that I was told in school, looking out over the very scene of this catastrophe, and I have believed from my infancy that Helig went down with his palace, cursed for his own and the sins of his ancestors, while only the harpist and the innocent peasants escaped up the hill to Trywyn-yr-Wylfa, where you could sit looking out over the low spring tides at the ruined palace foundations. I cannot tell a Silure from a Brython or a Goidel, or a Beaker person from any of them, and am finally disabused of the idea that I ever had any sense of chronology. I still have a mental image of naked, smoke-shrouded druids leaping around on the shores of Ynys Môn, alarming the armour-clad Romans, but I expect I'm wrong about that too. I suspect that Tacitus was wrong, since I no longer trust historians. They are only human, after all: their views biased and fragmented, their vision limited according to their preconceptions. Nor do I know quite why I was so concerned to attempt to capture some of this history. I think it may be due to a recent conversation I had with an American I met on a train. Not only was he unaware of the history of Wales – he did not know of its separate existence, and it was he who told me that the word on the street in the United States of America was that Oxford University had been closed down. If misconceptions such as this can be held coeval with the non-event, how will the facts be represented in the future when they will have become 'history'? This, I suppose is why the world has so many 'legends', a less didactic and sweeter word for the happenings of the past, offering legitimate scope for either scepticism or credulity according to the temperament of the listener. Of the million legends of Wales, each has a different version, and in the end only their essence matters. For a sense of place it is necessary to listen to the poets – the people, both native and those just passing through.

Here came my next problem. I have gained the impression over the last year that every Welshman who ever lived has said something worthy of restating, something witty or beautiful or profound, and that a good proportion of the rest of the world has recently visited the country, making notes as it went.

Almost more than any other country, Wales is difficult to understand and describe; its language known, on the whole, only to its own people. After the early waves of invasion it was largely unvisited by tourists until the eighteenth century when Defoe, Swift, Johnson et al. came to criticize the hostelries and mountains – particularly Penmaenmawr, the pass round which seems to have equally terrified and annoyed them. 'Horrid', 'hideous', and 'awful' were adjectives commonly used of mountains before the Romantic movement saw them in a different light, and the coach passengers grumbled all the way to Holyhead. Borrow prided himself on his knowledge of the country but he was not generally much liked by the inhabitants and was taken in by the legend of the hound, Gelert, which had been invented by the owner of the local pub to encourage customers. Later travellers saw more clearly the fascination and the beauty of the land, and yet in all their writings is a sense of surprise, of faint wonder that a place like Wales could exist – so close to England and so different. No longer outraged or fearful

of the historical threat, they remain diverted and slightly puzzled – uncomprehending of the native complexities, the depth
and richness of the culture. A good example of the more exas-
perating type of observer is one Mavor who toured the country
in 1806 and wrote: 'The Welsh do not like to have their
peculiarities recorded, or to have reflections passed on their
mode of acting and thinking; yet, surely, they ought to take in
good part what is intended for their welfare, and learn to mend
what may not have struck them as an impropriety or a disadvantage, till it was pointed out to them.' However, I think we
can discount the opinions of Mavor since he greatly admired a
poet – gloriously named Pratt – who penned the following: 'O
give the heirs of poverty their cots, Attach them fondly to their
native spots.' This was quoted apropos the poor of Merioneth
about whose welfare Mavor had chosen to worry himself.

I have heard visitors express surprise that the farmer's
brother, wandering in the orchard, lost in thought, is – say – a
Regius Professor of Greek, and yet when I was a child it had
long been accepted that the Welsh standard of education was
higher than the English and I got the impression from our
teachers that, while much of the world was ignorant of Wales,
their pupils were not to be allowed to be ignorant of the rest of
the world. There was, at that time in some quarters, a feeling
that Welsh was a dying language and should be allowed to
expire, thus freeing the people to take their place in the modern
world. That idea is now dead and Welsh is taught in all Welsh
schools, though the language is still under threat.

It has been suggested that, in this anthology, I have not made
enough of Wales's contributions to the world; of its academics,
its politicians, its lawyers, bridge builders, artists, singers,
actors, sportsmen, its regiments, and indeed I haven't. It would
take several more volumes than the several I have already gone
mad trying to compress into one. I may as well confess now
what is doubtless obvious – that my own view of Wales is
limited and somewhat partisan. Although my mother's family
comes from South Wales, until a few years ago I had never been
further south than Caernarvon, and when I was a child and a
little South Walian appeared in the National School he might
have dropped off the moon. This sense of locality is, I think, an
important element in the Welsh character. While many leave,
many stay in the same spot all their lives without feeling the

need of change; for there is something here I cannot describe – something like a vertical sense of tradition, of nourishment and sufficiency: something which obviates the need for outside diversion, travel or entertainment, for extended means of expression. I should not care to be pressed too closely to explain what I mean by this, but it is a very strong feeling. Perhaps the phrase I am looking for is genius of place. I left when I was seventeen but came back as soon as I was able, and while I have been 'abroad' three or four times I never quite saw the point. What there is to know about life – and death – is somehow more easily learned here. For one thing Wales abounds in sacred places, both pagan and Christian: there are holy wells and shrines, the ways the pilgrims walked, and the bones of saints lie under the ground. Wales was once dedicated to Our Lady and later it was the Bible that helped keep alive the language, and there is something immeasurably ancient yet vital in the landscape – something which makes you think of God.

On another level – and there are so many levels in the matter of Wales – there are the ghosts and fairies and fabulous beasts, the corpse candles which foretell a death and which – so one legend has it – were begged of the Lord by Saint David so that his people might take warning and repent in time. There are the *Cwn Annwn*, the hounds of hell who range the middle air; the monsters who lived in lakes, emerging to eat people; the dragons, the witches, the wise men; the maidens who also lived in the lakes and sometimes married the sons of men only to return in a huff to the water when their husbands inadvertently offended them. There's the thing that breathes outside our house on the long summer evenings and strikes a non-existent anvil behind the barns, and the people who talk in our parlour when we have all gone to bed.

There are parts of the world where the veil between this mode of existence and another is fragile and transparent. Your patterns of belief can imperceptibly change, and while, in London, you might hesitate before discussing the advisability of putting out a nightly bowl of milk for the *Tylwyth Teg*, down here the idea doesn't seem half so odd. It was still a custom in living memory and I understand its motivation very well. Material 'progress' is culturally impoverishing and custom should not lightly be discarded as though faith and old awarenesses were biodegradable. I make no apology for this

excursion into Celtic twilight. I like it in there. Many of my
friends say I have a fossilized view of the country and it must go
forward with other countries into the future, but this too often
means that all countries become indistinguishable from one
another, with chain-stores, hypermarkets and restaurants;
homogenized and soulless. There must be other ways of keeping a nation alive, but I do not know what they might be. Eco-
nomics is another subject I failed to grasp. I have never come to
terms with the modern world and I never will, since I cannot
see the necessity for violent and ruinous change – the afforestation, for instance, that has destroyed forever a whole way of
life, swallowing up the hill farms, altering the ecology and
obscuring the hills. (Wynford Vaughan Thomas somewhere
quotes a farmer who, acknowledging the harshness of life on
the outlying farms, said that if the cheap motor car and TV had
come twenty years earlier, which would have involved only
minor change, the young people would not have left and the
hills would have stayed under sheep.) Then there's the astonishing coastal motorway which would have baffled the people
of Helig-ap-Glannawg, as, fleeing from the flood to the Point of
the Doleful Hill they got mown down by the traffic, and the
very dodgy nuclear plant at Trawsfynydd. I could go on complaining, but opinions vary on the question of change and
mine is not the only view.

The literature of Wales speaks for itself. A lifetime could be
spent reading nothing else, and still its treasures and its
mysteries would not be fathomed – let alone the wit, the common sense and the wry, curious insights that are unlike those
of any other nation. From the earliest bards to the poets of
today, the oral tradition has stood them in good stead and you
can almost hear the words uttering themselves from the page.
The quality of inspiration, that in the preacher is called *hwyl*,
can sometimes be transferred to the written word, and Welsh
poetry more than any other repays reading aloud – even in
translation.

For the rest I have included snippets of this and snippets of
that – anything that I found of irresistible interest to myself.
What else could I do? Some will find the section on food irrele-
vant, but I am almost as interested in what people eat as in
what they say, and having read with pity years ago the list of
rations for the inhabitants of Beaumaris gaol, I was later

xvi

shaken to realize that that was more or less what they'd have had if they'd stuck by the laws and stayed at home. Diet throughout Britain has happily improved since the turn of the century, but the recherché dishes being produced in some restaurants and described as 'Welsh' would not have been recognized in most farmhouse kitchens. I wanted to put in our own recipe for rowan jelly but I forgot and now it's too late.* I also wanted to put in all the *Books of Wales*, the whole of Giraldus Cambrensis (Gerald of Wales), the whole of *The Mabinogion*, of Arthur Bradley, Gwyn Thomas and R. S. Thomas, and many, many others – poets, journalists, travellers, even the warring historians. I wanted above all to evoke the Wales that I know – perhaps a self-indulgent and ultimately frustrating aim for some of it has gone and some of it changed, but I have recognized it in what I have been reading – of home life and *Eisteddfodau*, and sheep trials and school, rain, chapel, fable, *hiraeth*, mountainside and sea.

I only wish I could explain more clearly what I meant – that the country has a unique and magical quality, and in some aspects is not to be easily distinguished from heaven.

* Rowan jelly got in after all.                                        A.T.E.

# THE ANTHOLOGY

# I

# LANGUAGE, CHARACTER, CLIMATE

Their Lord they shall praise,
Their language they shall keep,
Their land they shall lose
Except wild Wales.

TALIESIN
*Destiny of the Britons*, 6th century

*The Welsh Alphabet*

Consonants: b, c, ch, d, dd, f, ff, g, ng, h, l, ll, m, n, p, ph, r, rh, s, t, th.
Vowels: a, e, i, o, u, w, y.
Welsh has two genders only: masculine and feminine.

Bill poster in a Clwyd hotel

*Pronunciation*

The vowel *u* . . . in Welsh is sounded as the English *ĭ*, the *y* is sometimes sounded as a *u* and sometimes as an *ĭ*. Griffith, for example, is both Gruffydd and Gryffydd in the same page of comparatively recent writers. Owen, again, is Owain, Oweyn, and has other variations. Modern Welsh names have, of course, settled down to a uniform method of spelling, but in the writing of times not recent there is nothing of the kind. Of all known tongues, Welsh is one of the hardest to acquire. To any resident in North Wales, who has presumably a fair lease of life before him, the effort would be well worth making. But assuredly not for anyone otherwise circumstanced. That, however, is no reason at all why English people who regularly frequent the Principality should not master a few leading canons of pronunciation. It would save them infinite trouble in finding their way about, to say the least of it, and prevent them from making themselves at times entirely ridiculous. It would enable them, not only to imitate the ordinary sounds with sufficient accuracy for general purposes, but to recognize those occasional words with which no Saxon tongue can hope to grapple, and thus recognizing, to go warily and without pretension. It would not, I am sure, take anyone more than a quarter of an hour to permanently grasp the fact that a double *d* was the English *th* as sounded in the word *breathe*, that an *f* was invariably a *v*, and an *ff* an *f*, and that the letter *c* was always hard. The much-vexed *ll* is too obvious to be ignored. There are many receipts for it, but if the alien will place his tongue against the back of his front teeth and blow slightly, it is the most that any Welshman could expect of him. The vowels and diphthongs would be a greater tax upon the memory, but the effort is perhaps worth making. The *y* is troublesome because, as I have already remarked, it is sometimes pronounced as a *u* and sometimes as an *i*, according to whether it occupies the first or last place in a word. Mynydd, for instance, a mountain, phonetically spelt would be munnith. The *w*, which looks to the uninitiated so hopeless in print, is simply *oo*. This profound dissertation on the Welsh language is getting too prolonged, but having got so far I should like to rub in the useful fact that the Welsh *aw* is pronounced *ow* as in 'now', and also that the emphasis is nearly always on the penultimate, which gives, I think, a special resonancy to the language. An example of both these rules may aptly be found in the name, Trawsfynydd, which becomes to the ear Trowsvúnnith. The Welsh *th* is sounded as in the word *death* in contradistinction to the *dd*, which, I have said, is as in the word *breathe*.

ARTHUR BRADLEY
*Highways and Byways in North Wales* (1898)

If there are any who for the sake of preserving uniformity would prefer to compel our people to learn the English language rather than have the Scriptures translated into our tongue, I would wish them to take care lest their zeal for unity stand in the way of truth . . . lest by promoting concord they retard religion . . . How foolish it is to suppose that the prohibition of God's word in his mother's tongue spurs any man to learn a foreign language . . . Unless religion is taught in the language of the people there will be neither knowledge nor understanding of it.

BISHOP WILLIAM MORGAN (1545–1604)
in *William Morgan and His Bible* (1988)
Isaac Thomas

(Bishop Morgan translated the Bible into Welsh at Llanrhaeadr-ym-Mochnant, completing it in 1588.)

The translation of the Bible into the Welsh or British tongue which by Act of Parliament should long since have been done is now performed by one Dr Morgan and set forth in print.

*Acts of the Privy Council*, 22 September 1588

*Llanrhaeadr-ym-Mochnant*

This is where he sought God.
And found him? The centuries
Have been content to follow
Down passages of serene prose.

There is no portrait of him
But in the gallery of
The imagination: a brow
With the hair's feathers
Spilled on it; a cheek
Too hollow; rows of teeth
Broken on the unmanageable bone
Of language; in this small room
By the river expiating the sin
Of his namesake.

**4**

The smooth words
Over which his mind flowed
Have become an heirloom. Beauty
Is how you say it, and the truth,
Like this mountain-born torrent,
Is content to hurry
Not too furiously by.

R. S. THOMAS

*Strangers in their own land*

'Wales' and the 'Welsh' are disparaging terms for a country, a people and its language. The words derive from an ancient Germanic word *wealas* 'foreigner', applied by the incoming Anglo-Saxons to the resident British who were henceforth strangers in their own land. The Welsh are not alone as receivers of such cavalier treatment, for speakers of Germanic languages have often used kindred words to describe other people on their own ground. The Norsemen called the French *Valskr* and the Dutch describe their near-neighbours, the French-speaking Walloons of Belgium, as *Waalsch*. The Slavs have a related word, *Vlach*, to describe Romanians, who speak a Latin language.

The Welsh call themselves *Cymry* 'fellow-countrymen', their country *Cymru* and their language *Cymraeg*, words related to the Old British *combrogos* 'compatriot', recalled in Cambria and in Cumbria, one of the last bastions of Celtic in England. Welsh, which with Gaelic is defined as 'insular' Celtic to distinguish it from the continental variety, is nevertheless almost identical to the language of Gaul; its differences from the Celtic of Ireland are signs of a separation more ancient than their division in the British Isles. Where historically Gaelic used the *qu* or *k* sound, the Welsh and the Gauls used *p*, a difference displayed in the words for 'son' (Gaelic *mac*, Welsh *map*, now *mab*) and 'head' (Gaelic *ceann*, Welsh *pen*) among others.

The Welsh vocabulary as a whole is replete with words which show its antique lineage and its distant cousins.

VICTOR STEVENSON (Editor)<br>*Words* (1983)

The great change which transformed British and converted it into Welsh and its sister dialects was the loss of the endings of stems and words by which, for example, the four syllables of the British *Maglo-cunos* were reduced to the two of the Welsh *Maelgwn*.

J. MORRIS-JONES (1864–1929), *A Welsh Grammar* (1913)

It was a change as complete and as definite as the growth of French or Italian from Latin, but owing to the almost complete lack of datable evidence in contemporary manuscripts, charters, etc., no one knows when it took place. Some scholars believe that it must have been accomplished by the fifth century, others hold that the seventh is early enough.

SIR IFOR WILLIAMS (1881–1965)
*The Beginnings of Welsh Poetry* (1972)

*On translating Welsh Poetry (cywydd)*

Bedwyr, this frantic burden
Severs wholly me from men.
It's what makes me not notice
The too much time that I miss.
So hard – the hazard is huge
I deal against a deluge
While a dotty world yet wags
Trumps from its thousand handbags! –
Tomorrow and tomorrow,
Each day's a leech, lays me low:
So hard, to string in English
The tied Welsh that I would wish
And scan without cynghanedd,
Heart's clamour, labour of lathe,
Hammer-stroke – how I'm stricken! –
To give, I'm at it again,
A mirror of its merit
To the cywydd wild with wit.

TONY CONRAN

Wenglish folk are seldom ill; they are sometimes 'bard' and are truly far from well when 'bard in bed' and 'under the doctor'.

The word 'piece' when used to mean a round of bread and butter provides another example of the way in which words are put to use, and 'piece' is a word which evokes a treasured memory of childhood – that of sitting around the table at meal times. The prepared 'mound' of bread and butter, often cut in 'cwlffs' or 'cwlffyns' had already disappeared with a rapidity which testifies to the keen appetites of 'growing boys and girls' – and still more was needed! In turn, we children would say, 'Piece please, Mam' and another helping of basic food was procured. What a fundamental part of childhood bread and butter was! There were very few items of food with which it was *not* essential to eat bread and butter. It was a childhood ambition of mine – shared with many others, surely – to be able to eat tinned fruit (tin frute) without having to include its obligatory accompaniment!!

It is the way in which words like 'moithered', 'bard', 'peaky', 'rough', etc., etc. are pronounced and strung together which, together with the emotional content in word-delivery, impart a unique flavour to Wenglish. This is due, in part at least, to the fact that we are such a splendid ethnic mix 'round 'ere, and it matters not whether your grandparents or great-grandparents came from Dowlais or Dublin, from Lampeter or Leominster, from Bangor or Birmingham, from Trawsfynydd or Timsbury – they all contributed to that marvellous mixture called South-Walians. The Davieses and the Donavons, the Bevans and the Battrams, the Cadwalladers and the Colemans, the Howellses and the Hobbses met, courted, married and inter-married, giving the 'ethnic brew' a pungency of flavour and filling the valleys with a lilting 'lingo' of a special kind which even the great exodus of the depression years could do little to diminish.

JOHN EDWARDS
*Talk Tidy* (1985)


GALLTVADOG, April 9, 1750.
Dear Brother,—I received yours of yᵉ 17th and 24th March, and am obliged to you. Digon a digon ynghylch predestination, etc. I do not wonder at anything the wrech can say or do. I had the

kindest letter from her you ever saw by last post – a mere rascal, the spawn of Lucifer and the Queen of Hell. Gwrda Amral Griffin; gwnewch gymwynas i chwi eich hunen, na rupiwch, na brenin, na brenines, dyna fal y mae pawb o'r rhai synwyrol yn gwneuthur; a da fuasai i minneu pei gwneuthwn felly, mi gollaf o achos bod yn lled onest. Gwych yw'r Phœnix snuff, a iacha wragedd gwallgofus. Gyrrwch lwyth o hono i Aberystwyth, da bod Meirian mewn order. I am sorry for poor Ben Jones.

*The Morris Letters*, Vol. I
ed. J. H. Davis (1907)

*Split*

'What's Welsh about it?'
asked the grocer in Carmarthen.
'Just a thing about a tree.
It could be written by anybody
in Swindon or Slough.'


'Oh no' I said. 'Look here.
It says the author once took
a steamer from Weston
to Mumbles on St David's Day.
That makes him Anglo-Welsh.'


(Indeed the credentials were thin
and getting thinner. Who next
would we stick our label on?
I saw posterity slot us
with the Swedish-Finn and Flemish-Walloon.)


The grocer chortled: 'In that case
anybody can join then? Even
me. Except that I went
the other way from Porthcawl.'
He resumed his slicing of ham.

I felt as if I'd been hit
in the face with the Mabinogion.
This happened to me in Carmarthen.
It was one of the sadder moments
in my Anglo-Welsh life.

JOHN TRIPP (1927–86)

## I am Taliesin. I sing perfect metre

I am Taliesin. I sing perfect metre,
Which will last to the end of the world.
My patron is Elphin . . .

I know why there is an echo in a hollow;
Why silver gleams; why breath is black; why liver is bloody;
Why a cow has horns; why a woman is affectionate;
Why milk is white; why holly is green;
Why a kid is bearded; why the cow-parsnip is hollow;
Why brine is salt; why ale is bitter;
Why the linnet is green and berries red;
Why a cuckoo complains; why it sings;
I know where the cuckoos of summer are in winter.
I know what beasts there are at the bottom of the sea;
How many spears in battle; how many drops in a shower;
Why a river drowned Pharaoh's people;
Why fishes have scales,
Why a white swan has black feet . . .

I have been a blue salmon,
I have been a dog, a stag, a roebuck on the mountain,
A stock, a spade, an axe in the hand,
A stallion, a bull, a buck,
A grain which grew on a hill,
I was reaped, and placed in an oven,
I fell to the ground when I was being roasted
And a hen swallowed me.
For nine nights was I in her crop.
I have been dead, I have been alive,
I am Taliesin.

ANONYMOUS, 13th century
trans. Sir Ifor Williams

It is thought that the Welsh language is richer, more carefully
pronounced and preferable in all respects in North Wales, for
that area has far fewer foreigners. Others maintain that the
speech of Cardiganshire in South Wales is better articulated
and more to be admired, since it is in the middle and the
heartland of Wales. . . .

In their narrative poems and declamations they are so inven-
tive and ingenious that, when using their native tongue, they
produce works of art which are at once attractive and highly
original, both in the choice of words and the sentiments
expressed. You will find many poets in Wales, bards, as they
call them, who devote their energies to this kind of composition:

Stern bards, who many an austere epic song have sung.

More than any other rhetorical figure they delight in allitera-
tion, and especially that which links together the initial letters
or syllables of words:

>*Dychaun Dyu da dy unic.*
>*Erbyn dibuillh puilh paraut.**

GERALD OF WALES (*c.* 1146–1223)
*The Description of Wales* (1194)
trans. Lewis Thorpe

My father's family came to the Rhondda from Carmarthen,
leaving farmwork for the attractions of a miner's wage. They
were thoroughly Welsh, worshipping at the Welsh Congrega-
tional Church in Penygraig, and speaking only in Welsh to
each other . . . My mother was quick to recognize the advantages in being bilingual but no matter how often she asked him
to speak to us in Welsh he always refused . . . One of my regrets
is that my spoken Welsh is faulty because I never used it at
home.

GEORGE THOMAS
*Mr Speaker* (1985)

---

* In modern Welsh this reads:
>*Dichon Duw da i unig.*
>*Erbyn di-bwyll pwyll parod.*

What are the qualities that distinguish early Welsh writing?
. . . However filled with light and shadow, with humour,
pathos and magic, we discover them to be, all is clean and sheer
and shaped by the fine dry hand of a craftsman . . . Many still
underwrite a conception of old Welsh literature no more accu-
rate than early eighteenth-century conceptions of the blood-
swilling viking, skulls, snake-pits and all. The Four Branches
are not wind-filled, obfusc, gloomy, extravagant, whimsical,
stuffed with sentiment, or garnished with romance. They are at
once delicate and strong, rich in emotion but devoid of
emotionalism, magical yet matter-of-fact, and their atmosphere is that of rainbow-hued Dyfed and Gwynedd. They are as
remote from mysticism as from realism. They show a great love
of colours and contrasts, so that at times the texture of narrative
appears impregnated with a purity and soft brilliance of greens,
blues, reds and yellows. Above all they are strong and trans-
lucent.

If now I praise Snorri for the clarity of his style, for the charm
which accompanies his precision and resilience, I shall be
puzzled to express adequately the difference that every reader
will find between the Welsh writer and the Icelandic. The
Icelander's page is lit with a dry intellectual light; the
Welshman's is refulgent with imagination. What in Snorri is a
clear beam, in his fellow, is a warm glow.

GWYN JONES
from *Saga-Book* XIII, No. 1 (1946)


*From Exile*

It's bright the icy foam as it flows,
It's fierce in January great sea tumult,
It's woe's me the language, long-wished-for speech
For the sake of tales, would be sweet to my ear.

Ability in English I never had,
Neither knew phrases of passionate French:
A stranger and foolish, when I've asked questions
It turned out crooked – I spoke North Welsh!

On a wave may God's son grant us our wish
And out from amongst them readily bring us
To a Wales made one, contented and fair,
To a prince throned, laden nobly with gifts,
To the lord of Dinorwig's bright citadel land,
To the country of Dafydd, where Welsh freely flows!

DAFYDD BENFRAS, 13th century
trans. Tony Conran

From yon high prospect now I've ventured down
And stand delighted in my native town;
But whence the noises that assail mine ear?
What crowds before me with their goods appear?
'Tis market day – loud dealers strain their lungs
And High Street echoes with two different tongues:
The Welsh and English there alternate cry
'Rhai'n, rhai'n, yw pethau rhad' – 'Come buy, come buy!'
Now strangers hail raw natives as they meet,
Who cry 'Dim Saesneg', wanting power to greet.
Some few with signs their various bargains end,
Some curse the tongue they cannot comprehend.
But such as landlords more perfection reach –
They know each language and converse in each:
What should be foreign they pronounce quite well –
Scarce aught were better save the drink they sell.

JOHN JONES (1788–1858)
from *Holywell*

After dinner, the talk was of preserving the Welsh language. I
offered them a scheme. . . I recommended the republication of
David ap Rhys's Welsh grammar . . . the sound of Welsh, in a
continued discourse, is not unpleasant.

SAMUEL JOHNSON (1709–84)
*The Diary of a Journey Through North Wales in 1774*

12

'I must say I quite share the opinion of my brother Saxons as to the practical inconvenience of perpetuating the speaking of Welsh.'

MATTHEW ARNOLD (1822–88)
*On the Study of Celtic Literature* (1867)

Those of us who wonder how our grandparents came so easily to abandon their native language, and our natural heritage, at a time when it seemed to be prospering as never before, should consider the correspondence between Matthew Arnold and that ubiquitous Benthamite busybody, Hugh Owen. In the eighteen sixties Welsh dissent, Welsh speaking dissent, was poised to become an independent political force. Arnold with his life-long fear of Irish Fenianism could not have been unaware of this. And the Welsh at that time were organized in a way that was still beyond the capability of the Irish. Throughout the first half of the nineteenth century chapels had been going up at the rate of one a fortnight. At first Welsh dissenters had been content to confine themselves to theology. Unlike the *science of origins* that so took Arnold's fancy, theology was an exacting discipline. In their own language this people possessed on a popular level an extraordinary ideological network and a language which supported such a variety of newspapers, magazines, encyclopaedias, pamphlets, and books could hardly be described as dying. Every chapel and every meeting house was a potential political cell. Arnold understood this. As an Inspector of Schools it was part of his duty to be aware of any hidden threat to the uniformity of the State. He was as much devoted as his father had been to the concept of the State as a God-ordained, mystical, and sacred entity. From Hegel they derived that notable Teutonic ideal that States and the Laws of States, were nothing less than Religion manifesting itself in the relations of the actual world.

EMYR HUMPHREYS
from 'Arnold in Wonderland', in *Miscellany Two* (1981)

The Welsh language is the curse of Wales. Its prevalence and the ignorance of English have excluded and even now exclude the Welsh people from the civilization, the improvement and

the material prosperity of their English neighbours. Their anti-
quated and semi-barbarous language, in short, shrouds them in
darkness. If Wales and the Welsh are thoroughly to share the
material prosperity and . . . we will add, the culture and moral-
ity of England, they must forget their isolated language, and
learn to speak English and nothing else. For all purposes,
Welsh is a dead language . . .

Editorial, *The Times*, 8 September 1866

When you add to what might be called the natural and inherent difficulties of the necessary mountain climbing in Wales,
those of the Welsh language, you have a combination that is
beyond words to describe. Even the veriest tyro a-visiting
Wales will tell you that the language defies all description and
the most conscientious efforts to master it . . . If anyone feels
disposed to criticize an alien because he is unable to speak
Welsh, then let him go and test its difficulties for himself, its
long words, its savage consonants, its poor little vowels lost like
some bleating lamb upon rocky mountainsides.

MARKS
*Gallant Little Wales* (1912)

*The Welsh Not*

Word soon went around that a new boy, and a native one at
that, had come to school. The eyes of several cruel children
were upon me – I knew about them all, most of them were
loud-mouthed children from the village – they are still the
same. The teacher had told me, quietly, not to speak a word of
Welsh; but those evil boys were doing everything they could to
make me shout and, at last, they succeeded. I lost my temper,
and began to speak my mind to the traitorous cur who devised
how to annoy me. As soon as I spoke my strong Welsh, everyone laughed, and some string with a heavy wooden token
attached to it was put about my neck. I had no idea what it was;
I had seen a similar token about a dog's neck to prevent it from
running after sheep. Had this token been placed about my neck
to prevent me from going home? Midday, the hour of release,

**14**   came at last. The schoolmistress came there with a cane in her hand. She asked some question, and every servile child pointed his finger at me. Something like a smile came over her face when she saw the token about my neck. She recited to me some long riddle, of which I could not understand a word, she showed me the cane, but she did not touch me. The token was removed and I later understood that it had been placed about my neck because I had spoken Welsh.

That token was placed about my neck hundreds of times after that. This is how it was done: when anyone heard a child speaking a word of Welsh, he was to tell the teacher, then the token was placed about the neck of the speaker; and it was to remain about his neck until the person wearing it heard someone else speaking Welsh, then it would be put about his neck, poor soul. At the end of the school-day the one wearing it was to receive a blow with a cane across his hand. Evey day the token, as if by its own volition, found its way from every corner of the school to my neck. This is a comfort to me to this day: I never once attempted to have peace from that token by transferring it to someone else.

SIR OWEN M. EDWARDS (1858–1920)
from *The Bells of Memory* (*Clych Atgof*, 1906)
in *The Dragon's Pen* by Bobi Jones and Gwyn Thomas

*S4C*

There's a brand-new phenomenon in Wales,
    A television channel *yn Gymraeg*,
On which the Welsh-speakers now can view
    *Pobol y Cwm* and *Gwely a Brecwast*
        And *Dick Van Dyke*.

It's been a long time coming. It wasn't easy
    To get the government to open Channel Four.
It took three decades of protest and petition
    Before they'd broadcast *Rhaglen Hywel Gwynfryn*
        And *Mary Tyler Moore*.

It just may be that what will save the language
  Is children watching Sianel Pedwar Cymru
And growing up to be, on *Smyrffs*, *Wil Cwac Cwac*,
  *Sêr* and *Arolwg* and *Here's Lucy*,
    Americymry.

JOSEPH P. CLANCY

*A Welsh wordscape*

1

To live in Wales,

Is to be mumbled at
by re-incarnations of Dylan Thomas
in numerous diverse disguises.

Is to be mown down
by the same words
at least six times a week.

Is to be bored
by Welsh visionaries
with wild hair and grey suits.

Is to be told
of the incredible agony
of an exile
that can be at most
a day's travel away.

And the sheep, the sheep,
the bloody flea-bitten Welsh sheep,
chased over the same hills
by a thousand poetic phrases
all saying the same things.

To live in Wales
is to love sheep
and to be afraid
of dragons.

A history is being re-lived,
a lost heritage
is being wept after
with sad eyes and dry tears.

A heritage
that spoke beauty to the world
through dirty fingernails
and endless alcoholic mists.

A heritage
that screamed that once,
that exploded that one holy time
and connected Wales
with the whirlpool
of the universe.

A heritage
that ceased communication
upon a death, and nonetheless
tried to go on living.

A heritage
that is taking
a long time to learn
that yesterday cannot be today
and that the world
is fast becoming bored
with language forever
in the same tone of voice.

Look at the Welsh landscape,
look closely,
new voices must rise.
for Wales cannot endlessly remain
chasing sheep into the twilight.

PETER FINCH

Another characteristic reminiscent of the reputation of the **17**
medieval Welshman is the amount of humour that runs
through ordinary conversation. Much time is devoted to teas-
ing and bantering, and the stratagem called *taro'r post i'r pared
glywed* (striking the post for the wall to hear) is a popular
method of conveying inoffensive criticism as well as a means
of innocent amusement. In its simplest form it involves
twitting one of the persons present without alluding specifically to him, thus, 'It is surprising how some people . . .' But it
can be made into a fine art involving the use of metaphors,
puns and other devices.

The average countryman is very modest and even self-
effacing regarding his own qualities and possessions. Yet com-
petitive boasting, usually half jocular, is a traditional means of
entertainment. This has given rise to a series of humorous
stories of the *celwydd glân golau* type (clear obvious falsehoods),
in which the setting is usually the hearth of some farmstead in
the district. Thus, a group of farmers gathered round the fire
were extolling the virtues of their sheep-dogs in an endeavour
to draw an old fellow known to glory in his own possessions,
while he sat sullenly in the corner trying to devise a story that
would silence them. At last he told them of the occasion when
he asked his men to get up early next day to fetch the sheep
from the mountain for shearing. They did so, but as soon as
they had left the farm they met the sheep coming along the
lane with the dogs behind them. 'The dogs must have heard
me talking to the men the night before!'

ALWYN D. REES
*Life in a Welsh Countryside* (1975)

*On the Welch*

The guile and softness of the Saxon race
In gallant Briton's soul had never place;
Strong as his rocks, and in his language pure,
In his own innocence and truth secure:
Such is the bold, the noble mountaineer,
As void of treason as he is of fear.
He scorns supplanting arts and crafts as base,
But like his Hero ancestors he loves the manly chase.

His soil abounds with nature's choicest store,
His mountains' entrails stuffed with precious ore.
Yet sordid avarice could ne'er invade
The well-tuned soul, for love and music made.
Music and amorous poetry inspire
The natural Bard as soon as genial fire.
With equal appetite his lively mate
(Blooming and fair as nature's unsoiled state)
Affords him Joys as vigorous as their blood,
When with delight they calm its raging flood.
Scarce fancied blessings could with his compare,
Did he not with us griping bondage share;
But till (as fatal prophecies have spoke)
By his roused valour all our chains are broke,
Silent he lies beneath the galling yoke.
So hidden mines their horrid fate conceal,
Till well-tim'd fire the mighty force reveal:
At heaven and Liberty the powder aims
And mounts in glorious and destroying flames.

ANONYMOUS (the Brogyntyn Poet)
late seventeenth century

'The Welsh have the labour, and strangers the profit.' This begets an anxiety in every generous mind, that the present race should rouse from their lethargy, and make use of the advantages which the all-bountiful hand of Nature has so profusely strewed before them. They may have their valleys as so many forests of waving corn, judiciously intermixed with pastures, covered with herds of lowing kine; they may have their hills whitened with improved breeds of sheep, to enable them to increase their manufacture in a threefold degree; they may make their mountains verdant with evergreen plantations variegated with the autumnal russet of the deciduous oak, that valuable component in Britain's bulwark, while their bowels are pregnant with the ores of various metals; they have perennial streams issuing in every direction; and to crown the whole, the ocean offers its service, to waft their exports abroad, to return them the profits of barter, at many safe and commodious harbours; and to supply them with fish, along a line of two hundred miles of beautifully variegated shores.

GWALLTER MECHAIN (WALTER DAVIES, 1761–1849)
*Agriculture of North Wales* (1810)

'The people among whom I grew up spoke with a boisterous artistry. On certain levels of deprivation, life and speech cease to be cautious and hedged-in; humour then can express itself without inhibitions. Life in the valleys when I was a boy was a precarious and disquieting thing which encouraged an amazing vitality on people's tongues. We talked endlessly. That was one way of keeping up our spirits in a universe that did not seem very encouraging. A cracked world and a love of the poets gave us all the spiritual incentive and mechanical facility we needed. If we lacked sixpence for the pictures we could always float on a sea of metaphor in a session of high Socratic debate under a lamp-post in Porth Square or outside the Tonypandy Empire. Our imaginations had a ferocious quality. They roamed through our cosmos like hungry wolves, free to feed on whatever they fancied, finding nothing to make them fall back into a reverent hush. There's another thing. People tell me there are comic undertones in even my most sombre imagery. I can easily believe it. Humour is a sense of the incongruous or absurd, an aggravated sense of the contrast between man's divine promise and his shambling, shabby reality. There was enough incongruity between the way my people lived in the Rhondda of my early manhood, and the way in which they would have wanted to live, to have nourished at least ten thousand humorists of the first rank. But of course about the humour produced from such a situation there will be hints of the most extreme savagery; and the artist into whose spirit it may have entered too deeply will find his main task to be the rendering of his anger bearable to himself and acceptable to others.'

GWYN THOMAS (1913–81)
Radio interview with Glyn Jones (1950)
in *The Dragon Has Two Tongues* by Glyn Jones (1968)

**20**    The Welsh are quite incapable of directing one anywhere.
Mention a place a mile from their home and perhaps they
know it; two miles away and they have heard of it in myth and
legend; three miles and it might as well have been Dar-es-
Salaam. But lacking in any notion of honesty, and desiring to
seem helpful and wise, they invent elaborate directions for
getting there . . . They are poets and romantics and they have
fertile imaginations; their tongues run away with them and
consequently they send the unfortunate traveller about ten
miles out of his way.

MOORE
*Tramping through Wales* (1931)


Near the lake of Talyllyn in a sequestered part of Merioneth, I
was entertained for upwards of three days by a family of young
people with an affectionate and fraternal kindness that left an
impression upon my heart not yet impaired. The family consisted of four sisters and three brothers, all grown up and all
remarkable for elegance and delicacy of manners. So much
beauty and so much native good breeding and refinement, I do
not remember to have seen before or since in any cottage,
except once or twice in Westmorland and Devonshire . . .

It has often struck me that a world-wearied man, who
sought for the peace of monasteries separated from their
gloomy captivity – peace and silence such as theirs combined
with the large liberty of nature – could not do better than
revolve amongst these modest inns in the five northern Welsh
counties . . . Here is the eternal motion of winds and rivers . . .
Happier life I cannot imagine than this vagrancy, if the
weather were but tolerable.

THOMAS DE QUINCEY (1785–1859)
*The Confessions of an English Opium Eater* (1821)


Welsh rain . . . it descends with the enthusiasm of someone
breaking bad news. It comes down in a constant cataract. It
blots out sea, sky and mountain. Vast shapes from the beginning of the world that tower to the clouds are as if they had
never been. The rain is like a separate element. A man can lose

himself in it as if lost in fog. It flies, abetted by its companion the wind, to the left and to the right. It even blows upward over the edge of high places. It runs round corners with the wind. It finds its way up your sleeves and down your neck. It sings a song on the roads as it runs, a miniature stream, to join other rivulets until it forms a little mountain torrent. In the hills it comes rushing through the heather-stems to fall in hundreds of tiny waterfalls – hundreds of Lilliputian Bettws-y-Coeds – over stone walls upon the mountain passes. And a man looks at it in amazement and thinks that Owen Glendower must have been at his tricks again. In such wind and rain was the tent of King Henry IV blown down when the English armies were seeking the Welshman. And no wonder the whisper went round that he could control the elements; for rain in Wales can seem directed by some malignant producer, someone bent on drowning the earth and wiping from the mind of man all memory of dry places.

H. V. MORTON
*In Search of Wales* (1932)

[1252] A year after that, in the summer, the earth withered with the over excessive heat of the sun, so much that it gave hardly any of its wonted fruit, and the sea and the rivers gave not their fish as they were wont, and the trees gave not their wonted fruits. And towards the end of the autumn of that year there came so much rain that it covered the face of all the earth, after it had hardened, so that it could not absorb so much water, because of its great dryness. And on account of that so great were the floods that they submerged many houses and rent the trees and the orchards and broke the mills and caused many other losses.

from *The Chronicle of the Princes*
trans. Thomas Jones (1952)

### The Sheep Say Nothing

Rain is the hills' weather;
Then they loom through the cloud, grey
*Marie Célèstes,*
Laden with silence,
    The captain
Gone,
The crew
Lost, stumbled off into nothing, the hiss
And froth
Of the heather, the green
Bowing waves
Of the fern.

JOHN BARNIE

### from *My Square Mile*

Once again the rain has come to sadden the city's streets. Cardiff rain is different from the rain that falls in Flintshire. It doesn't whip against the windows, nor does it whirl drunkenly in the wind's eddies, nor pummel old men's backs and blind old ladies' spectacles. Neither does it fall through the sun's sieve in small, warm drops to tickle the faces of lovers and

moisten the noses of little dogs. No. Cardiff rain drips brownly
from the sky, staining buildings and pavements with its filth.

SIÔN EIRIAN
trans. Meic Stephens
in *A Cardiff Anthology*, ed. Meic Stephens (1987)

from *Winter and Warfare*

Wind piercing, hill bare, hard to find shelter;
    Ford turns foul, lake freezes.
  A man could stand on a stalk.

Wave on wave cloaks the land's edge;
Shrill the shrieks from the peaks of the mountain;
    One can scarce stand outside.

Cold the lake-bed from winter's blast;
    Dried reeds, stalks broken;
  Angry wind, woods stripped naked.

Cold bed of fish beneath a screen of ice;
    Stag lean, stalks bearded;
  Short evening, trees bent over.

  Snow is falling, white the soil.
  Soldiers go not campaigning.
  Cold lakes, their colour sunless.

  Snow is falling, white hoar-frost.
  Shield idle on an old shoulder.
  Wind intense, shoots are frozen.

  Snow is falling upon the ice.
  Wind is sweeping thick tree-tops.
  Shield bold on a brave shoulder.

  Snow is falling, cloaks the valley.
  Soldiers hasten to battle.
  I go not, a wound stays me.

Snow is falling on the slope.
Stallion confined; lean cattle.
No summer day is today.

Snow is falling, white the mountain's edge.
Ship's mast bare at sea.
A coward conceives many schemes.

ANONYMOUS 13th-century manuscript
trans. Joseph P. Clancy

from *Beneath the Barley: a Note on the Origins of Eleusinia*

I believe it was in November of that autumn of 1880 that I set
out one morning to walk to Newport; for no particular reason
that I can remember. Probably there had been a slight frost in
the night; the day was shining and splendid, and there was a
briskness in the air that made the walk – it would kill me now –

go very well. I had climbed up the long hill from Llantarnam, and was on my way towards Malpas when I saw the mountain, from Twyn Barlwm to the height above Pontypool, all a pure, radiant blue under a paler blue sky; and the sun shone on the farm houses and cottages of the mountain side, and made the whitewashed walls shine gloriously as if they were marble. I experienced an indescribable emotion; and I always attribute to that moment and to that emotion my impulse towards litera-ture . . .

ARTHUR MACHEN (1863–1947)
in *The Collected Arthur Machen* (1988)

*Cwm Bryn-Arw*

I came down into the valley –
The sun dizzied the air,
The earth breathed through its deep
Brown nostrils; trees

Crackled into life; a curlew
Spurred itself round
The green bowl of the hills;
A red grouse snapped

Clean from the bracken.
There were no doubts,
A Yellowhammer burst into flames
In the twigs of a bush –

How could it be otherwise?
Water was the hill's tongue
Licking the stones
And finding them good.

Safety is a poor net,
Coming down from the hills
Through the pouring blue,
In the hands of the light.

JOHN BARNIE

The water is hard in the well
But it never fails:
The clifftop fields are infinite salt
When the gales flock and pummel
Roof and farmstack and holt:
But the worm speaks well
Of the earth, the pheasant
Is heavy with praise in the lane:
The sea-birds, for all their grieving,
Gamble and dive at the nape of the storm:
And man embroiders his tales.
Hard hands have not kept it, this puissant
And sacred endeavour, nor high
Heads either this old domain.
It is one engrossing work, this frail
Commerce of souls in a corner,
Its coming and going, and the mark
Of the temporal on it. It is one
Coherent work, this Wales
And the seaway of Wales, its Maker
As careful of strength as
Of weakness, its quirk and cognomen
And trumpet allowed for
The whole peninsula's length.
It is one affirmative work, this Wales
And the seaway of Wales.

ROLAND MATHIAS
from *Tide Reach* (Section X)


*Synopsis of the Great Welsh Novel*

Dai K lives at the end of a valley. One is not quite sure
Whether it has been drowned or not. His Mam
Loves him too much and his Dada drinks.
As for his girlfriend Blodwen, she's pregnant. So
Are all the other girls in the village – there's been a Revival.
After a performance of Elijah, the mad preacher

Davies the Doom has burnt the chapel down.
One Saturday night after the dance at the Con Club,
With the Free Wales Army up to no good in the back lanes,
A stranger comes to the village; he is, of course,
God, the well known-television personality. He succeeds
In confusing the issue, whatever it is, and departs
On the last train before the line is closed.
The colliery blows up, there is a financial scandal
Involving all the most respected citizens; the Choir
Wins at the National. It is all seen, naturally,
Through the eyes of a sensitive boy who never grows up.
The men emigrate to America, Cardiff and the moon. The girls
Find rich and foolish English husbands. Only daft Ianto
Is left to recite the Complete Works of Sir Lewis Morris
To puzzled sheep, before throwing himself over
The edge of the abandoned quarry. One is not quite sure
Whether it is fiction or not.

HARRI WEBB

*Cymru*

My great agony, my bliss – my anxiety,
    My lovely paradise;
I love her bitterly too,
And hate her affectionately always.

ALAN LLWYD

# II

# FOOD, DRINK, HEALTH

*Rheese's Song*

...  let us tell yee
of some provision for the bellie:
As Cid, and Goat, and great Goates mother,
   and Runt, and Cow, and good Cowes Vther.
And once but taste o' the Welse-mutton,
   your Englis-s'eep's not worth a button.
And then for your Fiss, s'all shoose it your diss:
   looke but about, and there is a Trout.

Chorus. 
{
A Salmon, Cor, or Chevin,
Will feed you six, or seven,
As taull man as ever swagger,
With Welse-hooke, or long dagger.
}

BEN JONSON (*c.* 1573–1637)
from *For The Honour of Wales*, a Masque (1617–18)

*If you come my way that is . . .*
Between now and then, I will offer you
A fist full of rock cress fresh from the bank
The valley tips of garlic red with dew
Cooler than shallots, a breath you can swank

In the village when you come. At noon-day
I will offer you a choice bowl of cawl
Served with a lover's spoon and a chopped spray
Of leeks or savori fach, not used now

In the old way you'll understand. The din
Of children singing through the eyelet sheds
Ringing 'smith hoops, chasing the butt of hens;
Or I can offer you Cwmcelyn spread

With quartz stones, from the wild scratchings of men;
You will have to go carefully with clogs
Or thick shoes for it's treacherous the fen,
The East and West Marshes also have bogs,

Then I'll do the lights, fill the lamp with oil,
Get coal from the shed, water from the well;
Pluck and draw pigeon with crop of green foil
This your good supper from the lime-tree fell.

A sit by the hearth with blue flames rising,
No talk. Just a stare at 'Time' gathering
Healed thoughts, pool insight, like swan sailing
Peace and sound around the home, offering

You a night's rest and my day's energy.
You must come, start this pilgrimage,
Can you come? – send an ode or elegy
In the old way and raise our heritage.

LYNETTE ROBERTS

Mr Hugh Williams spoke as to Llanfair Mathafarn Eithaf, and the adjoining parishes of the Anglesey Union, to the effect that some of the farmers there live 'on bread-and-milk' for breakfast, on 'potatoes with buttermilk, and potatoes with butter' for dinner, adding that some get salt meat, but very seldom any meat except salt meat, that is to say, bacon and beef. He went on to say that they have bread-and-butter and tea in the afternoon, and porridge and buttermilk for supper. Lastly, he said that 'there are many farmers who cannot afford to get a piece of fresh meat once a year'. . .

Mr Ivan Thos. Davies, at Bala, stated it as his opinion that the hill farmers have much the same fare now as he had when a boy on a farm, and that fare he described as follows: 'First of all we had in the morning bruised oatmeal cake and buttermilk; then we had some bread-and-butter and tea. For dinner we had bacon and potatoes. For tea, at about three or four o'clock, we used to have a lot of *sucan*, followed by a cup of tea. *Sucan* is a kind of thin flummery, or something like that. Then we had porridge or bread-and-cheese and buttermilk for supper.' . . .

Mr David Rogers, farming in the parish of Forden, in Montgomeryshire, spoke to the following effect as to his own farm: They had breakfast at six o'clock, which in the case of the men consisted of broth; between nine and ten they had a meal which he called a bait; then came dinner, with mutton or beef, or whatever meat there might be; and between four and five in the afternoon came another meal, involving cold meat, cheese, and butter; and, lastly, there was supper. He remarked that in harvest-time his men had meat at all their meals except breakfast, and that the meat was fresh; but he was of opinion that they had not always fared so well.

Nevertheless it is a tradition, probably of long standing in other parts of Wales, that the farmers of Montgomeryshire near the English borders fared, comparatively speaking, better than those of other parts of the Principality, say, for instance, Cardiganshire. In this latter county it used, in the days before the making of the railway connecting Aberystwyth with Shrewsbury and Oswestry, to be related of them that it was their custom to begin dinner with the pudding ever since one of them had chanced to die before reaching that course. The alleged change was supposed by a people who rarely tasted pudding to embody the rule of securing the best thing first.

SIR JOHN RHŶS and DAVID BRYNMOR-JONES
*The Welsh People* (1900)

*Dietaries* (Beaumaris Gaol)

## Class 1

Prisoners confined for any Term not exceeding Three Days

|  | MALES | FEMALES |
|---|---|---|
| *Breakfast* | 1 pint of Oatmeal Gruel | 1 pint of Oatmeal Gruel |
| *Dinner* | 1 lb of Bread | 1 lb of Bread |
| *Supper* | 1 pint of Oatmeal Gruel | 1 pint of Oatmeal Gruel |

## Class 5

Prisoners employed for hard labour for terms not exceeding Three Months
SUNDAY, TUESDAY, THURSDAY AND SATURDAY

|  | MALES | FEMALES |
|---|---|---|
| *Breakfast* | 1 pint of Oatmeal Gruel | 1 pint of Oatmeal Gruel |
|  | & 6 oz of Bread | & 6 oz of Bread |
| *Dinner* | 4 oz Cooked Meat | 3 oz of Cooked Meat |
|  | without bone | without bone |
|  | 1 lb of Potatoes and | ½ lb of Potatoes and |
|  | 6 oz of Bread | 6 oz of Bread |

1879 Dietaries Table, Beaumaris Gaol

*Beti Jones's Supper*

But, to return to the subject of the ordinary everyday meals of the farmer's family and the various kinds of 'spoon-food' that could be made, I think this is the appropriate place in which to tell the story of the famous supper prepared by Beti Jones, y Ceunant . . .

The story goes that Beti Jones had tired of cooking different kinds of food for her very numerous children. She had twenty-five of them, and each one demanded a different supper. This was too much and Beti Jones, her patience exhausted, resolved to teach her brood a lesson. She was a woman of character and originality, and the method she adopted to solve the supper problem was characteristic. She asked the children, beginning with the eldest and ending with the youngest, what they would like for supper.

'Robin, what will you have for supper tonight?' 'Porridge,' said Robin.

'Nel, what will you have?' '*Siot*.'

'Mari, what will you have?' 'Posset.'

'Dic, what will you have?' 'Hot buttermilk and bread.'

'Siân, what will you have?' 'Whey.'

'Twm, what will you have?' 'Flummery,' said Twm.

'Sionyn, what will you have?' 'Cold *siot*.'

'Cit, what will you have?' 'Bread and milk.'

'Dai, what will you have?' 'Milk gruel.'

'Abraham Ephraim, what will you have?' 'Bread soaked in small beer.'

'Hannah Deborah, what will you have?' 'Oatmeal gruel.'

'Jacob Henry, what will you have?' 'Potatoes in buttermilk.'

'Ruth Salomi, what will you have?' '*Picwsmali*' [oatcake soaked in hot buttermilk, another form of *siot*].

'Charles Edward, what will you have?' 'Turkey pie' [bread, with a little butter, pepper and salt, and boiling water added].

'Humphrey Cadwaladr, what will you have?' 'Junket.'

'Claudia Dorothy, what will you have?' 'Bread and water.'

'Margaret Alice, what will you have?' 'Water posset.'

'Goronwy, what will you have?' 'Cold buttermilk and bread.'

'Arthur, what will you have?' 'Caudle.'

'Blodwen, what will you have?' 'Broth.'

'Gwladys, what will you have?' '*Brewis*.'

'Rhys, what will you have?' '*Siot* posset.'

'Corwena, what will you have?' 'Wheat flour gruel.'

'Caradoc, what will you have?' 'Toast and milk.'

'Llewelyn, my little one, what will you have?' 'I'll have porridge, like Robin.'

'Good lad,' said Beti Jones, 'you'll make a man yet.'

'No, I'll have whey, like Siân. No, flummery, the same as Twm.'

Having thus ascertained the wishes of all her children Beti
Jones disappeared into the back-kitchen without making any
kind of comment and without the usual scolding, which surprised the family, for it was quite out of character. However,
Beti remained out of sight in the back-kitchen for a considerable time, and when she reappeared in the living kitchen it
was with the baking pan in her arms. This she placed on the
kitchen table, and then she began carrying in the vessels in
which she had prepared the various foods demanded by her
brood. When all had been collected she poured the contents
into the baking pan, stirring the whole mess up with the
porridge stick, a job calling for a good deal of muscular
strength. This done, she spooned the resulting mess into the
bowls from which the children ate, filling each bowl according
to her knowledge of each child's requirements and capacity,
and finally placing them along the table before her astonished
offspring. There were some faint attempts at rebellion, but Beti
was a resolute woman and stood over her brood, porridge stick
in hand like a truncheon, until all had been eaten. That cured
them of finicky fancies about their food, and the story was a
standing warning to us children of a later generation.

HUGH EVANS (1854-1934)
*Cwm Eithin* (*The Gorse Glen*, 1931)
trans. E. Morgan Humphreys

*Sgotyn*
(Bread in Water)

This is still a favourite with older country folk:

bread
salt and pepper
boiling water
Break a slice of bread into a bowl, pour boiling water over
it and add salt and pepper to taste. Serve immediately.

BOBBY FREEMAN
*First Catch Your Peacock* (1980)

The Welsh, like the Irish, have only a limited number of dishes which can accurately be called 'national', and these, in the majority of cases, are somewhat rural, and often merely local. Mrs D. Dearle, who is an authority on Welsh cookery, writes: 'You will appreciate that cooking in the outlying villages and farms is of a very plain nature, and practically all the cakes, scones, etc., are done on the bakestone, except when bread-making is in progress. In most places bread is baked in a brick oven made hot with a wood fire, the ashes then being raked out and the bread put in. The oven door is then sealed with clay for about two hours. After the bread is baked, tarts and buns are then cooked; after this rice puddings are left in the oven to cook slowly, and served cold with the midday meal. The midday meal mainly consists of boiled meat or bacon with vegetables, the liquid then being flavoured with leeks and thickened with oatmeal for broths.'

And so it has been for many generations, and the Welsh seem to have been particularly indifferent to the art of cooking. 'Tea and bread and butter' seems to be the national institution, and the amount of both which is consumed is amazing.

COUNTESS MORPHY
*English Recipes: Including the Traditional Dishes of Scotland, Ireland & Wales*, (c. 1930)


*Lobsgows*
(Stew)

Put 1½ lbs of neck of mutton in a saucepan with just enough water to cover, bring to the boil and skim. Then add 2 coarsely-chopped onions, ½ lb of carrots, cut in dice, ½lb of turnips, also cut in dice, and 1 small swede. Season with pepper and salt, simmer gently for another ¾ of an hour. Coarsely-chopped cabbage is sometimes added to this dish.

COUNTESS MORPHY
(*ibid*)

Drink for drink comes to me
from his vineyard, from his fair hand;
and poetry, eloquent of longing,
and music. We get glory.
A sweet fair quiet concert,
then pipes and dancing every day.
Couplings secure the rooftree,
each rafter safely coupled in . . .
Four sweet lofts joined together,
where travelling poets sleep . . .
Spirits and finest bragget,
all liquors, white bread and wine,
with meat and fire in the kitchen . . .
There'll be no lack of gifts,
no fault, no famine, no shame,
no thirst ever in Sycharth.

IOLO GOCH (*c.* 1320–98)
trans. Gwyn Williams

It is thought (by the Welsh) that delicious dishes for fighting
men are cheese and butter with half-cooked flesh, which they
often eat after only squeezing the meat in the cleft trunk of the
tree; these things take the place of bread, and a milky liquid the
place of wine.

Raiding our land . . . these savages slaughtered pitilessly
young and old, parents and children alike.

GUILLAUME LE BRETON, 12th century

The following is the bill of fare at the 'entertainment' given by
Sir Watkin Williams Wynn at Wynnstay to celebrate the coming of age of his son in April 1770:
30 bullocks; one roasted whole; 50 hogs, 50 calves, 80
sheep, 18 lambs, 70 pies, 51 guinea fowls, 37 turkeys, 12
turkey-poults, 84 capons, 24 pie-fowls, 300 chickens, 360
fowls, 96 ducklings, 48 rabbits, 15 snipes, 1 leveret, 5

bucks, 242 pounds of salmon, 50 brace of tench, 40 brace of carp, 36 pike, 60 dozen of trout, 108 flounders, 109 lobster, 96 crabs, 10 quarts of shrimps, 200 crawfish, 60 barrels of pickled oysters, 1 hogs-head of rock-oysters, 20 quarts of oysters for sauce, 166 hams, 100 tongues, 125 plum-puddings, 34 rice-puddings, 7 venison pies, 60 raised pies, 80 tarts, 30 pieces of cut pastry, 24 pound cakes, 60 Savoy cakes, 30 sweetmeat-cakes, 12 backs of bacon, 144 ice-creams, 18,000 eggs, 150 gallons of milk, 60 quarts of cream, 30 bushels of potatoes, 6,000 asparagus, 200 French beans, 3 dishes of green peas, 12 cucumbers, 70 hogs-heads of ale, 120 dozen of wine, brandy, rum, and shrub rock work shapes, landscapes in jellies, blancmange etc.; a great quantity of small pastry; 1 large cask of ale which held 26 hogsheads. It is thought that there were at least 15,000 people at dinner in Sir Watkin's park all at the same time.

*Archaeologia Cambrensis* (1864)

. . . in the field, we should have been pleased with the plainest meal a hungry man can have, which is, I suppose, barley bread and a pale 'double Caermarthen' cheese, which you cut with a hatchet after casting it on the floor and making it bounce, to be sure that it is a double Caermarthen. And yet I do not know. For even a Welsh hymnist of the eighteenth century, in translating 'the increase of the fields', wrote avidly of 'wheaten bread', so serious was his distaste for barley bread. But it was to a meal of wheaten bread and oat cake, and cheese and onions and cucumber, that we came in, while the trembling splendours of the first stars shone, as if they also were dewy like the furze.

EDWARD THOMAS (1878–1913)
*Wales* (1905)

### A Cheese for the Archdeacon

Here's a good piece of cheese (I perhaps might have kept it)
But I hope the Archdeacon will kindly accept it
Nor suppose I deem wanting in bara a chaws –
A chroesaw – the Cloisters, a liberal house.

To remain in my larder it's rather too nice
For a part has already been eaten by mice.
So my worthy Archdeacon (I once more repeat it)
You will do me a kindness to help me to eat it.
   It's moist and it's mild, and without too much boasting
I think it's a capital cheese for toasting.
It's not much decayed, nor strong in its savour:
Though for some it is rather too flat in its flavour.
And because it's too weak for to please every palate,
It perhaps may suit better when eaten with salad.
When cold or when toasted its taste is so mild
It will please the most delicate lady or child.
It will do when you dine, or perchance when you sup,
With a dainty swig of your Warden's cup.
Or else for a change, if you're in the habit
To eat of the same, it will make a Welsh rarebit.
When dining on mutton, and pastry, and fish,
It will make macaroni – a very good dish.
And should any remain when your appetite's sated,
With that let your mouse-traps be properly baited.
   To conclude, and no longer continue this rhyme
Or I fear I might trespass too long on your time,
These poor silly lines, Sir, I beg you'll excuse,
And accept the respects of your curate, T. Hughes.

THOMAS HUGHES (1818–65)

### Bara Brith

*Ingredients:* 1 lb of flour, 6 ozs of sugar, 6 ozs of butter, 2 eggs, 3 teaspoons of baking powder, 6 ozs of currants or sultanas, ¼ pint of cold tea, a pinch of salt.

*Method:* Rub the butter into the flour, add the sugar, the salt, currants or sultanas, and mix all thoroughly. Beat up the eggs with the cold tea, and stir into the mixture. Finally add the baking powder. Turn into a well-greased tin, and bake in a slow oven for 2 hours. (You can soak the dry ingredients overnight in the tea.)

Stew down 3 parts rowan berries to 1 part crab apple. Drip
through a jelly bag, then add 1 lb sugar to every pint of juice and
boil and boil until it gels.


### Crempog Cymreig

Make a batter with ½ lb of flour, 1 oz of sugar, 1 teaspoon of
baking powder, a pinch of carbonate of soda, and sufficient
milk to make it of the consistency of cream. Beat well. Lightly
grease a hot girdle and drop a spoonful at a time of the mixture
on this, turning as soon as one side is lightly coloured. To serve,
do not fold the pancakes. They are eaten with jam and butter.

COUNTESS MORPHY
*English Recipes: Including the Traditional Dishes
of Scotland, Ireland & Wales* (c. 1930)


We used to visit farms for crempog teas and I used to eye the
huge pot of melted butter, in which lurked the small round
pancakes, with apprehension. I knew I could never eat enough
to satisfy the farmer's wife, and always when I had consumed
about six I could take no more. Unfortunately one's manhood
was judged by one's capacity to down a vast number of
crempogs, and I always failed abysmally in the eyes of the
parish.

'Well, well, you are no good,' complained one old body. 'Your
father could do twelve, Master Johnny could do twenty and
your grandfather twenty-four.'

I was humiliated and hardly a member of the rector's family
any more.

'Dduw, Master John, only six? Well, well, you're hopeless.'

There would be laughter and cheerful goodbyes, but I crept
away, a six-crempog boy.

KYFFIN WILLIAMS
*Across the Straits* (1973)

squints across a sprouting field,
chews at a leaf, then weighs your crop
to the nearest bag.

Soft cap down to the eyes
and what had been somebody's suit
held by baling cord;
he is pigmented with dirt
as if washing would have drained
away the year's knowledge.

The whole county waits:
in April the Pembrokeshire Earlies come
a stiff, dark green out of the ground.
Jack and his tribe pour
like Winter rats from their cottage.

Jack stops at the stile,
pushes the cap back to the perch of his head,
then walks along a row to what becomes
the centre of the field.
He delivers a potato from the earth,
soil spilling from the web of tubers,
shaking from the clumps.
He scrapes through dirt and skin;
the sweet flesh goes between his leather lips,
a nugget lodging in the jags of his teeth.

He closes his eyes on the taste –
it is the soil crumbling, the crush
of frost, the rain carried in on the sea,
the sweat of planting.

He holds the ridged sweetness to his nose,
between finger and thumb it glistens,
the rarest egg, the first
potato and the last.

TONY CURTIS

40

## *Eog*
### (Salmon)

For this, freshly caught salmon must be used. As soon as the salmon is caught and killed, it should be crimped. Make incisions from the head to the tail. Stand in cold water for 1 hour. Then put in a fish kettle, cover with cold water, add 4 ozs of salt and a few tablespoons of vinegar – sufficient to make the water sharp. Put on the fire and, just before the water reaches boiling point, pour it into a saucepan, and place the strainer containing the fish over it. Let both cool together and stand in a cold place for 12 hours. Now replace the fish in the fish kettle, cover with the same water and, when the water is again about to come to the boil, remove the fish and serve. The water should never be allowed to reach boiling point in this method of cooking.

COUNTESS MORPHY
*English Recipes: Including the Traditional Dishes
of Scotland, Ireland & Wales* (c. 1930)

## *Caws Pobi*
### (Welsh Rarebit)

Welsh toasted cheese, and the melted cheese of England, called 'toasted cheese', are as different in the mode of preparation as is the cheese itself . . . Cut a slice of the real Welsh cheese made of sheep and cow's milk, toast it at the fire on both sides, but not so much as to drop; toast a piece of bread, less than a quarter of an inch thick, to be quite crisp, and spread it very thinly with fresh cold butter on one side (it must not be saturated with butter), then lay the toasted cheese upon the bread and serve immediately on a very hot plate; the butter on the toast can, of course, be omitted if not liked, and it is more frequently eaten without butter.

LADY LLANOVER
*The First Principles of Good Cookery* (1867)

We make an exceedingly good toasting cheese, – and as the process is much abridged from the foregoing, I mention it.

Take thirty gallons of milk from the cow. You will colour it with annatto, by rubbing it on a tile with milk, so that it be well mixed. You will take as much annatto as you may think will colour it to your liking. Add to it as much rennet as will coagulate it. In about an hour's time, it will be fit to take out the whey from it. This is done by pressing the skimmer upon it, and touching it as little with the hand as possible. Press as much of the whey from it as you possibly can: put it under the press, turning it and changing the cloth twice a-day. In four or five days, it will be fit to take from the press; then lay it on a smooth stone, and rub it well over with salt: do this for three days, and treat it afterwards as other cheeses. The vats for these cheeses should not be more than three inches in depth. Five or six holes bored in the sides of all vats is a great improvement.

THOMAS JOHNES
*Cardiganshire Landlord's Advice to his Tenants* (1800)

*Penamnen, Dolwyddelan*
between Betws-y-coed and Blaenau Ffestiniog, Gwynedd.

Slender Alis, I never saw her table
Without, in a twinkling, the linen spread on it.

Lewys Môn, early 16th century (?)
ENID ROBERTS
*Food of the Bards* (1982)

I fynde wrytten amonge old gestes, howe God mayde Saynt Peter porter of heven, and that God of hys goodnes, sone after hys passyon, suffered many men to come to the Kyngdome of Hevene with small deseruynge; at which tyme there was in heven a great company of Welchmen, whyche with their crackynge and babelynge troubled all the other. Wherefore

**42**   God sayde to Saynte Peter, that He was weary of them, and that he wolde fayne have them out of heven. To whom Saynte Peter sayd:

'Good Lorde, I warrente you, that shal be done.'

Wherefore Saynte Peter wente out of heven gates and cryed with a loud voyce, *'Cause bobe'*, that is as moche to say as rosted chese, whiche thynge the Welchemen herynge, ranne out of heven a great pace. Saynt Peter sawe them all out, he sodenly wente into heven and locked the dore and so spaned all the Welchemen out. . . .

*Mery Talys* (1525)
Collected by John Skelton (*c.* 1460–1529)

The way to make a Welshman thirst for bliss,
And say his prayers daily on his knees
Is to persuade him that most certain 't is
The moon is made of nothing but green cheese;
And he'll desire of God no greater boon
But place in heav'n to feed upon the moon.

JOHN TAYLOR

from *An Invitation to Dyddgu*

Maiden, radiant and gifted,
Dyddgu with the smooth dark hair,
I invite you, a melancholy hide-out,
To the meadow of Manafan.

No feeble invitation befits you,
No glutton's invitation to a cottage,
No dish in payment for reapers,
No corn, no mixed fresh meal,
No share of a farmer's dinner,
No Shrove Tuesday meat feast,
No spread for a Saxon with his friend,
No churl's son's feast at his first-shave.

I promise nothing, a good result,
For my golden one, but a nightingale and mead;
A light-toned grey-backed nightingale
And a sturdy sweet-languaged thrush.

DAFYDD AP GWILYM (*c.* 1320–70)
trans. Bobi Jones in *The Dragon's Pen* (1986)


*Cawl Llaeth*
(Buttermilk Soup)

Melt 1 oz of butter in a saucepan and stir in 1 oz of flour, but without browning. Add gradually ½ a pint of warm buttermilk, and stir, over a very slow fire, till the mixture is quite smooth and free from lumps. Add 1 quart of hot veal stock, and simmer for 15 minutes.


For dinner we had salmon and leg of mutton; the salmon from the Dee, the leg from the neighbouring Berwyn. The salmon was good enough, but I had eaten better; and here it will not be amiss to say, that the best salmon in the world is caught in the Suir, a river that flows past the beautiful town of Clonmel in Ireland. As for the leg of mutton it was truly wonderful; nothing so good had I ever tasted in the shape of a leg of mutton. The leg of mutton of Wales beats the leg of mutton of any other country, and I had never tasted a Welsh leg of mutton before. Certainly I shall never forget that first Welsh leg of mutton which I tasted, rich but delicate, replete with juices derived from the aromatic herbs of the noble Berwyn, cooked to a turn, and weighing just four pounds.

'O its savoury smell was great,
Such as well might tempt, I trow,
One that's dead to lift his brow.'

Let anyone who wishes to eat leg of mutton in perfection go to Wales, but mind you to eat leg of mutton only; Welsh leg of mutton is superlative; but with the exception of the leg, the

mutton of Wales is decidedly inferior to that of many other
parts of Britain.

GEORGE BORROW (1803–81)
*Wild Wales* (1862)


*At the Beaufort Arms in Monmouth*

'What can you give me inside half an hour?' I ask. 'Anything
you like, sir,' the woman answers with unblushing effrontery,
and a respectful cordiality delightful to see in such a connexion. I am tempted to ask for buckwheat cakes, prairie chicken,
roast saddlecocks, and watermelons, but compromise with
'How about a fowl?' 'Fowl, sir? Take about an hour to cook a
fowl, sir.' But it is idle to defer the climax of this thrilling – or
grilling – tale. I had chops for dinner.

WIRK SIKES
*Rambles and Studies in South Wales* (1880)


The little inn at *Tan-y-Bwlch* appears from a very high summit
of a mountain over a lovely woody vale, as a small white speck.
The inconveniences of the vile road we had hitherto past, had
fatigued us beyond measure, and we began to reckon upon the
comforts of good beds and a good supper; we had indeed a dispute, whether we should order chickens or chops: but our morti-
fication on drawing up to the door can hardly be conceived,
when mine host with a petrifying phiz approached us, to say he
had no room to receive us. Indeed there are, as I understand, but
two beds to be occupied here with any degree of convenience.
We had no other remedy than, if possible, to reach *Festiniog*, three
long Welsh miles, at nearly dark, and with horses entirely
knocked up. These three miles of as steep road as any we had yet
passed, we had to walk (for our horses could scarcely move the
carriage) in the dark. We reached the inn (as it is called) at
*Festiniog*, which we had nearly passed, mistaking it for a barn or
out house. I addressed myself to an ancient female, who had
every appearance of a Welsh weird sister, and demanded if we
could have beds? After telling us, that she supposed we only
came there, because there was no accommodation at *Tan-y-*

*Bwlch*, – with seeming reluctance she agreed we should pitch our tents for the night here. There is no kind of asylum within 17 miles of this place; therefore we were not a little satisfied at being under any kind of roof, as the rain had been incessant for many hours. Bad therefore, as the best room was, we secured it, ordered a peat fire to be lighted, and inquired what provision was to be had. The old lady waited on us, to what she called the larder, in the approach to which we were nearly necessitated to creep on all fours. The appearance of its contents could certainly not vie with the Bush at *Bristol*. In a small deal packing case lay a small leg of starved mutton, and a duck ready dressed; each of which, from their cadaverous hue, and their effect on our olfactory nerves, had not been near the fire for a fortnight.

WIGSTEAD
*Tour to Wales* (1800)

*Pickled Puffin – Anglesey Delicacy*

The young ones . . . are pickled for sale by the renters of the island and form an article of traffic peculiar to this neighbourhood. The oil is extracted from them by a peculiar process and the bones are taken out after which the skin is closed round the flesh and they are immersed in vinegar impregnated with spices.

REVD WILLIAM BINGLEY (1774–1823)
*North Wales Excursions* (1798 and 1801)

The young puffins before they are quite feathered, are fledged and opened and strew'd with pepper and salt and Broiled and Eat pleasant enough. But the nice way of managing them is to Pickle them, and these are sent as rarities for ye Tables of the Great.

'Puffins which pickled bring profit.'

LEWIS MORRIS (1701–65)

The first time that I came to Llanberis, being somewhat
fatigued with traversing the adjacent mountains, I went to . . .
rest myself and obtain some refreshment. It was just at the dinner hour, and a scene was exhibited altogether novel to me. At
one table was seated the family of the house consisting of the
old host, his wife, and their son and daughter, eating their
bread and milk, the common food of the labouring people here:
a large overgrown old sow was devouring her dinner, with considerable dissatisfaction on account of the short allowance,
from a pail placed for her by the daughter in one corner; whilst
I was eating my bread and butter, with an appetite steeled
against niceties by the keenness of the mountain air, at a table
covered with a dirty napkin, in the other corner. This scene,
however, induced me always afterwards to bring with me
refreshments from Caernarvon, and enjoy my dinner, in quiet,
in the open air.

REVD WILLIAM BINGLEY (1774–1823)
*North Wales Excursions* (1798 and 1801)

I was introduced to the worthy representative of this long line,
who gave me a most hospitable reception, and in the style of
any Ancient Briton. He welcomed us with ale and potent beer,
to wash down the Coch yr Wden, or hung goat, and the cheese
compounded of the milk of cow and sheep. He likewise
showed us the ancient family cup, made of a bull's scrotum, in
which large libations had been made in days of yore. The family lay in their whole store of winter provisions, being inaccessible a great part of the season by reason of snow. Here they
have lived for many generations, without bettering or lessen-
ing their income, without noisy fame but without any of its
embittering attendants.

THOMAS PENNANT (1726–98)
*Tours in Wales* (1778 and 1781)

This Pillar is called Mail Coach Pillar and erected as a caution to mail coach drivers to keep from intoxication and in memory of the Gloucester to Carmarthen Mail Coach, which was driven by Mr Edward Jenkins on the 19th day of December in the year of 1835, who was intoxicated at the time and drove the mail coach on the wrong side of the road and going at a full speed or gallop met a cart and permitted the leader to turn short around to the right hand and went down over the precipice 121 ft, when at the bottom near the river it came against an ash tree, when the coach was dashed into several pieces. Colonel Gwynne of Glanbran Park, Daniel Jones, Esq., of Penybont and a person of the name of Edwards were outside and David Harris, Esq., of Llandovery, Solicitor, and a lad of the name of Kernick were inside passengers of the mail coach at the time and John Compton, guard.

I have heard it said that where there is a will there is a way. One person cannot assist many, but many can assist a few, as this pillar will show. It was suggested, designed and erected by J. Bull, Inspector of Mail Coaches, with the aid of thirteen pounds sixteen shillings and sixpence received by him from forty-one subscribers in the year 1841.

The work of this pillar was executed by John Jones, Marble and Stone Mason, Llandarog near Carmarthen. It was repainted and restored by Postal Officials in 1930.

**48**  I never cease to marvel at the contrast between public and private cooking in Wales. There are now some delightful exceptions to the general rule that public cooking in Wales is a form of self-inflicted gastronomic penance. The *Good Food Guide* lists them in lyric prose and the tourists flock to them. But they have no connection with any form of Welsh cuisine. And far too often you find yourself in establishments where the food served to the visitor represents the Welsh revenge for the defeat of Owain Glyndwr.

WYNFORD VAUGHAN-THOMAS
*Madly in All Directions* (1967)

### The Hostess of the Ferry Inn

I keep the custom of the Ferry, a tavern none can blame, a white-robed moon giving sweet welcome to him that comes with silver.

'Tis my desire to be, to all men's content, a faultless world to my guests, and to sing among them in familiar converse as I pour out the mead.

GWERFUL MECHAIN (*c.* 1462–1500)
trans. Sir H. Idris Bell

# III

# EARLY HISTORY, INVASION, BATTLES

'An old and haughty Nation, proud in arms.'

MILTON (1608–74)
*Comus*

Amid earth and rocks, like an old dog,
Death was gnawing on a bone
Three thousand years at Bryn Celli Ddu.


Till the sun was hacked into its belly
And time shovelled from the skeletons
And grey echoes of a race's early life laid bare.


There was no sound of mortality scuttling
Grossly, horribly, angularly among the stones;
In the analysing of the darkness it left there quietly.


And those who once walked Môn, their quality went
Through the earth, green to the grass and bright to the water,
Their lives were washed by the rain, the sun drank up their
    pain.


Their life went astray in the wind,
Was lost in the long time
Stretching between us and what used to be.


But their being is in our blood,
A crimson secret pumping through our hearts,
A bond of living, a grasp of recognition.


And such poor things as we
Against the muddled strength of death
Pierce the grave's armour with our ancestors' remains.


(Bryn Celli Ddu is an ancient burial mound in Anglesey. It is
thought to date from c. 2000–1500 BC. Archaeologists have dug
there this century.)

GWYN THOMAS
trans. Joseph P. Clancy

*Man 2:*  You're telling me that these chaps (Beaker Folk,
          weren't they? Correct me if I'm wrong) brought a spot
          of dolce vita with them from where they came
          from and enlivened every corner of Wales with it.
          What more can you ask for when a thing is useful
          and soothes the eye? Not like a design award
          to a teapot that scalds your hand and won't pour.
          What about about their houses? Had they evolved
          cosy shacks with a bronze knocker on the door,
          folksy earthenware or pewter platters? They had
          the materials, didn't they, and the ingenuity.

*Man 1:*  They still built more permanent houses for the dead
          than for the living. Nothing remains of their dwellings
          but there's no need to think that their wooden
          houses or clay and wattle structures weren't
          as snug as you'd need. They buried their dead now
          on the hills where they raised stone circles, *cistfeini*
          covered with low tumuli only slightly
          modifying a skyline. High places of the dead.

*Girl:*   Whose is the four-square grave
              barrowed on the hill,
          ashes under an urn?
              I cannot tell.

*Man 2:*  Garn Wen, White Cairn, grazed ridge which limits
          my living space, (How can you know where you are
          without hills, how live in a flat featureless
          land?) the holy white stones all taken away
          to catch the moon or starlight and mark
          a gate or wall for night returners, the grave
          exposed and robbed, lipped now with shouting slabs
          against rain, sheepdung and shepherd's unconcern.
          But always the dead. Let's have a little more about
          the living, their everyday things, their life.

*Man 1:*  It was clearly of some elegance, at least for the chiefs.
          Bronze razors and tweezers suggest care

for the appearance. Then ornaments of bronze, gold, jet
and amber. A fine gold torque to circle
the bare shaved neck of the well-dressed man,
holiday wear, not for the sport of hunting.
Those Bronze Age men loved air and space to make
burial such a culmination to their horizons.
They were hunters before the coming of war to our land,
flighting the expendable flint-tipped arrow
over thicket and rock; the woodlands of Wales
were rank with game and only slightly shrunk
by the newly cast and sharpened axehead.

GWYN WILLIAMS
from *Foundation Stock* (a radio poem for three voices)

'. . . the strong and warlike nation of the Silures . . .'

TACITUS (AD *c.* 56–*c.* 115)

Scapula had . . . decided on the conquest of Wales and the pursuit and destruction of Caratacus.

As the Roman general gazed across the Severn into the Welsh interior, he must soon have become aware of the enormity of the task he was about to undertake. He had no friends across the border and, in particular, he had a dangerous, determined and dedicated enemy in the Silures, whose loyalty to Caratacus had already been proven . . . Silurian territory in the west . . . reached at least as far as Swansea; in the north, it included the ranges of the Black Mountains and the Brecon Beacons; and in the south, it was bounded by a fertile coastal strip overlooking the Bristol Channel. Scapula would have been particularly interested in the terrain of the eastern boundary, which lay across his front as he sought to advance westwards. Here the tribal border probably extended as far as the Severn, for it would have been strange if they had not brought the Forest of Dean, with all its natural resources, under their influence at this time. In addition to the obstacle imposed by the Forest, Scapula's path was also obstructed by three major rivers, the Severn, with its tributaries the Wye and the Usk, both

of which joined the main stream at its mouth, where it flowed
into the Bristol Channel. All three rivers presented formidable
obstacles to any advance by land along the line of the coast but
were navigable for considerable distances. A Silurian *oppidum*
lay situated at Llanmelin, on ground to the west of Chepstow,
lying between the Wye and the Usk, with clear views across the
Severn estuary to the mouth of the Avon. It is thus evident that
as long as the Silures occupied this position and dominated the
forest areas between the Usk and the Severn, then the use of the
latter river would be a constant source of troubles to the
Romans. Scapula's prime task must have been to seize this
area. . .

JOHN PEDDIE
*The Roman Invasion of Britain* (1987)

**54**     Agricola decided to reduce the island of Anglesey, from the
occupation of which Paulinus had been recalled by the revolt
of all Britain . . . As the plan was hastily conceived, there was no
fleet at hand; but Agricola's resource and resolution found
means of getting troops across. He carefully picked out from his
auxiliaries men who had experience of shallow waters and
had been trained at home to swim carrying their arms and
keeping their horses under control, and made them discard all
their equipment. He then launched them on a surprise attack;
and the enemy, who had been thinking in terms of a fleet of
ships and naval operations, were completely nonplussed.
What could embarrass or defeat a foe who attacked like that?
So they sued for peace and surrendered the island.

TACITUS
*The Agricola* (AD 98)
trans. H. Mattingly (1970)

They had one *Archipræsul,* or chief *Druid* among them – *His
præest* Unus, says *Cæsar;* and where was he, but where they all
flock'd unto him? And where did they flock, but to the Isle of
*Mona*? Where *Tacitus* says, they were seen in great Numbers.

HERE indeed *Tacitus* finds them out, as if his Pen, having
taken the Hint from *Cæsar,* had travell'd all the conquer'd Prov-
inces of *Britain* in quest of these *Druids,* and of the Place of their
Abodes and Studies: And at last, by tracing the Steps of *Paulinus
Suetonius* over a small Arm of the Sea, he fell on the very Spot
and Place before hinted; and there at the first dash, gives us an
Army of them: For mentioning there the *Britains* resisting the
landing of *Romans* into the Island, he says, their Army (meaning the *Brittons*) was surrounded by another Army (for he
describes them no less) of *Druids,* of both Sexes, Men and
Women, for they had (it seems) their Nuns and Sisterhood in
that Order: *Druidæque circum, intercursantibus fœminis,* are his
words: And these too appear'd in such Numbers, that he calls
them *muliebre & fanaticum Agmen,* i.e. a Squadron of Virago's
and Madmen.

THE *Men-Druids* shewing *here* (no doubt) some part of their
usual Behaviour at their sacred Ceremonies, i.e. *Sublatis ad
Cælum manibus diras preces fundendo,* in pouring of Vollies of Exe-

crations and Curses, with their hands lifted up to Heaven, on
the insulting *Romans*: as the Women did theirs also, viz. *In
modum Furiarum, veste ferali, Crinibus dejectis, faces Præferendo*, i.e.
in running about like Furies with burning Firebrands in their
hands, clad in fearful Habits, with their hair waving and dang-
ling behind them.

THIS very Passage of the *Historian*, with unprejudic'd Men,
will render it hugely probable, that this was the very Place, and
these the very Persons of the famous *Druids*; and that that may
appear yet to any one more plain and evident; let me only ask,
if these *Druids* chief Seat and Residence had been in any other
Part of the then conquer'd *Britain* (and indeed what Part of it
the *Roman* Army, one Time or other, had not reach'd unto?)
how it came to pass that we had not some Account, in some
Author, of such an Appearance of these *Druids*, playing their
last Game (*Pro Aris & Focis*) as we have it by *Tacitus*, in this Isle of
*Mona*? I need not press the Question, 'tis so unlikely, that I
think no satisfactory Answer can be given it.

*Mons Antiqua Restaurata* (1723)

### The Battle of Argoed Llwyfain

There was a great battle Saturday morning
From when the sun rose until it grew dark.
The fourfold hosts of Fflamddwyn invaded.
Goddau and Rheged gathered in arms,
Summoned from Argoed as far as Arfynydd –
They might not delay by so much as a day.

With a great swaggering din, Fflamddwyn shouted,
'Are these the hostages come? Are they ready?'
To him then Owain, scourge of the eastlands,
'They've not come, no! They're not, nor shall they be ready!
And a whelp of Coel would indeed be afflicted
Did he have to give any man as a hostage!'

And Urien, lord of Erechwydd, shouted,
'If they would meet us now for our kinsfolk,
High on the hilltop let's raise our ramparts,
Carry our faces over the shield rims,
Raise up our spears, men, over our heads
And set upon Fflamddwyn in the midst of his hosts
And slaughter him, ay, and all that go with him!'

There was many a corpse beside Argoed Llwyfain;
From warriors ravens grew red,
And with their leader a host attacked.
For a whole year I shall sing to their triumph.

And when I'm grown old, with death hard upon me,
I'll not be happy save to praise Urien.

TALIESIN, late 6th century
trans. Tony Conran

## The Early Welsh Kingdoms

Could it be that the wonderful thing Maximus did for Wales
was to set up the administrative machinery that led to the formation of the early Welsh kingdoms?

It is likely that it was Maximus who sent the invitation to
Cunedda to settle in Wales – the date is right and it fits the
known facts. What is more significant is that Maximus figures
in several Welsh genealogies as well as his mention on the
Pillar of Eliseg.

The kingdom traditionally founded by Cunedda became
Gwynedd and extended to Anglesey. In the time of Gildas it
was ruled over by Maelgwn, who is described by the historian
as the 'dragon of the isles'. More is known about him than
about many early kings. His youth was devoted to the church,
but in the mid-sixth century he changed character and became
a ruthless heroic chieftain remembered by medieval Welsh
poets, celebrated by Taliesin and in the story of the *Dream of
Rhonabwy*. His people are also sometimes known as the
Venedotians, and his own seat was at Deganwy, a craggy rock

which now looks out across holiday homes and towards
Llandudno and the Ormes.

Maelgwn died of the 'yellow plague'. In later medieval
romance, the plague became a hideous monster, the 'yellow
spectre' which Maelgwn saw through a keyhole (translated by
J. E. Lloyd, *Outlines of the History of Wales*, Caernarvon, 1906,
p. 83):

> The strange beast shall come
> From the ladies marsh
> With vengeance for sin
> Upon Maelgwn Gwynedd
> Its hair and its teeth
> And its eyes shall be saffron
> And it shall bring death
> To Maelgwn Gwynedd.

In Gildas' time, Dyfed was ruled over by Vortepor, whose
ancestry can be traced back to Magnus Maximus . . .

The origins of the other Welsh kingdoms are less clear. Some
stemmed from the tribal organization of Wales, others traced
their dynasties to Roman times. *Gwerthrynion* takes its name
from its legendary founder Vortigern – *Buelt* also had a line
traced back to him . . .

By the seventh century Gwynedd emerged as the dominant
state in Wales, achieving prominence first under the leader-
ship of Cadfan (Catamanus). His tombstone is still preserved at
Llangadwaladr church in Anglesey and describes him as
'Catamanus, wisest and most renowned of all kings'. The proud
boast has an exotic ring about it, and echoes the phraseology of
the Byzantine court, hinting that forgotten splendours may
have coloured court life in seventh-century Wales.

LLOYD LAING
*Celtic Britain* (1979)

*The Hall of Cynddylan*

> Cynddylan's hall is dark tonight,
> No fire and no bed.
> I weep alone, cannot be comforted.

Cynddylan's hall is all in dark tonight,
No fire, no candle-flame:
Whose love, but love of God, can keep me sane?

Cynddylan's hall is dark tonight,
No fire, no gleam of light.
Grief for Cynddylan leaves me desolate.

Cynddylan's hall, its roof is charred and dark,
Such sparkling company sheltered here.
Woe betide him whose whole lot is despair.

Cynddylan's hall, the face of beauty fallen,
He's in his grave who yesterday stood tall.
With him alive no stone fell from the wall.

Cynddylan's hall, forsaken then tonight,
So snatched from his possession.
Death take me so and show me some compassion.

Cynddylan's hall, no safety here tonight,
On Hytwyth's high expanse
No lord, no soldiery, no defence.

Cynddylan's hall is dark tonight,
No fire and no music.
My tears carve out their ravage on my cheeks.

Cynddylan's hall is dark tonight,
No fire, the company's all gone.
My tears tumble down upon its ruin.

Cynddylan's hall, to see it pierces me,
No fire, roof open to the sky:
My lord is dead and here, alive, am I.

Cynddylan's hall, burned to the very ground,
After such comradeship,
Elfan, Cynddylan, Caeawc, all asleep.

Cynddylan's hall, anguish is here tonight.
Once it was held in honour:
Dead are the men and girls who kept it so.

Cynddylan's hall, too much to bear tonight,
Its chieftain lost, O
Merciful God, what can I do?

Cynddylan's hall, the roof is charred and dark
Because the Englishry wreaked havoc on
The pasture-land of Elfan and Cynddylan.

Cynddylan's hall is dark tonight,
I mourn Cyndrwynyn's line,
Cynon, Gwiawn and Gwyn.

Cynddylan's hall, my open wound,
After the bustle, all the mirth
I knew upon this hearth.

ANONYMOUS, 9th-century saga<br>trans. John Ormond

[1094] And the French brought a host to Gwynedd; and against them came Cadwgan ap Bleddyn, and he defeated them and drove them to flight, inflicting great slaughter upon them. And that battle was in Coedysbys. And at the close of that year the castles of Ceredigion and Dyfed were all taken except two castles, Pembroke and Rhyd-y-gors; and they were all razed to the ground and the spoils carried off by them, and Ceredigion and Dyfed were ravaged.

[1095] A year after that, the French ravaged Gower and Cydweli and Ystrad Tywi, and they remained waste. And in the middle of autumn William, king of England, moved a host against the Britons, but they sought a defence in their woods and their wilderness, and he returned home empty-handed and having gained naught.

[1108] A year after that, a folk of strange origin and customs, with nothing known of where they had been concealed in the

**60**  island for many years before that, were sent by king Henry to
Dyfed. And they occupied the whole cantref called Rhos, near
the estuary of the river called Cleddyf, and drove away all the
inhabitants from the land. And that folk had come from
Flanders, the land that lies near the Sea of Britain, because the
sea had overwhelmed the land and its bounds and had thrown
sand all over the ground, so that the whole land was unfruitful.

*The Chronicle of the Princes*
trans. Thomas Jones (1952)

### Welsh History

We were a people taut for war; the hills
Were no harder, the thin grass
Clothed them more warmly than the coarse
Shirts our small bones.
We fought, and were always in retreat,
Like snow thawing upon the slopes
Of Mynydd Mawr; and yet the stranger
Never found our ultimate stand
In the thick woods, declaiming verse
To the sharp prompting of the harp.

Our kings died, or they were slain
By the old treachery at the ford.
Our bards perished, driven from the halls
Of nobles by the thorn and bramble.

We were a people bred on legends,
Warming our hands at the red past.
The great were ashamed of our loose rags
Clinging stubbornly to the proud tree
Of blood and birth, our lean bellies
And mud houses were a proof
Of our ineptitude for life.

We were a people wasting ourselves
In fruitless battles for our masters,
In lands to which we had no claim,
With men for whom we felt no hatred.

We were a people, and are so yet.
When we have finished quarrelling for crumbs
Under the table, or gnawing the bones
Of a dead culture, we will arise,
Armed, but not in the old way.

R. S. THOMAS

The Welsh race has this characteristic throughout all its members . . . it resorts to the woods for homes and to war for peace. Easily angered, skilful in marching through intricate ways, the Welsh are not hampered by sandals for their feet nor by leggings; taught to endure cold, never inclined to give up toil; wearing a short tunic, they do not weigh down their body with armour, nor do they protect their side with a corslet nor their brow with a helmet . . . Rejoicing, as they do, in constant plunder and in bloodshed, it rarely happens that any of them die except through wounds; if any one can cast it up to a Welshman that a kinsman of his died without killing any man, he thinks it the greatest dishonour.

GUILLAUME LE BRETON, 12th century

### How the Welsh Can Be Conquered

Any prince who is really determined to conquer the Welsh and to govern them in peace must proceed as follows. He should first of all understand that for a whole year at least he must devote his every effort and give his undivided attention to the task which he has undertaken. He can never hope to conquer in one single battle a people which will never draw up its forces to engage an enemy army in the field, and will never allow itself to be besieged inside fortified strong-points. He can beat them only by patient and unremitting pressure applied over a long period. Knowing the spirit of hatred and jealousy which usually prevails among them, he must sow dissension in their ranks and do all he can by promises and bribes to stir them up against each other. In the autumn not only the marches but certain carefully chosen localities in the interior must be fortified

**62**    with castles, and these he must supply with ample provisions and garrison with families favourable to his cause. In the meantime he must make every effort to stop the Welsh buying the stocks of cloth, salt and corn which they usually import from England. Ships manned with picked troops must patrol the coast, to make sure that these goods are not brought by water across the Irish Sea or the Severn Sea, to ward off enemy attacks and to secure his own supply-lines. Later on, when wintry conditions have really set in, or perhaps towards the end of winter, in February and March, by which time the trees have lost their leaves, and there is no more pasturage to be had in the mountains, a strong force of infantry must have the courage to invade their secret strongholds, which lie deep in the woods and are buried in the forests. They must be cut off from all opportunity of foraging, and harassed, both individual families and larger assemblies of troops, by frequent attacks from those encamped around. The assault troops must be lightly armed and not weighed down with a lot of equipment. They must be strengthened with frequent reinforcements, who have been following close behind to give them support and to provide a base. Fresh troops must keep on replacing those who are tired out, and maybe those who have been killed in battle. If he constantly moves up new men, there need be no break in the assault. Without them this belligerent people will never be conquered, and even so the danger will be great and many casualties must be expected. What does it matter to an army of English mercenaries if their losses are great today? There is enough money to ensure that the ranks of battle will be filled again and more than filled tomorrow. To the Welsh, on the other hand, who have no mercenaries and no foreign allies, those who fall in battle are irreplaceable, at least for the time being.

GERALD OF WALES
*The Description of Wales* (1194)
trans. Lewis Thorpe

# OLD LAWS, KINGS, CASTLES

Three indispensables of a king: his priest to celebrate mass and to bless his food and drink; his bodyguard to execute his commands; his court judge to determine sentences. Three things which a king does not share with anyone: his treasurer, his hawk, and his thief.

*The Laws of Hywel Dda*, 10th–12th century

'Welshmen shall not have castles.'

from *The Statutes of Wales*
no. 4, Henry IV, c31

Hywel Dda, Howell the Good, was a grandson of Rhodri. He may well have taken Alfred as his model, and he certainly cultivated friendship with Wessex. Hywel was astute in statecraft, expanding his rule through a judicious marriage, and could be militant enough when the occasion demanded: on the death of his cousin in battle, he seized the kingdom of Gwynedd. Yet he is chiefly remembered for formulating a legal code based on the ancient laws which existed in Wales. He is said to have convened a great assembly at Whitland, Dyfed, attended by six representatives from each cantref (district) of Wales. Here, in Hendy-gwyn ar Daf, the White House on the Taf, Hywel and his lawyers conducted six weeks of negotiations which achieved the near-impossible: a consistent and unified legal code to apply throughout the country in place of the varying tribal laws and customs.

The laws survived Hywel's death, but the unity he had brought to parts of Wales did not. Peace never prevailed, because Wales, like England in this period, was divided into a number of small kingdoms whose rulers were generally more intent on pursuing their own quarrels than in making common cause. The years which followed Hywel's death saw further family quarrels and provincial feuds, usually over tenure of land, despite the new laws intended to eliminate this age-old problem.

from *Castles and Historic Places in Wales*
Wales Tourist Board (1974)

*From the Early Welsh Laws*

. . . A hundred cows for every *cantref* in his kingdom are to be paid as the fine for an insult to the king; and a rod of silver long enough to reach from the ground to the top of his head when he is sitting on his throne, as thick as his third finger, with three knobs at the top and three at the bottom, as thick as the rod; and a bowl of gold big enough to contain in it a full drink for the king, as thick as the finger-nail of a ploughman who has ploughed for seven years, with a golden cover on it as thick as the bowl and as broad as the king's face . . .

. . . Whoever kills the cat that guards the king's barn, or steals it, its head is to be set down on a clean level floor, and its tail is to be held up, and then wheaten grains are to be poured around

it until they cover the tip of its tail. Any other cat is worth four
legal pence . . . In law, essential qualifications of a cat are that
it should be perfect of ear and eye and tail and teeth and claws,
not singed by the fire; and that it should kill mice and not eat its
kittens, and should not be caterwauling every full moon . . .

## Concerning the Separation of Husband and Wife

If anyone send away his wife without lawful cause, and take
another in her place, by judgement the woman who has been
put out is entitled to come to her home, and be in her home
until the ninth day. And if on that day she is sent away, first let
all things which are hers go out from the house, and after the
last of the number, let her herself go out from the house.

The husband shall have all the pigs, the wife the sheep. The
husband shall have all the horses and mares, the oxen, and
cows, bullocks and heifers: the wife shall have the goats. Next
the household equipment shall be divided as follows: all the
vessels of milk, except one *baeol* are the wife's and all the
dishes, except one meat dish, that is *cigddysgl* are the husband's.
One cart and yoke are the wife's. All the jars and all the drinking vessels are the husband's. Of the bedding, the husband shall
have all the bedclothes which are beneath; the wife those
which are above. After he has taken another wife, the husband
is obliged to send the bedding to the wife whom he has
repudiated.

The husband shall have the cauldron, the brycan, and the
pillow and nithlen, and the coulter, and the wood-axe, and the
gimlet, and the fire-dog, and all the sickles except one, and the
gridiron. The wife shall have the pan and the tripod, the broad
axe and the sieve, the ploughshare and the one sickle, the flax
and the linseed, and the *trythgwd* except gold and silver. If there
has been anything of these two that is, *tlysau*, they shall be
divided into two equal parts, both as to linen things and as to
woollen things.

The husband shall have the barn and the grain and whatever
there is above ground and in the ground, and the hens and all
the geese and one cat; and if there are several [cats] all are the
wife's except the one, as stated above. The wife shall have the
meat which is salted and lying on the ground, and the cheese

**66**     that is fresh on the ground, but after the meats and cheeses are
hung up, the wife shall have none of them by right. The vessel
of butter, if it be not full, the wife shall have, and the ham likewise unless it be unbroached, and so much of the flour as she
herself can manage to bring in her own hands from the granary
into the house with the strength of her knees. Each one of them
shall have his personal clothing, except the cloaks, which
should be divided.

. . . A freeman's wife may give away her tunic and her mantle
and her kerchief and her shoes, and her flour and cheese and
butter and milk, without her husband's permission, and may
lend all the household utensils. The wife of a villein may not
give away anything without her husband's permission except
her headdress; and she cannot lend anything except her sieve
and riddle, and that only as far as her cry may be heard when
her foot is on her threshold . . .

      . . . An adult woman who elopes with a man and is taken by
him to a wood or a thicket or a house, and is violated and let go
again, if she complains to her family and in the courts, as proof
of her chastity a bull of three winters is to be taken and its tail is
to be shaved and smeared with fat, and then the tail is to be
thrust through a hurdle; and then the woman shall go into the
house and put her foot on the threshold and take the tail in her
hands; and a man shall come on either side of the bull with a
goad in the hand of each, to stir up the bull; and if she can hold
the bull she may take it for her insult-fine and as recompense
for her chastity; and if she cannot she may take as much of the
fat as sticks to her hands. A woman who gives herself up to a
man in wood or thicket, and is abandoned by the man to woo
another, and comes to complain to her family and to the courts,
if the man denies it let him swear an oath on a bell without a
clapper; but if he offers to make compensation, let him pay her
a penny as broad as her behind . . .

The Laws of Hywel Dda, 10th–12th century

Unfortunately no original version of the laws of Hywel Dda has
been preserved, but there are several manuscripts which cannot have been written later than the year 1200; two can be seen

in the showcases of the National Library at Aberystwyth, and from such documents historians have been able to visualize the system under which the Welsh lived until the time of the Tudors.

The state of society revealed is that of a tribal people, settled indeed upon the land, but retaining the outlook and instincts of a semi-nomadic race grouped according to ties of blood and kinship. The country was divided into 'commotes', which was the unit of local organization somewhat similar to the parish of today, these commotes themselves belonging to 'cantrefs', which were aggregations of two or more commotes. Within the commote the people were divided into three classes beneath the king, namely the free tribesmen, claiming connection by birth with the royal house of Cunedda, forming a large and aristocratic class of well-to-do free men; the bondmen, or servile tenants; and the strangers. These classes had each their own rights and their separate obligations; the king went on tour from one commote to another, when the bondmen bore the brunt of the trouble caused by his arrival with a small army of servants, huntsmen, horses and dogs. The wealthier people, who paid their dues in cash, also lived a roving life, moving their flocks from summer pastures on the hills to lowland winter grazing grounds; they kept their own flimsy structures on the higher grounds for summer dwelling places as well as the homesteads in the valley, a fact borne out by the innumerable recurrences of the words *hafod* (summer lodging) and *hendre* (homestead) in Welsh place names.

The spirit of the commote was widely different from that of the English manor. The manorial system was bound up with the idea of the village; but in Wales there were neither villages nor towns of any sort for centuries after the people had settled down. With the instinct of the herdsman, the Welsh had scattered themselves each on their own pastures; owing to the difficult nature of the ground, with its dingles, streams and precipitous slopes, the formation of a village as a centre for the community never appealed to them, and so we see that the small family farm, which is the agricultural unit of the present, has its roots in the most distant past. To conjure up a picture of the ancient commote is to describe a scene not very different from the aspect of the countryside today. Imagine a little valley winding among the foothills of any of the great mountain tracts, and let us see how historians fancy the scene as Hywel Dda depicts it. On the lower lands stood the homesteads of the free tribesmen, with the lands which they were cultivating and their grazing grounds and patches of woodland. Farther afield were the cottages of the bondmen, the poorer folk, situated on the less fertile slopes; and above these, again, was the uncultivated hill, where rights of grazing were in common, where the tribesmen would send their herds in the summer months, and from which from time to time newcomers would try to carve a squatter's holding. Centrally placed within the commote would be the Llan, the enclosure set apart for the support of the monks whose headquarters were one of the Celtic monasteries, and near it would be the demesne lands of the lord of the district, tilled by the services of the bondmen. The holdings of the tribesmen would be fairly large isolated farms, and the cottages of the bondmen tended to be grouped into small 'townships' – little clusters of houses too small to be described as villages but often in later ages marked by a chapel, a smithy or a public house. This is the Wales of today, just as it was the Wales of Hywel Dda; except where the feudal system was introduced in Norman times – as in the Vale of Glamorgan and Pembroke – the countryside of Wales has kept its characteristics of isolated farms and scattered cottages, the natural organization of an old semi-nomadic stock.

Apart from the layout of the countryside, the Welsh laws and customs were totally different from anything seen in England. There was a democratic, almost communistic spirit about the practices of the Welsh; property was conceived as common stock to be enjoyed by all, and from among the innumerable regulations concerning every class of individual and their respective rights we may notice in passing that the smith and the bard were the most important officials at Court, and that divorce was obtainable on sufficient grounds by either party without loss of status. The laws of inheritance, however, were quite the most important in creating and preserving a unique form of society. The English custom of primogeniture, the inheritance of the possessions by the eldest of the family, was unknown; the Welsh followed the principle of Gavelkind, which involved the subdivision of property among all the children equally. The laws were slightly different for bondmen and tribesmen, but the conception was the same; everyone was entitled to a share of the means of subsistence, so everything was lumped together and equally divided whenever a death occurred.

This was really the principle of the herdsman; among a nomad people flocks and herds could be divided ad infinitum, for the heirs could move off to fresh fields with their cluster of beasts, and in time they would increase and replenish the earth. Gavelkind, applied to a settled people, did, however, prove to be the weakest spot in the Welsh system. When grazing grounds were no longer unlimited, the continual subdivision of property meant smaller and smaller holdings, and the only escape from endless re-splitting was for some members of the family to renounce their share of the possessions. By medieval times this seems to have been fairly common, and probably accounts for the continuous supply of landless men of independent character who provided the great Welsh contingents of fighters on foreign fields. Ten thousand red-robed Welsh infantry and archers fought at Falkirk for Edward I, and twelve hundred Carmarthenshire men joined the Black Prince for Crecy and the siege of Calais. They were armed with bows and arrows, or long, light spears; the pay of the men was twopence a day, and their own chaplain and surgeon accompanied the force.

Gavelkind had other and less picturesque effects; it meant periodic inter-tribal strife, as the holdings of the more populous groups grew smaller, it encouraged the marriage of cousins and the inbreeding of a community already by isolation too much inclined in that direction, and it finally led to the most meagre holdings and individual poverty on the land.

EILUNED and PETER LEWIS
*The Land of Wales* (1937)

*The Choice Things of Man*

His King just, his Lord generous;
His Horse vigorous, his Greyhound swift,
His Hawk full of desire, his Land fertile,
His Oxen strong, his Sheep of a good breed,
His Swing long: his Victuals healthy,
His Drink pure, his Fire bright,

70 His Clothes comfortable, his House dry,
His Bed easy, his Wife chaste; his Maid notable, his Servant
    industrious,
His Son orderly, his Kinsman affectionate,
His Neighbour without deception; his Mill near,
His Church far off; his Spiritual Father wise
And his God merciful.

An ancient Welsh maxim in translation

### The Reign of Gruffudd ap Cynan

. . . He was renowned and famous both in lands far away and in those near to him. And then, he multiplied every kind of good thing in Gwynedd, and the inhabitants began to build churches in all directions there, and to set woods and plant them, and to make orchards and gardens and encircle them with fences and ditches, and to make walled buildings, and to support themselves from the produce of the earth in the manner of the Romans. And Gruffudd, too, made great churches for himself at the chief courts, and built courts and honourably gave continual feasts. Indeed, he made Gwynedd glitter then with whitewashed churches as the heavens with stars . . .

. . . He took a wife, Angharad by name, daughter of Owein son of Edwin, who the wise men of the kingdom say was of noble birth, well-grown, with fair hair, large-eyed, of fine shape, with queenly figure and strong limbs and well-made legs and the best of feet, and long fingers and thin nails; kindly and eloquent, and good at food and drink; wise and prudent, a woman of good counsel, merciful towards her kingdom, charitable to the needy, and just in all things . . .

ANONYMOUS, 12th century

### The Death of Llewellyn ap Gruffudd (Lluwellyn the Last)

The object of Llewellyn's sudden journey from North Wales to Aber Edwy, was to enter into consultation with some of the chief persons of the district, whom he was anxious to engage in his service against the English sovereign, whose forces were then invading the principality in different quarters. On his arrival, however, at Aber Edwy, he found himself fatally disappointed; for instead of meeting friends, he perceived that he was nearly surrounded by the forces of his enemy. Edmund Mortimer and John Giffard, having had intimation of his road, marched to meet him with a large body of troops from Herefordshire. Considering, from the numbers of the enemy, that resistance would be in vain, Llewellyn withdrew with his men (some represent him as attended but by a single squire) to Builth; and as the ground was covered with snow, he is said to have had his horse's shoes reversed, in order to deceive his pursuers. This is the tradition still preserved at the place, which adds, that the smith, whose name was Madoc-goch-min-mawr, 'Red-haired wide-mouthed Madoc', betrayed the secret to the English commanders. Llewellyn succeeded in passing the bridge at Builth, and breaking it down before the arrival of his pursuers. (Some state, however, that he merely retreated across it.)

Having thus missed their prey, the English party returned down the river, and crossed eight miles below at a ferry known to some of them, and still called Caban Twm Bach, or Little Tom's Ferry-boat. (The question is, whether this was from the right or left bank, and whether it was in consequence of the destruction of the bridge at Builth.) It is supposed that the garrison of Builth, overawed by the presence of so large an English force in the neighbourhood, refused to treat with the Welsh prince; and that he, in consequence, immediately proceeded to the westward, with the view of returning to North Wales, or of gaining Caermarthenshire. He ascended the vale of Irvon on the southern side, for about three miles, and crossed the river above Llanynis, over a bridge called Pont-y-Coed, or the 'Bridge of the Wood'; at which place some accounts represent him as having previously left the principal part of his troops. Having reached the opposite bank, he stationed the few troops who had accompanied him on the northern side of the river, where the ground was peculiarly favourable for defending the passage. On the arrival of the English forces, they made a fruitless attempt to gain the bridge; but a knight of the party, Sir Elias Walwyn (a descendant of Sir Philip Walwyn of Hay), discovered a ford at some distance, where a detachment crossed the

72 river. These coming unexpectedly on the rear of the Welsh troops, routed them without difficulty. Llewellyn himself, either in the flight, or while watching the movements of the main body, who were still on the other side of the river, was attacked unarmed in the melée, in a small dell, about two hundred yards below the scene of action, from him called Cwm Llewellyn, or 'Llewellyn's Dingle', by one Adam Francton, who plunged a spear into his body, and without further noticing his victim, joined in the pursuit of the enemy. On his return, probably with the view of plundering the slain, he discovered that the person whom he had wounded (for he was still alive) was the Prince of Wales; and on stripping him, a letter in cipher and his privy seal were found concealed about him. Francton, overjoyed at perceiving whom he had in his power, immediately cut off his head, and sent it to the King of England: the body was dragged to a little distance, and buried in a place still known by the name of Cefn-y-Bedd, or Cefnbedd Llewellyn, 'the Ridge of Llewellyn's Grave', near the banks of the Irvon.

THEOPHILUS JONES (1759–1812)
*History of the County of Brecknock* (2 vols., 1805 and 1809)

from *The Death of Llywelyn ap Gruffudd*

I've lost a lord and I grasp a long fear,
for a hand has killed the lord of the court . . .

A lord who was roofstone where the Welsh gather,
   of the line which should hold sway in Aberffraw.
Lord Christ, how grieved I am for him!
True lord, deliverance came by him.
His fall came from the heavy sword-stroke,
from the long swords crushing him down . . .

The heart is chilled under a breast of fear,
lust shrivels like dry branches.
See you not the way of the wind and the rain?
See you not the oaks beat together?
See you not the sea stinging the land?
   See you not the truth equipping?
See you not the sun sailing the sky?

See you not the stars have fallen?
Do you not believe God, demented men?
   See you not that the world is in danger?
A sigh to you, God, that the sea may come over the land!
   Why are we left to linger?
There's no retreat from the prison of fear,
   there's nowhere to dwell, alas for the dwelling!
There is no counsel, no lock, no opening,
   no way of delivery from terror's sad counsel.
Each retinue was worthy of him
and every warrior stayed about him,
every dogged one swore by his hand,
every ruler, every province was his;
every district, every homestead's invaded,
every clan and line now falls.
The weak and the strong were kept by his hand,
every child now weeps in his cradle.
Little good it did me to be tricked
into leaving my head on, with no head on him.
A head which, falling, made panic welcome;
a head which, falling, made it better to give up;
a soldier's head, a head for praise henceforth;
a leader's head, a dragon's head was on him,
head of fair, dogged Llywelyn; it shocks the world
   that an iron stake should pierce it.
My lord's head, a harsh-falling pain is mine,
my soul's head, which has no memorial;
a head which owned honour in nine hundred lands,
   with the homage of nine hundred feasts;
a king's head, iron flew from his hand;
a king's head, a proud hawk breaching a gap;
a regal head of a thrusting wolf,
may the head of heaven be his patron!
A magnificent lord, a blessed host with him;
splendidly eager to voyage to Brittany.
True regal king of Aberffraw,
may Heaven's blessed kingdom be his abode!

GRUFFUDD AB YR YNAD COCH, 13th century
trans. Gwyn Williams

It is as difficult to get a definite idea of Owen's character from the bards who saw him and sat at his table as it is from the English chroniclers who associate him with storms and magic. It is easy to make a list of details – he was the people's golden sword, his gifts were coats of mail, he well understood the intricacies of alliterative song, stern was he towards those of alien tongue, but the defender of the oppressed men of South Wales. Iolo describes him while longing for his appearance to deliver Wales – for his tall form, for the three lions azure on his golden shield. But the personality of Owen remains far off and mysterious. His sons fought and fell in battle – he was at few battles, if at any. We see him in council, tall and majestic, but even there he is the personification of political dreams rather than a real man. It may be that he tried to surround himself with mystery; every disappearance as well as every appearance increased his influence. Had he the superstition which is the shadow of fatalism? He consulted a seer when at 'Merlin's city, now called Carmarthen', and was told that he would be taken under a black flag. A soldier who helped to defend Calais, and who wrote a history of Wales in the turmoil of a busy soldier's life over a century later, came from the fringe of Owen's country. He gives the facts of Owen's life as they had been warped and confused by popular tradition, and the various popular beliefs about the causes of his disappearance – that he could not pay his mercenaries, that he really died, that he had lost faith in his mission. One early morning the Abbot of Valle Crucis was walking along the hillside above the abbey, and praying. Owen Glendower appeared and said:

'Sir Abbot, you have risen too early.' 'No,' answered the Abbot; 'it is you who have risen too early – by a hundred years.'

And Glendower knew that he was not the Owen that prophecy had spoken of, and he disappeared.

In England Owen Glendower was known only from the descriptions of those that hated and feared him. One proof of his greatness is that in English tradition the prejudices against him disappeared. In Shakespeare his belief in magic remains; his boasts of a poetic gift which enabled him to frame to the harp 'many an English ditty lovely well', and of his power to summon spirits from the vasty deep, are contrasted to his disadvantage with the rough manners of hasty, swearing Hotspur. But the final contrast is between the arrogance of the English custodian of Welsh castles and the dreamy, mystical leader of Welsh rebellion. On the one side are:

> Harsh rage,
> Defect of manners, want of government,
> Pride, haughtiness, opinion, and disdain,
> The least of which, haunting a nobleman,
> Loseth men's hearts, and leaves behind a stain
> Upon the beauty of all parts besides.

On the other hand, many of the best qualities of a ruler are described in the final English verdict on Owen Glendower:

> In faith, he is a worthy gentleman,
> Exceedingly well read, and profited
> In strange concealments, valiant as a lion,
> And wondrous affable, and as bountiful
> As mines of India.

SIR OWEN M. EDWARDS (1858–1920)
in *Land of My Fathers* (1915)

*The Rebellion of Owen Glendower*

The news of the victory of Bryn Glas spread at incredible speed throughout Wales; and to Master Sparrow's revolutionary delight vast numbers of armed peasants, many of them travelling at their own charges, gathered to the Prince's standard from every quarter.

Before August of 1402, though both Glyndyfrdwy and Sycharth had long been blackened ruins, Owen had several separate armies, amounting in all to over ten thousand men, whose bivouac fires, moving as if by magic through all parts of Wales, caused desperate appeals to reach King Henry.

From Abergavenny and Usk, from Cardigan, from Caerleon, from Carmarthen, from Newport, from Cardiff, and even from Gwent, these cries for help came.

Owen's own hopes were as much increased as Master

Sparrow's, and his purposes as much strengthened and hardened, by this accession to the cause of what was practically the
whole mass of the common people of Wales. It *was* a peasants'
revolt, as Robert Whitney had predicted it would be, and
though no castle of any importance had yet fallen into their
hands, the local peasants of Glamorgan and Gwent and even of
Cardigan had avenged themselves with delicious joy for three
centuries of contempt by pillaging and burning every single
mansion where the landlord was an Englishman or a pro-
English Welshman.

JOHN COWPER POWYS (1872–1963)
*Owen Glendower* (1941)


. . . Owen Glendower, according to his accustomed manner,
robbing and spoiling within the English borders, caused all the
forces of the shire of Hereford to assemble together against
them, under the conduct of Edmund Mortimer, Earl of March.
But coming to try the matter in battle, whether by treason or
otherwise, so it fortuned that the English power was dis-
comfited, the Earl taken prisoner, and above a thousand of his
people slain in the place. The shameful villainy used by the
Welshwomen towards the dead carcasses was such as honest
ears would be ashamed to hear and continent tongues to speak
thereof. The dead bodies might not be buried without great
sums of money given for liberty to convey them away . . .

HOLINSHED
*Chronicles* (1585)


There is a somewhat comic story related of the family of Owen
Tudor, the husband of Henry the Fifth's widow, Catherine of
France, whose mother, it seems, resided in Anglesea. Although
of high blood, their fortunes do not appear to have allowed the
family to live according to English ideas of rank. Catherine had
announced her intention of marrying the young Welshman,
who first gained her good graces by a combination of agility
and awkwardness; for, in dancing before her, not being able to
recover himself, in a turn, he fell into her lap as she sat on a

little stool with many of her ladies about her. The match she proposed to herself was considered beneath her dignity, owing to the supposed obscurity of Owen Tudor's birth. A deputation of English lords was therefore sent to Anglesea to report the style of his mother's living. They found themselves in as great perplexity as Sancho in reporting his interview with Dulcinea, for the matron was discovered sitting in a field surrounded by her goats and eating a dried herring on her knees, having no other table.

The lords did not dare to relate the case exactly as they found it, for the fair Catherine had already made her election, and they saw the ill policy of too strictly adhering to truth: their account, therefore, ran as follows:

They said 'the lady was seated in state, surrounded by her javelin men, in a spacious palace, eating her repast from a table whose value was so great, that she would not take hundreds of pounds for it.'

The queen became the wife of this illustrious lady's son; but still reports of the meanness and vileness of his relations were brought to her ear, and she urged him to send for some of those chiefs of whom he boasted, that she might judge for herself of their dignity and importance. Owen, confident in the superiority of his lineage, sent for two of his cousins from Anglesea, Ivan ap Meredudd and Hywel ap Llywelyn, who accordingly arrived in all their savage pomp, and were presented to his bride. Catherine, surprised at their manly beauty, strength, and goodly nature, spoke to them with great affability; but after trying them in several languages, discovered that all but the native British was unknown to them, on which she laughed and exclaimed, 'that they were the goodliest dumb creatures she had ever beheld.'

COSTELLO
*North Wales* (1845)


To bring order to those parts of Wales not controlled by the government at Westminster, Henry VIII held a meeting with the Border barons at Shrewsbury in 1534 and then established Rowland Lee as Lord President of the Marches. Under him all those who had committed crimes in Wales were tried in the nearest English county and he was given the power to put down crime by capital punishment. He was one of Thomas Cromwell's men and in a letter to his master he said, 'If we should do nothing but as the common law will, these things so far out of order will never be redressed.' In another letter he describes how an outlaw was 'brought in in a sack, trussed on a horse, and hanged on a gallows for a sign on market day in the presence of three hundred people'. Of any outlaw he grimly jokes, 'If he be taken he playeth his pageant.' Good fun for the English counties of the borderland, where they were not short of this kind of entertainment in Bishop Lee's day. Ludlow was his official base but he had another near Shrewsbury where he had a manor. And of course he held courts up and down the Border. He disliked the granting to Wales of Justices of the Peace and said of this in 1536, 'If one thief shall try another all we have here begun is foredone.' He showed little sympathy with traditional Welsh ways and it is said that it was he who first compelled Welshmen to shorten their names and use only the last element as a surname. But the Welsh continued to call themselves *ap* this and *ap* that up to the end of the century. In a play called *Sir John Oldcastle* (c. 1600) by Drayton and others, Davey, who has been involved in a Welsh clan quarrel at Hereford, offers as his surety for bail 'her coozin ap Ries, ap Evan, ap Morrice, ap Morgan, ap Lluellyn, ap Madoc, ap Meredith, ap Griffin, ap Davy, ap Owen, ap Shinken Shones'. All one person, of course, but the judge, whether unfamiliar with the Welsh way of naming people or fancying himself as something of a wit, as judges are apt to do, abruptly says, 'Two of the most sufficient are enow.' (He meant the most well-off.) But I blame Henry VIII, not his servant Rowland Lee, for my present surname, which one of my daughters has lately renounced.

GWYN WILLIAMS
*The Land Remembers* (1977)

## Dunraven Castle

There is little doubt that in the fortress of Dyndryvan Caractacus held his court; for, on the death of his father (and his uncle, Manawyden, having relinquished his claim to the throne – 'though it was his of right, according to the true

principle of the sovereignty' – in favour of one 'so much super-
ior to himself'), the civil sovereignty and war sovereignty were
united in the person of a sage and soldier, so eminently quali-
fied to uphold the glory, and maintain the independence, of his
subjects. The Welsh are naturally proud of a ruler, whose
renown has endured for seventeen centuries, and to whom history refers in all her records, as the model of a 'patriot, hero,
king'. It is, therefore, no common ground we tread, when we
visit the Castle of Dunraven, and examine the few remains of
thick walls, built by the Normans, above foundations which
the Britons raised.

The rocky headland on which the castle stands is called
'Witches' Point': why we were unable to ascertain. An old
watch-tower, modernized into a pretty view-house, stands on
the verge of an adjacent cliff. The land here slopes upward; and
along these high lands, it is said, in times happily gone by, the
wreckers placed false lights to lure unhappy mariners upon the
merciless rocks underneath. There is a tradition, indeed, that a
later Lord of Dunraven, 'one Walter Vaughan', having lost by
extravagance his paternal estates, throve by this wicked practice, until Providence returned the poisoned chalice to his own
lips – his two children having perished close beside the home
they had left as merchant voyagers, their own father's hand
having guided the light that wiled their vessel among the
breakers.

S. C. HALL
*The Book of South Wales* (1861)

### Rhyd-y-gors Castle, Pembroke Castle

[1096] A year after that, died William fitz Baldwin, who had
established the castle of Rhyd-y-gors by command of the king
of England. And after his death the garrison left the castle
empty. And then Brycheiniog and Gwent and Gwynllŵg did
homage to the French, and the French moved a host to Gwent
and after they had gained naught they returned home empty-
handed. And the Britons slew them in the place called Celli
Tarfawg. And thereupon the French led frequent raids into
Brycheiniog and thought to destroy the land completely. And
when they had failed to have their will in aught, they returned

home; and then they were slain by the sons of Idnerth ap Cadwgan, Gruffudd and Ifor, in the place called Aber-llech. The castles, however, still remained intact, with their garrisons in them.

In that year Uchdryd ab Edwin and Hywel ap Goronwy and many other leaders and the war-band of Cadwgan ap Bleddyn went to the castle of Pembroke and despoiled it completely, and ravaged the land; and they returned home with vast spoil.

*The Chronicle of the Princes*
trans. Thomas Jones (1952)

*Manorbier Castle*

. . . About three miles from Pembroke Castle is the fortified mansion known as Manorbier – there the house stands, visible from afar because of its turrets and crenellations, on the top of a

hill which is quite near the sea and which on the western side reaches as far as the harbour. To the north and north-west, just beneath the walls, there is an excellent fishpond, well constructed and remarkable for its deep waters. On the same side there is a most attractive orchard, shut in between the fishpond and a grove of trees, with a great crag of rock and hazelnut trees which grow to a great height. At the east end of the fortified promontory, between the castle, if I may call it such, and the church, a stream of water which never fails winds its way along a valley, which is strewn with sand by the strong sea winds. It runs down from a large lake, and there is a water-mill on its bank. To the west it is washed by a winding inlet of the Severn sea which forms a bay quite near to the castle and yet looks out towards the Irish Sea . . . This is a region rich in wheat, with fish from the sea and plenty of wine for sale. What is more important than all the rest is that, from its nearness to Ireland, heaven's breath smells so wooingly here.

GERALD OF WALES
*The Journey through Wales* (1191)
trans. Lewis Thorpe

*Cardigan Castle*

[1220] In that year, about the feast of Ieuan y Coed, Llywelyn, prince of Gwynedd, gathering to him the princes and leading men of all Wales, moved a mighty host against the Flemings of Rhos and Pembroke because of the frequent attacks they made upon the Welsh against the Welsh, and for violating the terms of the peace and the truce which the king and the leading men of England had made between the English and the Welsh. And on his first expedition he took by force the castle of Cardigan, which first the Welsh had destroyed and then the Flemings had repaired. And after the castle had been taken by force, some of the garrison were slain, and others burnt and others bound in prison; and the castle was all thrown to the ground.

*The Chronicle of the Princes*
trans. Thomas Jones (1952)

We are being authorized by the Parliament to view and consider what garrisons and places of strength are fit to be demolished, and we finding that the Castle of Haverfordwest is not tenable for the service of the State, and yet that it may be possest by ill-affected persons, to the prejudice of the peace of these parts, these are to authorize and require you to summon . . . ye inhabitants of the towne and country of Haverfordwest, and that they forthwith demolish the workes, walls and towers of the said Castle, soe as that the said Castle may not be possesst by the enemy, to the endangering of the peace of these parts . . . If a speedy course be not taken to fulfil the commands of this warrant, I shall be necessitated to consider of settling a garrison.

OLIVER CROMWELL, 1648

### *Caernarvon Castle*

That most magnificent badge of our subjection.

THOMAS PENNANT (1726–98)
*Tours in Wales* (2 vols., 1778 and 1781)

### *Powys Castle*

The venerable Powys Castle is going fast into decay. The buildings are in a state of dilapidation; the gardens and grounds are neglected and the pride and ornament of the park is being removed for the sake of the timber. What the hand of time is doing for the one, the hand of avarice is doing for the other; so that at no distant period the beauty and magnificence of Powys will be no more.

EVANS
*Tour through North Wales* (1798)

How aweful is the silence of the waste,
Where nature lifts her mountains to the sky.
Majestic solitude, behold the tower
Where hopeless Owen, long imprison'd, pin'd,
And wrung his hands for liberty, in vain.

J. M. W. TURNER
(in the Catalogue for the Royal Academy
Exhibition, 1800. Turner exhibited
a picture of Dolbadarn Castle)

## Harlech Castle

Harlech Castle, on Cardigan Bay, is twin brother of Carnarvon
and Conway, to which it certainly bears a strong family likeness, being ornamented with very similar round towers at each
corner; the entrance is likewise between two circular turrets,
and an extensive open court stands in the middle. This was the
last fortress in Wales that held out for Charles I; and the garrison did not yield till only twenty-eight men were left alive. One
tower is called after Margaret of Anjou, who found a refuge
here during her adversity; and we saw some frightful dungeons
within the walls, which had probably served as a prison and a
tomb to many brave princes and bards during those early times
when it was as customary to shut men up twenty or thirty years
in darkness and solitude, as now to lock up a rebellious child
during ten minutes in a closet.

The principal staircase here had entirely fallen down, which
I was not perfectly inconsolable to perceive, because in every
ruin there generally is a narrow tottering ascent, scarcely prac-
ticable, and quite in the dark, which tourists are expected to
grope and scramble up at all hazards. If the stairs of every
ancient keep-tower I have mounted in my time could be piled
one above another, they would go a considerable way towards
reaching the moon. A—— at last succeeded in rummaging out
what he considered a tolerable flight of steps; indeed, he cares
so little to encounter a mile of ruinous perpendicular stairs, that
if he passed a day on the tread-mill it would apparently be a sort

of rest to him. I was on the point of yielding to my fate, and took *le premier pas*, when the guide unexpectedly interposed, declaring, that though 'some gentlemen of great steadiness had been known to reach the summit of that tower in safety, he never could scale it himself, and dared not undertake now to accompany us on the enterprise'. This very rational view of the subject appeared so convincing, that I gladly retraced the three steps I had already mounted, while A— — unflinchingly proceeded to escalade the castle with a degree of steadiness that an engineer might emulate, and soon emerged on the highest pinnacle of a crumbling battlement, whence he probably saw a very extended horizon of sea.

C. SINCLAIR
*Sketches and Stories of Wales and the Welsh* (1834)


## Penrhyn Castle

The first day at Bangor must inevitably be devoted to the black marble castle of Penrhyn, recently built by Mr Pennant, with magnificence worthy of those old feudal times, when great men kept troops of retainers, and lived in a patriarchal way, having all their sons, their sons' wives, and their families, domesticated in the house. Now a very large house is seldom filled above once or twice in a year, looking cold and desolate at all other times; therefore it can scarcely create surprise that few such ornamental palaces as this are built in the present day. The park is surrounded by a high massy wall – the gates so strong that those of Newgate are a joke to them – and the castle itself used to be more inaccessible to intruders than any enchanted palace in the 'Arabian Nights' . . .

C. SINCLAIR
*Sketches and Stories of Wales and the Welsh* (1834)


## Conway Castle

Conway is admirably situated and every view around it is worthy of the painter's pencil. We proceeded immediately to the castle, the ruins of which are extremely extensive and grand. Near the entrance we were annoyed by a swarm of children

who rushed out of the neighbouring houses, begging for 'a ha'pence, pleace, ma'am; a ha'pence, pleace, sair', words which they were taught to utter in a whining tone and which they continue repeating as long as they dare follow a party of strangers in defiance of any remonstrance on their parts. This is a very common nuisance in some parts of Wales and it is a matter of regret that the cottagers do not foresee what a deep and lasting mischief they are doing to their children by initiating them into such degrading practices which are conducive only to idleness and poverty.

SMITH
*Guide to Bangor* (1835)

*Newport Castle and Chepstow Castle*

A gentleman who has fallen into bad ways and sunk to be a crossing-keeper can hardly look more disreputable and shabby than does Newport Castle. Its towers have been reduced in height, modern windows knocked through the walls, and large portions destroyed. The building, such as it is, dates to the fourteenth century . . . Similarly Chepstow Castle. The poor, half-ruined castle took to beer and became a brewery.

S. BARING GOULD
*South Wales* (1905)

### At Strata Florida

This afternoon on the edge of autumn
our laughter feathers the quiet air
over tombs of princes. We idle
in an old nave, lightly approach
old altars. Our eyes, our hands
know fragments only; from these
the Abbey climbs and arches into the past.
We look up and find
only our own late August sky.

Ystrad Fflûr, your shadows fall
benevolently still on your ancient lands
and on us too, who touch your stones
not without homage. Take our laughter
on your consenting altars,
and to the centuries borne up
by your broken pillars, add
the light weight of an hour
at the end of summer.

RUTH BIDGOOD

# V

# FARMING, DROVING, FISHING

*Agricultural Proverb*

January will strike down.
February will despoil a giant.
March will slay.
April will flay.
May will raise the heart.
June will make a merry door-way.
July, a merry cattle-fold.
August, a merry host.
September rejoices the birds.
October, – cheerful is social intercourse.
November begins the lamentation.
December, – beware its anger.

*Iolo MSS* (Welsh Manuscript Society, 1848)
trans. Taliesin Williams

Rhos-y-grug was a poor farm. As with most farm-names in the district, the name, meaning 'the moorland of the heather', was a good description of the farm itself. Originally the place had been a *ty unnos*, a 'one-night' house, built in the days when a man could become a house-owner if he could build his house on common land overnight to the extent that smoke could come out of the chimney by morning. Tradition had it that it was Daniel's great-grandfather who had dug up the land, 'every inch of it', and had taken from the earth the stones that he had used for the boundary walls around the fields. However, the fields were still the preserve of the heather, and Daniel used to love quoting an old piece of doggerel:

> Gold 'neath the fern-leaves,
> Silver 'neath the gorse,

and then in a deep, doleful voice,

> Famine 'neath the heather.

Daniel was a bachelor about forty years old at this time, living with his widowed mother; she always used to refer to him as 'this boy of mine' even when he had become a grown man. In the eyes of the neighbours, the son was rather aimless as a farmer. Instead of ploughing properly he would merely scratch the surface of the land. He would also sell a bullock before fattening it and do as little as he could to help nature with the tasks that came with the seasons of the year. After blundering through some sort of a day's work, Daniel's pleasure would be to leave everything at the end of the day to go to the village shop or the smithy for a chat with anybody who happened to be there. Rhos-y-grug was a secondary thing and, after the sermon delivered by the man from America, the poor destitute crops, the crooked trees, and the stony fields (stones always seemed to come from somewhere all the time) were far less real than the gold of Havilah and the bdellium and the onyx stone.

T. HUGHES JONES
from *The Squire of Havilah*
trans. T. Glynne Davies in *The Penguin Book of Welsh Short Stories*
ed. Alun Richards (1976)

... a well-balanced man who combines rectitude, industry and sound farming with a range of other interests and accomplishments is a man to be taken seriously. He is known as a *dyn o bwysau* (a man of weight), or a *dyn o farn* (a man with judgement) whose opinion on any matter is valued and quoted.

I have been told by several people who have studied Welsh farming from a technical standpoint that the upland farmer tends to be conservative in his methods, unambitious and often even lazy. This view overlooks the fact that he has not yet completely succumbed to the materialistic values of the modern world which tends to measure everything in terms of production and profit. Such judgements which measure one society by the standards of another are, of course, quite unscientific. The countryman is content with a relatively low standard of living only to the extent to which prestige in his community is not determined by economic factors. It is not always easy for an observer, obsessed with the value which the modern world attaches to 'efficiency', to appreciate that to many a Welsh farmer, even today, writing a poem or an essay for an *eisteddfod*, or attending a drama practice or a preaching festival may be more important than producing surplus wealth. There is hardly a farmer in Llanfihangel who would suffer the loss of face involved in carrying hay on Sunday, however tempting the weather. Loss of crops is preferable to the loss of status which would result from unfaithfulness, not only to one's God, but to the standards cherished by one's forebears. Again, the countryman is fond of conversation, and his status is affected by the number of friends he has outside the locality. Therefore, he may consider it well worthwhile to lose a day's ploughing in order to attend an auction, even though there is nothing he wants to buy or sell. There will be the exchange of news with friends from a wider area, and this will enrich the discussion on his own hearth and on the hearths of his neighbours during subsequent evenings. People who neglect the non-economic aspects of life are criticized by their neighbours on the ground that 'they think of nothing but the penny'.

ALWYN D. REES
*Life in a Welsh Countryside* (1975)


### Welsh Farmers' Wives

... in middle age, seem to me to develop a type so uniform and so prevalent that it is sometimes impossible to believe that a casual group of them are not all members of a single family. And a very good type it is, too – a sallow or slightly brown firm, capable face, with a good jaw, black eyebrows, and dark reso-lute-looking eyes, that give one the idea of being able to light with passion somewhat easily, and make one think, somehow, of those Welshwomen of old who did such wild work on Saxon corpses after Mortimer's defeat at Pilleth.

This suggestion, however, is an outrageous libel on the good ladies who bring their butter and chickens into Corwen market

from the valleys of Denbigh and Merioneth. The tall hats, I
need not say, have long disappeared. Caermarthen market,
twenty-five years ago, saw the last of them; but the Welsh-
woman still has a distinct look about her headgear. She is given
to wearing somewhat masculine hats of felt or straw, wearing
them not seldom, over a white cap. But this is, perhaps, rather
among the most humble class. The farmer's wife, too, though
her husband may only hold fifty or a hundred acres, comes into
preaching or market almost always in a trap of some sort, and,
as one knows well, this is a matter of thrift, not of display it is a
pleasant thing to note. A country of small farmers surely
breeds an admirable race of women! They are lifted above the
squalor and the hopelessness of the farm-labourer's life, and
yet, on the other hand, not, as a class, tempted to become social
hybrids. They may have to work hard, and even live hard, but
they have independence, at any rate, and a settled home, and a
good position in the rustic democracy, and, so long as the rent is
paid, may reasonably count, in Wales, on seeing their home
remain indefinitely in the family, and their children's children
succeed them. As to the maidens of North Wales, they show
beyond a doubt a high average of comeliness.

ARTHUR BRADLEY
*Highways and Byways in North Wales* (1898)

Mr Jenkin Thomas, son of a tenant farmer, living in the neighbourhood of Cardiff, gives the following description of the
house in which he was brought up: 'We were a family of thirteen – eleven children and our parents – living in this house on
the farm. There were three bedrooms in the house and two
front rooms, and a small back kitchen, a small pantry, and a
small dairy. In consequence, we, as a family, had to put three
beds in the same room, and seven of us slept in the same room,
and we had not room even to walk between these three beds.
We had to go over a bed to get into bed. The servant-men, in
consequence, had to sleep out in the buildings, and that was a
great inconvenience to us . . .'
    Miss Kate Jenkins, while speaking as to farms in the Vale of
Towy, and admitting that the buildings are on the whole
improving, instanced several bad cases known to her, adding,

as a general remark, that 'Welsh farmers will inhabit houses no English farmer would live in' . . .

Mr Thomas Davies, a tenant farmer, who gave his evidence at Llansawel, in Carmarthenshire, specified certain very poor buildings, and spoke in particular of one farmhouse as 'having one sleeping-room upstairs, where both the sexes sleep, with no divisions between them, no ceiling overhead between them and the slate roof, and the wind and the snow getting in through the crevices' . . .

SIR JOHN RHŶS and DAVID BRYNMOR-JONES
*The Welsh People* (1900)

*Agricultural Proverb*

A small bagful of March dust is worth a large bag of the king's gold.

A swarm of bees, if had in May, is worth eight oxen-load of hay.

A June swarm is good if healthy. A July swarm is not worth a straw.

If the grass grows in February, it will not grow much after throughout the year.

If the meadow grows in March, plenty will be seen to follow.

Happy our lot, if a mild April will clothe [with green] the ground and the branches of the grove.

A showery May will produce a loaded land of corn and hay.

The month of June, it is well if it be partly wet and partly dry.

It is poison to the horse and ox, if July be not dry.

*Iolo MSS* (Welsh Manuscript Society, 1848)
trans. Taliesin Williams

The Welsh have always been primarily shepherds and herdsmen and, as Rees has stressed, their homes, 'situated on the hill slopes at the edge of the woodlands, as described by Giraldus, were eminently suitable for a pastoral life'. But in the summer months the herds and flocks were frequently taken to the pastures on the higher ground. For this purpose the summer-house was necessary; this is the *hafdy* of the Laws, the *hafod* or *hafoty* as contrasted with the *hendref* or *gaeafdy* (winter house). Indeed, the Laws refer too to an autumn house, the *cynhaeafdy*. The *hafod* season in the Venedotian Code was from the beginning of May to August; in the Demetian, from the beginning of May to September; and in the 'Gwentian', from the beginning of May to the end of September.

The Laws have no details which make possible a reconstruction of the *hafdy*, but from the valuation, it is clear that the house was of a slight and even temporary character. This practice of transhumance however persisted throughout the ages and the many place-names testify to its former universality. Even today, in the sheep-farming districts of central Wales in particular, almost the whole household of some of the valley farms moves into a distant *lluest*, a moorland house often several miles away, for the sheep-washing and -shearing duties which extend over several weeks. As an example, this is the practice of several valley-farmers in the Llanbrynmair (Montgomeryshire) district who with members of their families and their servants migrate annually for a short period to the high sheep-walks of the Pumlumon uplands. Another modern development of the same tradition of transhumance is the widespread Welsh practice of 'wintering' flocks, which have spent the summer months on the moorlands, on the rich lowland of some of the valley farms often many miles from the holding of the farmer concerned.

IORWERTH C. PEATE
*The Welsh House* (1946)

*In Welsh Uplands*

Above the glowing rowan trees
A ploughshare rustles slowly through the stubble
Where Puw the ploughman, lean and puckered,
Plods on alone beneath benignant stars,
Breaking the sullen turf at night because
The rustic lore he lives by prophesies
A spell of mist and clogging rain tomorrow.

**94**

His old, white horse, Abednego,
Walks wearily like Puw,
Both wondering how soon
They'll reach the last long hedge-row
And stumble home to deep and dreamless sleep.

They have been here for centuries,
The man, the horse, the rustling plough,
Taming these harsh, high hills:
Undaunted mountain trio
United in a true poetic triad,
Deploying skill and strength and craft
Against the wicked whimsies of the weather,
And winning many battles overnight
By native wisdom and unending toil.

Puw and Abednego are both hill-born,
Descendants of those sinewy progenitors
Who fought the foiling elements,
Subdued the soil and fashioned
With cunning their clean furrows
Across these cloudy acres year by year,
Writing the runes of this Cistercian range.

The masters of these hills
Were tough and frugal, silent men,
Though eloquent enough in prayer
And turning up a poet now and then:
They usually died old and bent
But still unbeaten by life's labours
And proudly spurning any alien speech.

A. G. PRYS-JONES (1888–1987)


*The Black and White Sheep and the Blazing Tree*

. . . And then Peredur travelled on until he came to a beautiful
valley, and there was a river in the valley, and the sides of the
valley were wooded with fair smooth trees of equal height, and
there was many a fine meadow in the valley. And on one side

of the river there was a flock of white sheep, and on the other side a flock of black sheep; and when one of the black sheep bleated, one of the white sheep would come to them, and would become pure black; and when one of the white sheep bleated one of the black sheep would come to them, and would become pure white. And he saw a tree on the river bank, and one half of the tree was blazing up to its very top, and the other half in leaf and with its bark growing beautifully . . .

ANONYMOUS, 12th century
*The White Book Mabinogion* (1907)
trans. J. G. Evans

A small farmer of Llanyblodwel told me that his father always destroyed black lambs and that formerly the farmers killed all black sheep that came into their possession as they are under the impression that the evil spirit dwelt in them. When their black sheep were killed their owners went on their knees on the ground and prayed. The same farmer told me that every black animal was feared: black chickens and black cats were killed because they were the same colour as Satan.

REVD ELIAS OWEN (1833–99)
*Montgomeryshire Folklore*

*The Shearing*

When my life was thrifty, thrifty,
Soon my one sheep grew to fifty;
After that I lived for fun
And found my flock was back to one.

ANONYMOUS
Folk verses, 16th–17th century
trans. Glyn Jones

This was the Field. The white tents, the four hundred yards of grass, the hurdles, and the pens flashed at his eyes, the flags and the bright dresses of the women. The first dogs had already gone out. He was suddenly sober, a shepherd with a job to do. He knew that most of his fellow competitors disliked him, and that some of them feared him, but to be feared was honey on his tongue. He knew, too, how they hoped to see everything go wrong for him this afternoon: he wouldn't trust those scabs down the field not to loose a tough one when his turn came. They said it was the run of the game, the sheep a man had to work; he growled to think how often he got bad ones. Some of these farmers, squat, basin-bellied, fat-legged, he'd like to see them on the mountain. That's where you showed whether you could handle sheep, not on a green handkerchief like this.

He was a red-headed one from the farmstead up under Creigiau: the Rocks. A scurfy, thin-soiled place with the whole mountain for a sheep-run. Sometimes he had a woman up there, but never for long: they could stand neither the place nor

its tenant. The tall, black rocks rose up behind the cottage like a claw; the mountain sprawled away thereafter in bog and stream and the rush-hidden grass of the grazing grounds. Lonely – too lonely for everyone save him – too lonely sometimes even for him. That was when he would come to the town and haggle with some sly or trampled creature to come up for a week, a fortnight – no one had ever stayed longer than that. And they all left him the same way: they waited till he was far out on the mountain after sheep and then fled downwards, from home field to path, from path to mountain road, and so to where the lower farms spotted the slopes round Isa'ndre. Fled, they would say, as if the devil were behind them, a devil with big hands and red hair.

He lumbered his way to the stewards' table. There were thirty or forty dogs entered for the different classes, the air quivered with their excitement. Their merits and failings were as well known here as those of their masters, and even more discussed. He saw men eyeing his black-and-white bitch as she moved close behind him. 'Novice?' asked one of the Isa'ndre shepherds, jerking his thumb. 'Novice!' he sneered, and then, savagely: 'Open! The Cup!'

The Cup! That tall white silver thing on his shelf for a year, his name on it for ever. A wide smile covered his face and he looked down at the bitch. 'You better,' he said. 'You better, see!' Her tail went tighter over her haunches, her eyes seemed to lose focus.

They were ticking his name off at the stewards' table. They were looking down at the bitch, a fine-drawn, thin-faced youngster. 'You ought to have entered her for the Novice. It's not fair to a young 'un.' 'She's going to win,' he told them, grinning. 'She better!'

He was walking away, swinging his stick. Behind him they shook their heads, shrugged, went on with their business. He grew restive and arrogant among men who seemed always to be moving away from him. Crike, he'd show them.

And then he was out at the shepherd's post, and far down the field they were loosing the three sheep which he and his bitch must move by long invisible strings, so that his will was her wish, her wish their law. A movement of his fingers sent her out to the right on a loping run which brought her well behind the three sheep. She sank instantly, but rose at his whistle and

came forward flying her tail and worked them swiftly through
the first hurdle. No one of them attempted to break as she ran
them down towards the shepherd, turned them neatly round to
his right, and then at a wave of his stick fetched them down
past his left hand and so away to the second hurdle. They were
now running too fast, and he whistled her to a stalking pace
while the hurdle was still seventy yards away. The sheep
halted, their heads up, and at the whistle the bitch proceeded
with short flanking runs which headed them into the gap.

The shepherd was now five separate beings, and yet those
five integrated so that they were one. He was the shepherd, he
was the bitch, he was the three sheep together and severally; he
could hardly distinguish between them as aspects of himself.
The sheep had been turned across the field towards the hurdle
in front of the spectators' benches at a moment when a string of
children ran madly towards a stall selling drinks and ice-
cream. As they faced the benches, the shepherd could feel
alarm and irresolution grow in the sheep. The bitch felt it, too,
and showed by a short, furious spurt that she was worried. Her
worry moved simultaneously within the shepherd's mind.

The bitch steadied on his whistle, crouched, rose again, and
raced out to fetch a straggler back. At once a second sheep broke
away on the other side. By the time she had them once more in
a group her anxiety was apparent to every shepherd on the
field. They broke again and it looked as though they would pass
round the hurdle, but a fierce whistle helped her cut them off.
The pattern renewed itself; yet again the sheep faced the hurdle
and the fluttering benches behind, yet again the bitch sank in
their rear. The time was going by, she had lost the benefit of her
quick work at the beginning and the shepherd brought her
once more to her feet. She raced to their right, but grew confused on his signals and sank at the wrong time, letting a sheep
escape. The crowd began to laugh, for she seemed little better
than a fool to them now. She collected the sheep for the last
time, but they at once strung out across the face of the hurdle,
and at the shepherd's furious whistle she openly cringed and
began to creep away from the sheep. Hoots of laughter and
miaowings pursued her across the field; only the shepherds
were silent.

GWYN JONES
in *Shepherd's Hey* (1953)

Aye, lad, I sold the last batch of lambs at the mart yesterday. A
fair enough price they fetched too. Mind you, the ewes are
yearning: been bleating away all night long. I didn't wean the
lambs this year: only sold them off as they came ready. It's all
early lambs now. Aye, the poor old ewes are yearning. Like to
see them? I'm just going to have a look at them now.

Sheep are my life, you know. Fond of sheep I am. If I was a
poet I'd write an ode about sheep. The lambs are so pretty in the
spring, bouncing like snowflakes all over the meadow; I can
watch them for hours. A pity they have to grow. Still, there's
attractive about them at every age – like people, I suppose. Take
yearlings now; smart they are; in the bloom of life, as you might
say. A penful of warm wethers, out of breath after gathering;
there's nothing like pushing through them, feeling them,
enjoying them with the tips of my fingers. Kind old mother
ewes like these I'm going to show you now. A proper Samson
of a ram, head up, staring into the distance, pleased with himself after a good season's work. And the odd old barren that
couldn't take a ram, empty in a field full of in-lambs. Feel sorry
for them I do. Nature's hard on some.

Aye, I've got a barren or two every year. But I've got one – if
she's really mine – you'll see her in a moment – I've had her for
twenty years. Hard to believe, isn't it? Black she is, with two
curly horns like a Welsh ram. Curlier if anything. Where she
came from I haven't a clue. Perhaps you can explain it when
you see her.

ISLWYN FFOWC ELIS
from 'Black Barren' in *The Penguin Book of Welsh Short Stories*
ed. Alun Richards (1976)

from *The Boundary Fence*

According to the best geographical authorities, ancient and
modern, the parish of Llangernyw, in the county of Denbigh,
lies well within the confines of the temperate zone; but, sixty
years ago, two adjoining farms in the very centre of the parish
might well have passed as a slice of the tropics, – and that on
account of the abnormal and unneighbourly heat locally gen-
erated by the mutual antipathy of the two farmers. The farms
were known as Bodrach and Frwynos; and following a custom

of that part of the country, their neighbours familiarly called each farmer by the bare name of his farm. In the one case farm and farmer alike were called Frwynos, and in the other, Bodrach; but the farmers' actual names were Peter Hughes and Thomas Bevan.

For a period of thirty years there blew over the boundary fence between these two farms a constant tempestuous simoom; and a cool lull only came when notices had been served on both farmers by the only landowner in the parish – and the only owner of land all the world over, according to one old book – that they would have to move shortly, in accordance with the provisions of an ancient Allotments Act, into very small holdings under a yew tree's sombre but impartial stewardship in the parish churchyard.

On account of the preternatural heat already mentioned, the two farmers may be said to have lived in a little torrid zone of their own, in which the equator followed the zigzag line of the boundary fence; for it was in the immediate vicinity of the fence, on either side, that the rays were hottest. This equator was by no means an imaginary line, though the ease with which Peter's sheep crossed over it favoured the view that it was a fence in theory and not in thorns. And that apparently must have been the view held by many woolly philosophers in Peter's flock; for their idealism, as practically applied to the problem of the boundary fence, made Thomas Bevan's life on the other side of the fence scarcely worth living.

The boundary fence was a massive old earthwork, of a width that was reminiscent of defensive fortifications in the battles of long ago. In form it was zigzag, and, as seen from the other side of the glen, it resembled a giant snake wriggling its way down to the river below. But though its earthwork was wide and massive, it was ill-provided with anything in the shape of a regular and efficient hedge on top; and in that respect it fell far short of the ideal boundary fence. It was overrun with brambles in profusion; but these were no defence against the undesirable aliens of Peter's flock. Their only service was to act as a set of Custom House officers on the frontier, who did their utmost to delay the progress of the trespassers, and collected as much wool as they could conveniently carry; but they were not equal to the task of holding up the invaders indefinitely.

The boundary fence belonged to Bodrach, and nothing more

was expected of Peter Hughes than that he should dwell in peace on the other side; and that was the last thing anyone who knew Peter would expect him to do. As the fence belonged to Thomas Bevan it was his duty to repair it; and this he conscientiously tried to do many a time, but every attempt failed. To his great chagrin, Peter's flock were expert critics of anything in the shape of a hedge, and they found great delight in putting Thomas Bevan's repairs to the test under his very nose . . .

R. DEWI WILLIAMS (1874–1958)
in *Clawdd Terfyn* (1912)

*Ponies, Twynyrodyn*

Winter, the old drover, has brought
these beasts from the high moor's hafod
to bide the bitter spell among us,
here, in the valley streets.
Observe them, this chill morning, as
they stand, backsides against the wind,
in Trevithick Row. Hoofs, shod with ice,
shift and clatter on the stone kerb.
Steam is slavering from red nostrils,
manes are stiff with frost and dung.

Quiet now, last night
they gallivanted through the village,
fear's bit in teeth. Hedges were broken,
there was havoc to parked cars. Yet,
despite the borough council's by-laws
these refugees are welcome here.
Fed from kitchen and tommybox, they
are free to roam the grit backlanes,
only kids and mongrels pester them.
We greet them as old acquaintances
not because they bring us local colour,
as the tourist guides might say, but
for the brute glamour that is with them.
Long before fences and tarmac, they
were the first tenants of these valleys,
their right to be here is freehold.
Now, in this turncoat weather, as
they lord it through the long terraces,
toppling bins from wet steps, ribs
rubbing against the bent railings,
our smooth blood is disturbed
by hiraeth for the lost cantrefi,
the green parishes that lie beyond
the borders of our town and hearts,
fit for nothing now but sad songs.
These beasts are our companions,
dark presences from the peasant past,
these grim valleys our common hendre,
exiles all, until the coming thaw.

MEIC STEPHENS

*Horse Hysbys*

An old woman and her son and his wife live on a mountain in
comfort and want for nothing. The old woman is in a caravan.
The man and his wife are in a stone house and work a freehold
of nearly forty-three fertile acres, and they have a horse to help
them. This is the horse Hysbys, which means 'knowing'.

Puah is the old woman and Bensha her son, Bensha for

Benjamin. They are comers from the Rodericks, noted porthmen or cattle-dealers in back time, and before they settled on the mountain Puah and Bensha followed their trade and Hysbys took them about in the caravan.

Hysbys was in his prime then. He was as fast as a sunbeam, and his coat was so yellow that if he were in a field of ripe corn on a sunny day you would not know which was corn, which was Hysbys, which was sunlight. His coat lit the most desolate roads on the blackest nights and enabled him to bring his caravan to a sheltered gap where there was a spring of water and good pasture and easy granary doors.

Between the shafts he was boss. He travelled as he willed, trudge, amble, jog-trot, or trot, and he halted the caravan where he willed. A sharp word of command or a smart tug at his rein and he would prance and rear and do savage faces, or fall on the floor and make his legs stiff like a dying horse, or land the caravan in a bog and pretend he could not pull it out.

Stripped of his harness he was mild and gentle for a knowing horse who understood happenings. Bensha combed and brushed him and spoke friendly to him and gave him sugar to eat. But Puah took an advantage of his softness. She blamed him when there was no blame to be: the gap he had halted in was too close or too open, and sometimes for nothing she would tell him to stand still while she got a thick stick to beat him with, and though the stick was a thin twig and she hit him ever so lightly he trembled like a gate in a dry wall and wept for the unjust punishment. It was odd that such a knowing horse did not have the sense to know that as he showed off when he was boss of the caravan so Puah showed off when she was bossess of him.

CARADOC EVANS (1878–1945)
from 'Horse Hysbys and Oldest Brother'

### The Drovers

The Spanish fleet of North Wales, which brings hither that little gold and silver we have.

ARCHBISHOP JOHN WILLIAMS (c. 1640)

The small Welsh black cattle were hardy and tough and could stand up to the rigours of trekking over the rough, muddy and stony mountain tracks, along which they were driven in order to avoid the turnpike roads and the payment of tolls. Travelling at a steady rate of two miles an hour, the journey from West Wales to the English border took from twelve to fifteen days.

R. B. JONES
in *Country Quest*


### The Drovers (Heiptro Ho!)

A great feature of the droves was the noise they made. It was heard for miles and warned local farmers what to expect. The noise consisted of the shouting of the drovers combined, I suppose, with a certain amount of noise from the cattle. But it was the men's voices that chiefly attracted attention. It was something out of the common, neither shouting, calling, crying, singing, halloing or anything else, but a noise of itself, apparently made to carry and capable of arresting the countryside. The horsemen and two of the cattle acted as leaders to the rest, and the men kept calling and shouting the whole time. As soon as the local farmers heard the noise they rushed their cattle out of the way, for if once they got into the drove, they could not easily be got out again.

Reminiscence recorded by Caroline Skeel (1926)
quoted by Shirley Toulson, *The Drovers' Roads of Wales* (1977)


At three in the morning, two blacksmiths, a feller (or overthrower) and a helper started from Bala eighteen miles away carrying with them 480 shoes (*cw* in Welsh) and the necessary nails, hammers and knives. On reaching Dolgellau they set to work. The feller and his helper threw a rope round the bullock's horns; while the feller gripped the horns, the helper took hold of one foreleg, bending it at the joint. Then the feller twisted the horns and down went the bullock, being held firm

while the helper bound its legs. A piece of iron about three feet [91 centimetres] long with a point at one end and a fork at the other was pushed into the ground, the point downward and the rope from the forelegs to the hindlegs was placed in the fork. The bullock was then ready to be shod. The first blacksmith trimming the hoof and the second nailing on the shoes. The bullocks were from two-and-a-half to three years old and hard to throw. One of them, a huge black steer from Anglesey, actually dragged the feller and his helper through the river; they held fast however and in the end 'Merionethshire had Anglesey down on his back'. The master blacksmith got 10d for every steer shod.

HUGH EVANS (1925)
quoted by Shirley Toulson, *The Drovers' Roads of Wales* (1977)

When I set out a-droving
My Father said, You're mad,
Why leave the farm, why come to harm
And go for a droving lad?
But I saw the wide world beckon
Beyond the roads I knew,
And beyond the tower of Brecon
Fresh fields and pastures new.

> *Haip-trw-ho, haip-trw-ho!*
> *And a-droving we will go.*

Upon my sturdy pony
My saddle I did throw,
I whistled to my corgi-dog
And off we both did go,
I had a young man's longing
For new cities and new sins
So I set out a-droving
And that's how life begins.

> *Haip-trw-ho, haip-trw-ho!*
> *And a-droving we will go.*

Once past the Bwlch, they told me,
No Welshman ever comes back,
But my homeland could not hold me
And I took the droving track.
To taverns called The Feathers,
Welsh Harp and Prince of Wales
I rode through England's weathers
And drank deep of England's ales.

> *Haip-trw-ho, haip-trw-ho!*
> *And a-droving we will go.*

Great herds I drove to market
From many an upland farm,
I stored up many a sovereign
And I never came to harm.
I stood my round, I stood my ground,
Drank deep of many a glass,
And many a broad-beamed Saxon wench
I pleasured in the grass.

*Haip-trw-ho, haip-trw-ho!*
*And a-droving we will go.*

But now the railway's coming,
I see a cloud of steam,
I hear the rails a-humming,
I hear the whistle scream,
Its message to the drover
Is carried loud and clear,
It says, Your days are over
And the cattle trucks are here.

*Haip-trw-ho, haip-trw-ho!*
*But a-droving I shall go.*

I'm setting sail tomorrow
At the rising of the sun
And I'm going off to Texas,
Though they say I'll need a gun,
And I'll drive the Yankee long horns
Through lands that once were Spain's
As I drove the small black cattle
Through our green and narrow lanes.

*Haip-trw-ho, haip-trw-ho!*
*And a-droving I will go.*

HARRI WEBB

**108**    I obferved in the Dovey, two of the boats, called Coracles; thefe
are ufed chiefly in fifhing; they are five or fix feet long, and
three or four broad, or an oval fhape, and fo light that one man
may with eafe carry them on his fhoulders. They were the *vitilia
navigia* of Pliny, and were much in ufe amongft the antient
Britons. Their name was taken from their being formerly covered with *coria*, or hides. Camden fays, 'they were made of fplit
fallow twigs, interwoven, (round at the bottom), and on that
part next the water, covered with a horfe's hide'; but they are
now ufually covered with pitched canvas. They hold only a
fingle perfon, who can row himfelf with incredible fwiftnefs
with a paddle in his right-hand, whilft with the other he can
manage a net.

THOMAS PENNANT (1726–98)
*A Tour Round North Wales* (1778)

*Cockles and Mussels*

*Cockle Gathering*
The collecting of cockles [*cardium edule*: Welsh – *rhython, cocos* or
*cocs*] and mussels [*mytulis edulis*: Welsh – *cregyn gleision*] is of
great antiquity in Wales and there is extensive evidence from
prehistoric and Roman sites that shellfish was important in the
diet of early man. Throughout the centuries cockles and mussels, as well as other shore-living shellfish such as periwinkles
[*littorina littorea*: Welsh – *gwichiaid*] and limpets [*patella vulgata*:
Welsh – *llygaid meheryn* or *llygaid y graig*] provided the essential
protein in the diet of coastal people throughout Wales.
Shellfish occurred everywhere and were especially profuse
along rocky stretches of coast. They were very easy to collect
and the gatherers of shellfish required no elaborate equipment,
tools or great expertise to gather substantial quantities. To those
prepared to venture to the sea shore, no cost at all was involved
in harvesting vast quantities of shellfish, that were very easily
prepared for consumption in the farm or cottage kitchen . . .
In the Burry Inlet, according to Bulstrode in 1911: 'Along
the foreshore, there are to be seen numerous extemporized
fireplaces, banked up with sand on three sides to protect
them from wind and open in front. Upon these fires the cockles
are placed, contained in a large iron or tin cauldron, a small

quantity of water having been first poured into the saucepan to prevent scorching. As the cockles gape owing to the passage of steam from below, the sea-water contained between their shells is liberated and thus the cockles may be said to be literally boiled in their own liquor, this liquor being at the end of each boiling decanted almost entirely into another receptacle near, to be used subsequently for the process of washing the cockles . . . The cockles are kept on the fire until the water is actually boiling, when they are emptied into another receptacle and a fresh batch of living cockles placed in the cauldron. The boiled cockles are then riddled over a table, the soft parts passing through a sieve, the shells remaining behind. From time to time the cockles are washed in their own liquor and at the end of the process they are taken in a basket either to a neighbouring stream, to a spring, on to the foreshore or to a pump or tap . . . At the end of a day's work at Penclawdd, there may be seen numerous cockle wives sitting by the side of a rivulet which traverses the sands, awaiting their turn to wash their boiled cockles. The cockles when ready for market are wrapped in white cloths, placed in baskets or small wooden tubs and taken to the neighbouring market towns by the cockle wives, who may be seen in the early morning on the railway platforms with basket or tub deftly poised upon their heads. On Saturdays, a special train leaves Penclawdd for Swansea about 7 a.m., which is known as "the cockle train".'

In the western part of Carmarthen Bay, when the cockle gathering industry flourished in such places as Laugharne and Llansteffan, boiled cockles were usually heavily salted with 28 lb of salt being added to every 60 quarts of cockles.

Of course, attendance at market and vending from town to town still remains important despite modern methods of distribution. 'A generation ago, the Saturday morning train from Penclawdd to Swansea used to be a colourful sight: almost the whole female population of the villages would crowd on the platform dressed in Welsh costume – red and black striped dresses, black and white check aprons, grey plaid shawls and close-fitting cockle bonnets, with a starched white frill peeping out from under the brim – and the white cloths over their tubs and baskets would shine like so many fresh mushrooms. After selling their cockles they would return on the 2.30 train from Swansea.' Before the railway came to Penclawdd in 1863 the women used to walk the nine miles to Swansea market in bare feet with tubs of cockles balanced on their heads and it is said that a stream on the outskirts of Swansea known as *Yr Olchfa* (the washing place) was given its name by the cockle women because it was there that they washed their feet before putting on their boots before entering the town.

### Mussel Gathering

For centuries the most important centre of mussel gathering in Wales has been the Conwy estuary . . . In the nineteenth century, mussels in the Conwy were usually gathered for their pearls, and the history of pearl fishing in the Conwy dates back for many centuries. Spenser in his *Faerie Queene*, for example, wrote:

> Conway, which out of his streame doth send
> Plenty of pearles to decke his dames withall.

A local historian in 1835 gives details of the pearl fishing at that time:

'There are two kinds of mussels found in the Conwy from which pearls are obtained: *mya margaritifere* (*cragen y diluw*) and the *mytulis edulis* (*cragen lâs*). Those of the former species are procured high up the river, about Trefriw, and pearls scarcely inferior to the oriental ones are occasionally found in them . . . The other variety, the *cragen lâs*, is found in abundance on the bar at the mouth of the river and great quantities of the mussels are daily gathered by numbers of industrious persons. At ebb tide, the fishers, men, women and children may be observed busily collecting the mussels, until they are driven away by the flood. They then carry the contents of their sacks and baskets to *Cefnfro*, the northern extremity of the marsh, where the mussels are boiled: for this operation there are large crochanau or iron pots, placed in slight huts; or rather pits as they are almost buried in a vast heap of shells. The fish are picked out and put into a tub and stamped with the feet until they are reduced to a pulp; when, water being poured in, the animal matter floats, which is called *solach* and is used as food for ducks, while the sand, particles of stone and the pearls settle in the bottom. After numerous washings, the sediment is carefully collected and dried and the pearls, even the most minute, are separated with

a feather on a large wooden platter.' By the early 1880s pearl
fishing on the Conwy had ceased, but mussels were being gathered in considerable quantities for human consumption.

J. GERAINT JENKINS
*Cockles and Mussels – Aspects of*
*Shellfish Gathering in Wales* (1984)

### Catching the Gwyniad

The lake of Bala produces fine trout, perch, the gwyniad, an
alpine fish which runs from one to six pounds weight, and
some other species of fish in great abundance. We were all anxious to catch some gwyniads, the *Salmo lauaretus* of Linnaeus,
which seldom can be done by angling; but the civility and
attention of Mr Richards, which reflected honour on his master, enabled us to obtain several at one sweep of the net, and we
had them dressed for dinner. This fish is certainly very delicate;
but in point of flavour it is inferior to some others of its genus,
which the Welsh rivers and lakes produce. It dies, the moment
it is taken out of the water.

MAVOR
*Tour of Wales* (1806)

# VI

# HIRAETH, LOVE, SPORT

I am a man cut off, obscure, an exile from Môn, a stranger to our ancient tongue, strong-syllabled, a stranger to the sweet strains of the Muse. Full of care I am, ah me to speak of it! And full of longing, sunk in heavy-hearted sorrow.

GORONWY OWEN (1723–69)
from *Hiraeth am Fôn*
trans. Sir H. Idris Bell in *The Development of Welsh Poetry* (1936)

*Head in the Clouds*

Head in the clouds to you is a worn phrase
Weakly used to indicate disapproval
Of somebody else's ability to evade
Or ignore the day's burden and trial.

But to us who were born above Pencarreg
Head in the clouds is true, is simply true.
Nor all the brazen comfort of the sun
Can dissipate the clouds upon Penrhiw.

And if you say, as other friends have said,
That I walk always with my head in a cloud,
I am wilful enough to take you literally
And let your saying make me homesick and proud.

Homesick for clouded hills that never lose
The loom and shape they had when I,
My head in other clouds, trod their old paths
Too proud then to know that I too would die.

Proud now to know that when I have to die
My head has always been in clouds: first those
That still hang low over Pencarreg and Penrhiw,
And then the ones in which you shroud me close.

T. HARRI JONES (1921–65)

The elder children had crept in from the other room and sat around her in a ring, their white anxious faces raised.

So she sang for them, as she promised, an old Welsh folk song, *Pant Corlan yr Wyn*, about the shearing, and then gave them, as a special treat, a song called *Hen Aelwyd Cymru* (The Old Welsh Hearth), her heart full to brimming. Her breasts had gone out in the flood-tide of her emotion and the old *hiraeth* came up in her throat; her eyes were half shut in the longing, and her beautiful contralto voice, clear and low, went out with an infinite tenderness.

'There now,' she said at last, as she sent off the elder children to their room. 'That will be three-and-sixpence if you please. Front seats!'

As she tucked up the little one for the night he said, half awake:

'Our Meg . . . ?'

'Hush.'

'You're . . . not going to go away?'

'There's silly!' she whispered.

'Fine and nice,' he said, turning over drowsily, the songs still with him.

That was to be her recompense.

GERAINT GOODWIN (1903–41)
from 'Saturday Night'

### Hiraeth

Those first months in the autumn of 1942, I loathed the fogs, London's apparent offhandedness. I longed for the provincial friendliness of Welsh people. I wanted to hear a bit of Welsh spoken, or, at least, the accented sing-song voices that I knew so well with all their cosmic portentousness. At King's College I joined the Welsh Society and even gave a talk on Welsh poetry. I chanted William Barnes's translation of an anonymous ninth-century Welsh lament until tears of homesickness came into my eyes:

> Cynddylan's hall is all in gloom tonight;
> No fire, no lighted room:
> Amid the stillness of the tomb. . . .

DANNIE ABSE
*A Poet in the Family* (1974)

. . . We do find, constantly recurring, a note of *hiraeth*, that typically Welsh word which we can but inadequately render as 'longing': an intense, passionate yearning for that which we have not, for dead friends, vanished youth, the peace of heaven, some satisfaction which life can never give . . .

When we come down to modern days, the note changes a little, the *hiraeth* becomes more spiritual, more religious, and in doing so acquires a deeper intensity . . .

When this note of wistfulness is united with the delicacy of conception and the power of bare, direct, seeming-effortless and infinitely significant expression which are other characteristic gifts of Welsh poetry the resulting verses are at times

quite heartrending in their perfect simplicity . . . and in some
of the Welsh poems we have a feeling that the author is looking
with unacquainted eyes at a new world, coming for the first
time, and with wondering incomprehension, into the presence
of sorrow and death.

SIR H. IDRIS BELL (1879–1967)
in *The Development of Welsh Poetry* (1936)

The liking of Welshmen for Welshmen is very strong, and that
not only when they meet on foreign soil, as in London, but in
their own land. They do not, I suppose, love their neighbours
more than other men do, but when they meet a fellow-country-
man for the first time they seem to have a kind of surprise and
joy, in spite of the commonness of such meetings. They do not
acquiesce in the fact that the man they shake hands with is of
their race, as English people do. They converse readily in trains:
they are all of one family, and indeed if you are Welsh, not only
can you not avoid meeting relatives, but you do not wish to.
Small news about the coming and going of people travels
among them rapidly, and I have never got out of a train in
Wales without feeling that I shall meet someone whom I
should like to meet, on the platform or in the first street. They
like their own land in the same way.

EDWARD THOMAS (1878–1917)
*Wales* (1905)

### The Spear (Y Gwayw)

I saw her there, her fair hair
Pale as foam, as white water,
From head to toe perfection,
More radiant than day-dawn.
She watched the play of Noah
In the saint's church at Bangor.
World's wonder and non pareil,
Pure flower and my betrayal,
Just to see her is for me
Greatest gift; and agony.

I'm stabbed with a seven-edged spear,
Each edge a complaint to her
That I lie pale with poison,
The gift of the men of Môn.
Their envy is in my heart
And no man can pull it out.
No smith tempered this weapon,
No hand fine-ground its iron;
Without shape, without shadow,
A bitter barb brought its blow,
Subdued my splendour. I am ill
With love for Gwynedd's candle.
The long spear has pierced me,
My one thought is her beauty.
You may witness my weakness,
A sad boy with a white face,
Wearing her wounds in his heart,
Her painful skewer, her sharp dart.
She placed it there. I am killed
By a girl gold as Esyllt.

I'll wear her spear for an age,
Carry it in my rib's cage,
Endure the ache of the awl
Until death's dismissal.

DAFYDD AP GWILYM (c. 1320–70)
trans. Leslie Norris

*Love in a Welsh Climate*

The Welsh of my day were all for Love, but indulgence in it was
fraught with many perils, physical, social, moral and hypocritical. It was much easier for the Squire, especially if he was not
a fluent Welsh speaker, to enjoy a fair spread of sin – than for
the Welsh peasant. A communicating non-conformist, say a
Baptist or a Methodist – if caught out in illicit love, had to bear
the sanction of ex-communication by the minister, deacons
and the baptized members in congregation assembled. I remember one such transgressor being asked by the minister and

the deacons, if he had anything to say before being cast out. 'Well,' he said, 'the only difference between some of you and me is, that I was caught!' The Squire if he was C. of E. had an easy time; besides, he was usually financially able to compensate the female sharer of his pleasures. I remember as a schoolboy being shown a terrace of brick houses – each with a keystone of the arch above its front door in the shape of a most artistic Cupid, and being told that the rich owner of a brickworks had built them to house his brood mares, as it were, and the legend was that all passes by him at pretty maids were welcomed. There was one proviso – they did not enter one of these houses until there was ample external evidence that the connection had been fruitful. I have a faint memory of seeing an old gentleman standing at the door of his house studying form on market day. Physically he now needed a stick, but there was still a sparkle in the eye, as he doffed his three-quarter, not a top hat to the ladies.

It is of course quite untrue to suggest that the little maids in service at the Plas or mansion who were seduced were always the unwilling victim of the *Y Sgweier* or rich farmer; often there was collusion as well as mutual delight. The words the soldiers sang, 'She was poor but she was honest, Victim of the squire's whim, etc.', did not always apply. There were some men who were irresistible – often leading lights in church or chapel. Farmers hired maids and farm hands by the year – the hiring day being Michaelmas Fair on 10 November, when the future employer would seal the contract of service by an earnest *ern* of a shilling, sometimes 2/6 – paid as a rule to the parents of the girl or youth to be hired. If later the employer for some reason did not choose to have the servant he would tell him so, and he'd keep the *ern*. Likewise the servant was released by returning the *ern*. It was the easiest thing in the world for a bachelor farmer with a young housekeeper and perhaps another couple of milk-maids, to find his way into their beds without much trouble. Then there were affairs between the head carters or plough men, *y gwas mawr*, and maids on their own, or neighbouring farms. Girls were 'dated' at chapel, concerts, *eisteddfodau*, singing festivals, and at harvest time. There were some who believed that no maid was more easily seduced than she who had been to an emotional prayer meeting, or a sermon with a *hwyl*, or above all a singing festival. A good intake of

118 Handel or Bach would apparently lower the lady's defences
sufficiently for her to stoop to folly. Tutors at theological col-
leges would advise their students not to go a-courting on Sunday, an emotional day, when *les girls* were most inclined to be
permissive. During the winter months a singing rehearsal was
held after the evening service, to get ready for the singing festival the following June. The likely lads would escort the chosen
and willing back home to the farms often two or four miles
away with the last part of the journey nearly always down an
unmetalled rutted farm lane. There would be connivance by
the employer at the late arrival home of his maid servant. Then
there was the old established *Caru trwy'r nos* or 'Courting all
night'. The girl would leave a ladder conveniently placed near
or beneath her bedroom window and usually on a Saturday
night the man of her choice would arrive, clean-shaven and
smelling of scented soap, his Amlwch shag-tobacco-laden
breath disguised by the heavy exotic perfume of 'Sen-Sen'
cachous. He would strip to his vest and long drawers both of
heavy Welsh wool with a black vertical stripe in the drawers,
and then with the nice protection of a blanket between them
they'd commence to giggle and cuddle, protest and counterpro-
test, all very pleasurable no doubt. Occasionally the blanket
proved insufficient insulation, and some months later a hurried marriage would be arranged – with the whole community
rejoicing and congratulating the happy virile couple. Some of
the happiest and most successful marriages in Wales have
started on this basis.

JAMES WILLIAMS
*Give Me Yesterday* (1971)


*Saturday, 11 November, 1871*
This morning Catherine Price of the New Inn was married
to Davies, a young Painscastle blacksmith, before the Hay
registrar. What I call a gypsy 'jump the broom' marriage. The
wedding feast was at the New Inn which is now shut up as an
inn and abolished. As I passed the house I heard music and
dancing, the people dancing at the wedding. They were dancing in an upper room, unfurnished, tramp, tramp, tramp, to the
jingling of a concertina, the stamping was tremendous. I
thought they would have brought the floor down. They seemed

to be jumping round and round. When I came back the dance
seemed to have degenerated into a romp and the girls were
squealing, as if they were being kissed and tickled and not
against their will.

FRANCIS KILVERT (1840–79)
*Kilvert's Diary 1870–79*
ed. William Plomer (1977)

I wished her goodnight and went upstairs. But hardly had I
reached my little room than down below I heard the soft sound
of first the kitchen door and then the house door. Curiosity
aroused, I went to the window and, in the light of the moon
that to my advantage was veiled by the clouds, saw Sarah going
over the yard and to the half-open door of a shed from which
crept out a figure that – as it stood up – appeared to be none
other than – Owen. Truly, I thought, it wasn't only on my
account that she had remained sitting up so long! I hoped to be
able to be a witness of a Welsh pastoral scene in storm and rain;
but I had deceived myself, for the Phyllis of my farm had
devised things more comfortably. She came back again across
the yard, her faithful shepherd behind her, then into the house
and into the kitchen. But how my astonishment grew when,
instead of sobs, oaths and kisses, I heard only a sound which
indicated that Owen was taking off his boots and Sarah her
shoes. And truly – in stocking feet they came up the stairs, past
my chamber and into Sarah's little room opposite!

'No!' I cried out – 'that's too much! that goes beyond the
bounds of decency! that's unheard of! This girl of barely eighteen, with her childish eyes and modest behaviour, shy in
speech and conduct – Celts, Celts – I should have known that
it's in their blood. But what's that to me? Perhaps we are still
living in a paradise here, where the serpent has not yet spoken!'

I fell asleep, and when I woke the next morning, the sun was
already shining into my eyes. For after yesterday's storm, the
sky had brightened up again overnight, and all that was to be
heard was the murmuring of the cornfield and the sea. In the
garden, the open poppy flowers, with raindrops still sparkling
in them like diamonds, nodded up to the window of my room,
and behind the wet hedge at the bottom the sea was still quite
rough. But the sky was blue and the morning so bright that

across on Anglesey I could distinguish more clearly than ever before the rocks of the coast, the white walls of the houses, the church towers, woods and fields. I set out in good time, and the family, who had accompanied me to the front of the house, bade me fond farewell. Only Sarah couldn't comprehend why I, contrary to my usual custom, was so short with her. She stood on the step for a long time, looking after me in surprise; then she went pensively back into the house.

When I arrived, the schoolmaster was already standing at his garden gate; he stepped out and we walked straight on. I couldn't concentrate on anything until I had told him the strange story of the previous evening. 'Yes', I concluded, still a little upset, 'Caesar must have been right when he claims in his Commentaries that this people live together without difference of sex.'

The schoolmaster had listened to me, smiling, and then he began: 'You do the poor couple an injustice, dear sir! What you observed there yesterday you can see in every Welsh farm where there is a daughter who is courted by the son of another farm. With us it is the natural consequence of a love-affair seriously intended. Until today I have heard nothing of Sarah's and Owen's intention, but now I know with certainty that they will soon marry. For this nocturnal visit is a proposal of marriage, and if it is accepted, then there will not be long to wait for the wedding. This *Caru-ar-y-gwely*, called courting on the bed, is customary throughout Wales – the girl sits on her bed chatting with her beloved until the morning. But don't believe that anything unseemly happens; the girl – who doesn't think there is anything improper in a custom practised by her mother and grandmother before her – would flee in terror from the lover who abused this opportunity – indeed, he would have to think himself lucky if he got away without a bloody nose.

JULIUS RODENBERG
*An Autumn in Wales* (1856)
trans. William Linnard (1985)

As I was washing under a span
of the bridge of Cardigan
and in my hand my lover's shirt
with a golden beetle to drub the dirt,
a man came to me on a steed,
broad in shoulder, proud in speed,
and he asked me if I'd sell
the shirt of the lad I love so well.

But I said I wouldn't sell
for a hundred pounds and packs as well,
nor if the grass of two ridges were deep
in wethers and the whitest sheep,
nor if two hay meadows were choked
with oxen which were ready yoked,
nor if St David's nave were filled
with herbs all pressed but not distilled.
Not even for all that would I sell
the shirt of the lad I love so well.

ANONYMOUS, 16th century
trans. Gwyn Williams

Were all the peaks of Gwynedd
In one huge mountain piled,
Cnicht on Moelwyn,
Moel-y-gest, Moel Hebog,
And Eryri on top,
And all between us,
I'd climb them climb them
All!
To reach you.
O, how I love you!

Were all the streams of Gwynedd
In one great river joined,
Dwyfor, Dwyryd,
Glaslyn, Ogwen,
And Mawddach in flood,
And all between us,
I'd swim them swim them
All!
To reach you.
O, how I love you!

Were all the forts of Gwynedd
In one great fortress linked,
Caer and castle,
Criccieth, Harlech,
Conwy, Caernarfon,
And all in flames,
I'd jump them jump them
All!
To reach you.
O, how I love you!

See you Saturday,
If it's not raining.

MICHAEL BURN

Passing the Bagillt station, we next reach Holywell, or, in the Welsh, *Treffynon*, 'the Town of the Well', which derives this appellation from a remarkable spring that bursts out of the ground with such copiousness, and possesses such curative properties, real and imaginary, that tradition would have been strangely at fault if it had not connected its origin with some marvellous or supernatural event. Here, accordingly, in times far too remote for the control of history, lived the good St Beuno, a man of noble descent, who erected a Church on the spot, and educated his niece, Winifred, accomplished at once in beauty, and full of all piety and devotion. Caradoc, a neighbouring prince, kindled at the sight of the former quality, but was so wickedly indifferent to the latter as to pursue the fair virgin with unlawful love, and piqued at her refusal, in days when love-making was rather roughly practised, lopped off, as she was flying from his importunities, her beautiful head, which, bounding down the hill like a ball, rested at length, most fortunately, on a spot from its barrenness formerly denominated *Sychnant*, or the dry hollow, where burst forth, instantly, the stream which succeeding ages counted holy, that still, in all its marvellous gushing, we behold. Beuno, catching up the head of his niece, ran up the hill to where lay the fair body from which it had been severed, and after pattering an ave, adjusted it adroitly in its original position, when the virgin rose, beautiful as ever, none the worse for the adventure, but for a slight unavoidable trace around her fair neck, which served but to authenticate the miracle, and render her ever after a distinguished female saint and abbess of Gwytherin, in Denbighshire, where, at length, she died. As for Caradoc, of course he was struck dead, and swallowed up as he was making off, sword in hand, from the scene of his untoward amour.

PETER ROBERTS
*Cambrian Popular Antiquities* (1815)


*Song to a Child*

Dinogad's smock is pied, pied –
Made it out of marten hide.
Whit, whit, whistle along,
Eight slaves with you sing the song.

When your dad went to hunt,
Spear on his shoulder, cudgel in hand,
He called his quick dogs, 'Giff, you wretch,
Gaff, catch her, catch her, fetch, fetch!'

From a coracle he'd spear
Fish as a lion strikes a deer,
When your dad went to the crag
He brought down roebuck, boar and stag,
Speckled grouse from the mountain tall,
Fish from Derwent waterfall.

Whatever your dad found with his spear,                    **125**
Boar or wild cat, fox or deer,
Unless it flew, would never get clear.

ANONYMOUS, 7th century
trans. Tony Conran

At the head of the valley lies Cwm Trwsgl, with its great fox
earth, where we often found ourselves after a long day with the
Ynysfor Hounds. Everyone followed the hounds on foot, or
rather the few who were keen enough to put up with the ever-
changing weather and precipitous rocky slopes that made it the
roughest hunting country in Britain. I think I learnt most about
the mountains from following the Ynysfor Hounds.

Ynysfor takes its name from the small hill that was once an
island. That was, of course, before Maddocks built his great
embankment down at Portmadoc at the beginning of the last
century. The rocky and wooded mound that rises from the flat
land around it is about half a mile long and a quarter of a mile
wide. It has little bays and cliffs, but no sea has surrounded it
for a hundred and fifty years, and today only its name remains
to tell us that at one time it was one of the many wooded knolls
that, at high tide, became islands in what was possibly the most
beautiful bay in Europe. People have lived there since prehistoric times. The Phoenicians may have tied their boats there,
and later the Vikings must have found it a safe base for their
raids on the country around – a countryside that is rich in
Romano-British legend. There are the remains of an old fort on
one of the rocky outcrops, and the old house at Ynysfor was
probably built from its stone. The Hendy is typical of the older
type of Welsh house, with a big chimney a quarter of the way
along the roof, and a stepped gable end in which there is a
small dovecote. It stands above the stable yard and, like so
many old Welsh houses, has no view. The working Welsh
squire saw enough of the beauties around him throughout the
day, and all he needed from his house was comfort and protection. The Hendy of Ynysfor is certainly protected, tucked as it is
under the hill away from the south-west winds that drive up
from the sea.

It was to the old house that Jackie Jones came with his

hounds two hundred years ago to found the remarkable family of Jones of Ynysfor; they have hunted and followed their own hounds, and farmed and lived off their land as few Welsh landed families have done. Jackie Jones was the son of a parson, and was sent up to Oxford presumably to follow in his father's footsteps. But he had been born with a passion for the chase, and instead of ministering to the spiritual needs of the neighbourhood, he seems to have given up his life to hunting foxes, otters and pine-martens over the mountains and in the rivers around Snowdon. His hounds must have been pure Welsh, rough-coated, sometimes black and tan, with lovely voices. Today, the cry of the Ynysfor hounds still echoes among the cliffs of Cnicht, Snowdon, Lliwedd and Hebog. Jackie Jones started a tradition that he passed on to his son Evan who, in his turn, lived, farmed and kept hounds at Ynysfor until, on his death, a new era began with his two sons John and Richard.

John Jones it was who built the new house in 1865. On rising ground, facing the magnificent peak of Cnicht, there rose the present Ynysfor, a stone-built house with sharp-pitched roofs and gable ends. It stands firmly and confidently, no architectural masterpiece but a good house for its period. It was well designed and built, with a good hall and well-windowed rooms; the squirearchy had become more sophisticated and the glorious views were better appreciated. Here John Jones and Lydia his wife brought up two sons and eight daughters who, although amazing individualists, were undoubtedly of the Ynysfor stamp. Evan and Jack were the boys, and Cordelia, Bessie, Minnie, Annie, Dolly, Freda, Sybil and Miggs the girls. Ynysfor must have been a lively place at the end of the last century.

When I first knew Colonel Evan, Captain Jack and the Misses Minnie, Annie, Sybil and Miggs lived there. I used to go over often; in winter to hunt and in the summer to shoot crows and pigeons, to help Jack bring in the hay or just to be there to listen to the innumerable stories of the country round about and the people who had lived there. The family usually sat in the living room: Evan and Jack in the middle opposite the fire, while the sisters formed an outer semi-circle.

Meals were despatched with the utmost speed. Jack and I would come in from the fields when the stew pot was already in the dining room with a sister ladling out the contents. Before I could eat even a potato and a small piece of meat, the door would burst open and in would dash the raven-haired daughter of some tenant farmer with a large open tart, banging it down on the sideboard, and sweeping out again in a second. The tart eaten, Jack's voice would be saying, 'Well, John, there's that drain to be dug', as he wrung out his moustaches and disappeared through the back door. I followed him out into the fields again, stew and tart complaining from the depths of my stomach.

Sometimes I helped Jack feed the hounds. The slate-flagged kennels are two hundred yards from the house on the north side of the island, surrounded by rook- and magpie-filled trees. One of the trees is used as a giant gibbet for the carcases of horses, cows and sheep, strung up by a winch and left to hang and season in the wind and the sun. When the bones are picked clean by the hounds and terriers, they are thrown down the bank below the kennels to become a fearful cemetery where the rooks and magpies quarrel over the pickings.

I suppose the kennels are the heart of Ynysfor, for, without the hounds, the character of the house would go and it would become just another dwelling. There are trophies of the hunt everywhere. In the hall, the masks of foxes from Arddu and Aran snarl at a stuffed pine-marten, and, in the living room (the room which I always feel is most typical) are family portraits, a fine Dutch still-life and the white pads of a large dog fox. This fox I remember being killed above Llanaelhaiarn after a long hunt from Ynys.

KYFFIN WILLIAMS
*Across the Straits* (1973)

### Hold Hard, These Ancient Minutes in the Cuckoo's Month

Hold hard, these ancient minutes in the cuckoo's month,
Under the lank, fourth folly on Glamorgan's hill,
As the green blooms ride upward, to the drive of time;
Time, in a folly's rider, like a county man
Over the vault of ridings with his hound at heel,
Drives forth my men, my children, from the hanging south.

Country, your sport is summer, and December's pools
By crane and water-tower by the seedy trees
Lie this fifth month unskated, and the birds have flown;
Hold hard, my country children in the world of tales,
The greenwood dying as the deer fall in their tracks,
This first and steepled season, to the summer's game.

And now the horns of England, in the sound of shape,
Summon your snowy horsemen, and the four-stringed hill,
Over the sea-gut loudening, sets a rock alive;
Hurdles and guns and railings, as the boulders heave,
Crack like a spring in a vice, bone breaking April,
Spill the lank folly's hunter and the hard-held hope.

Down fall four padding weathers on the scarlet lands,
Stalking my children's faces with a tail of blood,
Time, in a rider rising, from the harnessed valley;
Hold hard, my county darlings, for a hawk descends,
Golden Glamorgan straightens, to the falling birds.
Your sport is summer as the spring runs angrily.

DYLAN THOMAS (1914–53)

*Children's Pastimes, Ebbw Vale, 1939*

When the four o'clock sun comes around and burns hot patches into the back of my jumper, Miss Stevens rings the home bell and I speed out from Pont-y-Gof Girls, double quick.

It is Whip and Top time and we are not allowed to play it in the yard. That is only for Strings and On-it and Last Man's Head Off.

I found the top I had last year in the boot polish box, under the cold slab in the pantry. It is still as good as a new one from Lloyds the Toy Shop up in James Street, except that some of the green paint has been whipped off the sides.

People throw down sweet wrappers and silver paper outside Idwal's Post Office, so I look in the gutter for bits and stick them on the top with condensed milk. When I whip the top, it spins the silver paper into a round rainbow.

Some girls put chalk, but silver paper shines better. When the condensed milk dries a bit, the paper whirls off, so I stick on different colours.

Gran says it is a waste of condensed.

Soon it will be time for Bowlies, steel hoops we push along with hooks on rods, which make sparks, and after that Bat and Catty.

The Catty is a stick sharpened at both ends, put in a hole you make with your heel in the dirt. You bang it with the bat and hit the catty hard when it flies up in the air, then mark with a cross where it falls and measure back with the stick to the hole. The one who has the most stick lengths is the winner. You can be knocked out of the game if someone hits your stick with a catty. Then they ask for 'Chance', and you have to put your stick across the hole for them to throw at. Mam maintains Bat and Catty is dangerous, because you can get a catty in your eye.

Grown-ups always find fault with our games.

If we tamp balls on to the roofs at the back of our Row it is 'Stop that! You'll have the slates off in a minute!'

When you miss a catch and the ball goes over the wall into gardens, especially Mrs Taylor's, you won't get it back. Her garden is a ball graveyard.

IRENE E. THOMAS

*Knappan (Cnapan)*

But being drawn to speak of the exercise of the body, I cannot overpass a game used in one part of this shire among the Welshmen, both rare to hear, troublesome to describe, and painful to practise, yet for the rarity thereof, I crave pardon to trouble you, and though somewhat long, yet as brief as I may. This game is called *Knappan*, and not unfitly, as shall be shewed, the game is thought to be of great antiquity, and is as followeth . . .

I will let you know that this *Knappan* happeneth and falleth out to be by two meanes, the one is a settled or standing *Knappan*, the day and place being known and yearly observed. Of these *Knappan* days in Penbrokshire there were wont to be five in number . . . And at these days and places were these games wont yearly to be exercised without any matchmaking or appointment, and therefore I call these standing *Knappans*. Other the like plays would oftentimes be by making of match between two gentlemen . . . which most commonly fall out to be the greatest plays, for in these matches the gentlemen would divide the parishes, hundreds or shires between them, and then would each labour to bring the greatest number, and would therein entreat all his friends and kinsmen in every parish to come and bring his parish wholly with him, by which means great number would most usually meet, and therefore against these matches there would also resort to the place divers victuallers with meat, drink and wine of all sorts, also merchants, mercers, and pedlers would provide stalls, and booths, some to play, some to eat and drink, some to buy and some to sell, and others to be seen (you know what kind I mean) great multitudes of people would resort beside the players . . .

Their matches are commonly made without stint of number, but as they happen to come . . . The companies being come together, about one or two of the clock, afternoon, beginneth the play, in this sort, after a cry made, both parties draw together in some plain, all first stripped bare, saving a light pair · of breeches, bare headed, bare bodied, bare leggs and feet, their clothes being laid together in great heaps under the charge of certain keepers appointed for the purpose, for if he leave but his shirt on his back, in the fury of the game it is most commonly torn to pieces, and I have also seen some long lock gallants trimly trimmed at this game, not by polling, but by pulling their hair and beards . . .

You shall see gamesters return home from this play with broken heads, black faces, bruised bodies, and lame legs, yet laughing and merrily jesting at their harms, telling their adversaries how he brake his head, to another that he strake him on the face, and how he repaid the same to him again, and all this in good mirth, without grudge or hatred. And if any be in arrerages to the other they score it up till the next play, and in the meantime will continue loving friends . . .

GEORGE OWEN, OF HENLLYS (1552–1613)
*The Description of Penbrokshire* (1603)

It has been argued that despite the differences in the two games, the *cnapan* tradition may well have predisposed the Welsh towards their love of and skill in rugby football. Be that as it may, the tradition persisted: in the Llandysul area of south Cardiganshire until 1922. Here was held on the first day of the Julian calendar a mass football match in which the goals were eight miles apart.

A game very similar to hockey and played with stick bent
and round at one end and a small wooden ball was known in
Wales as *bando*, a game known throughout the country in varying forms and still to be found in some areas. The earliest
example of the Welsh term *bando* occurs in a dictionary by
John Walters published in 1770–94. It was particularly popular
in the Cynffig-Margam district of the Vale of Glamorgan
where wide stretches of sandy beaches afforded ample room
for play. The 'Margam Bando Boys', at the turn of the
eighteenth–nineteenth centuries, were celebrated in song in
both English and Welsh:

> Due praises I'll bestow
> And all the world shall know
> That Margam valour shall keep its colour
> While Kenfig's waters flow.
>
> Our master, straight and tall,
> Is foremost with the ball;
> He is, we know it and must allow it,
> The fastest man of all.
>
> Let cricket players blame
> And seek to slight our fame,
> Their bat and wicket can never lick it,
> This ancient manly game.
>
> Our fame shall always stand
> Throughout Britannia's land;
> What man can beat us? Who dare to meet us?
> Upon old Kenfig's strand.

IORWERTH C. PEATE
*Tradition and Folk Life:
A Welsh View* (1972)

*London Welsh v. Bridgend*

> Then I got on the train, very late
> at night, Saturday, and lay on the seat,
> exhausted, as did the other man
> there, a little man, beady-eyed and
> with a pointed chin, and he pulled the

blinds down, and we lay, and just about
dozed off when bam! door opened,
in came half a rugby team, enormous
fellows, tipped me off the seat on the
filthy floor, then sat down, singing,
shouting, crashing on each other with
their beer cans, and one sat by the
beady man, running his fingers exquisitely
along the fellow's thigh-bone, through
his trousers, but in only a bawdy
way, friendly even, if you could believe
it, and they roughed, and one
arse in the corridor undid the fire
extinguisher, soaked us, and another
slammed the door, sat down again, kept
asking me the beady man's name, which
I didn't know, angry now, afraid even,
but decided to be sensible, and got
going, talked, had their beer, and they
got serious to meet me, a most
generous gesture, and a big man, older
than the others, kept deflecting the
attention of the bawdy one from the
beady one, the bawdy one trying to make
the beady one talk, which he couldn't,
in inhibition, and cringing fear, and I
felt sorry, but leant on the carriage arm,
with them, drinking, singing, yawning, and
hearing about his wife, from one of them,
till, at last, they were quieter, they had
won their match, they had had a good day,
and they dozed off, one on my shoulder, sixteen
stone, snoring loudly, but I finally dozed
off, at the train's rhythm, rattling
through the darkness, and I half-woke,
at times, saw a misty scene, as of Arthur's
knights assembled, swaying, brief white
faces, then dozed, felt the train stop
in my half-asleep condition, and men get
out, a shrieking porter, and banging doors,
then slept again, and then woke, two
hundred miles from London, they had

all gone, every one, bar the beady one, and I
sat, heavy, soggy, wanting lukewarm tea, and
saw, with my round eye and my mind's eye,
the aftermath of dawn, and the mess of the
twentieth century; the industry, the steel
works and the smelting works, a new day, for
better or worse in our hands, and the
carriage window, filthy, but a filter,
for that streaky, watery, nearly
light-blue, blue.

J. P. WARD

As every Welsh rugby fan knows, no match is more important
than the one against England. Regardless of whether a Triple
Crown or a Grand Slam is at stake, or whether the match is at
the Arms Park or Twickenham, the confrontation with the Old
Enemy is always special, something to savour, and greeted
with eager anticipation by player and supporter alike.

GARETH EDWARDS
*Most Memorable Matches* (1984)

*Cardiff Arms Park*

Only to hear some sixty thousand Welshmen
sing natural three-part harmony unrehearsed
while rugby giants battle on the field
is knowing that these men were never English.
The language changes, but the hearts do not.

To see red-jerseyed forwards lift themselves
and drive the startled Englishmen before them
as sixty thousand roar the anthem out
is seeing that this race was never conquered.
The valleys darken, but the fire lives.

To see this, all the same, is to regret
that sixty thousand with this splendid fire
urge fifteen on to drive the English back.
If only they would urge themselves like that.

ALUN REES

# VII

# LANDSCAPE, PLACES, TRAVELLERS

*The Seven Wonders of Wales*

Pistyll Rhaedr and Wrexham Steeple,
Snowdon's mountain, without its people;
Overton Yewtrees, Saint Winifred Wells,
Llangollen Bridge and Gresford Bells.

Traditional

. . . we sometimes see these Mountains [of Wales] rising up at once from the lowest Valleys to the highest Summits, which makes the Height look horrid and frightful, *even worse* than those Mountains Abroad.

DANIEL DEFOE (1660–1731)
*Tour Through the Whole Island of Britain* (1724)

### Directions for Visitors

If you want to see Wales,
Measure the long isosceles
Of Snowdon with your feet;
Fly your heart through the dappled trees
Of calm Cwm Cynfal; dip
Your fingertips into the lees

Of the old religion
At Holywell – and see the new
At pink Llantrisant mint.
Ascend the sacred avenue
Of Strata Florida:
Beyond the transept seek the yew,

The flame of evergreen
That streams up from dead Dafydd's bones,
And know that there, under
The sheep-cropped turf and tumbled stones,
Are clenched the corded roots
Stronger than new pence or old thrones.

RAYMOND GARLICK

### The Rivers of Merionethshire

'And since each one is praised for her peculiar things,
So MERVINIA is rich in mountains, lakes, and springs;
And holds herself as great in her superfluous waste,
As others by their towns and fruitful tillage graced.
And therefore to recount her rivers from their springs,
Abridging all delays, MERVINIA thus begins.'

DRAYTON

The principal rivers are, the Dee, the Maw, the Dovey, the
Dwyrhyd, and the Dysynni: there are also the Wonion,
the Traethbach, the *Maes y pandy*, the Dyffryngwn, the Diflas,
the Cwmceili, the Cowarch, the Twrch, the Llew, the Dee,
the Bychan, the Treweryn, the Lymauduon, the Eden, and the
Cain; besides a hundred other nameless streams. Merionethshire, and the neighbouring county of Carnarvon, may be truly
named the Paradise of anglers, the whole district being
diversified with woods, lakes, rivers, torrents, cataracts, and all
the varied decorations of nature in her wildest garb.

### The Dee
Has its source within a short distance of Bala lake, which it
soon enters a little below Llamrwchyllyn: issuing from this
extensive sheet of water near the town of Bala, it takes a north-
north-east direction through the beautiful vale of Edeyrnion,
and, afterwards passing the town of Corwen, flows through the
picturesque vales of Glyndyvrdwy and Llangollen into the
southern part of Denbighshire.

### The Maw
Rises in the mountains of the north-east part of the county, and
flows first southward, and then south-westward, by the village
of Llanvachrek, towards Llanelltyd, where it is joined by the
Wonion.

### The Wonion
Equal in size to the Maw, rises near the source of the Dee, at a
place called Drws y Nant, and, winding through a narrow valley in a less turbulent stream than is usual with rivers having a
mountainous origin, passes the town of Dolgelly. – *A beautiful
trout stream.*

### The Dovey
Rises at the foot of Aran Mowddwy, and flows southward
through the rich vale to which it gives its name; and passing by
the small town of Dinas Mowddwy, enters the western part of
Montgomeryshire, where it becomes the southern boundary of
Merionethshire.

*The Dwyrhyd*

Rises in the mountains on the northern side of the county, and
gradually losing its character of a mountain torrent as it
emerges into a more level district, flows in beautiful meanders
through the celebrated Vale of Festiniog.

GEORGE AGAR HANSARD
*Trout and Salmon Fishing in Wales* (1834)

### The River Ebbw

Springing from the coarse canvas of Llangynydir
streams embroider the moors with silver,
Nant Pwll Goch, Nant o Dyn Ty, and Ebwy Fawr,
Twisting, plunging under the skin tight surface of Carno
    Reservoir.

Through a shimmer of King Cups and velvet monkey musk
    at Glan-yr-afon,
gathering like housewives for a gossip,
joining Gantre Brook, Cwm Draw, Nant-y-Meddyg,
taking in Nant-y-Byg.

Industry washed its grimy hands
and the river ran brick and paynes grey.
Bearded barabits choked on scourings,
ochre mud flooded kitchens in lower Cwm,
stained settees and sideboards,
solidified in coconut matting.

Furnaces rusted,
Bessemer cooled,
Rolling Mills hissed to a steamy standstill,
left a steel corpse in a slag grave,
between the Domen and Mynydd Carn-y-Cefn.

The valley is grey with shadows of men waiting.

But underneath, the Ebwy is clear,
its arched culvert echoes with news of Waun-y-Pound and
    Rassau.
Put your ear to the ground and listen.

IRENE E. THOMAS

*Ogmore*

It is good to be back in Ogmore. Because of the American trip
we have not been here since October 6th. This time of the year
one can take an oxygen walk to Southerndown almost without
seeing anyone – for company there's only the sheep, the crows
and the gulls, and perhaps an occasional self-absorbed, solitary
dog. This morning we took the sand route at first, for the tide
was right; then we climbed up and over the rocks to the high,
breath-holding cliffs. We observed a sheep utterly motionless.
It seemed to be reading a red danger sign on which was written
DANGEROUS CLIFFS. To misquote Shelley: there is only one better
walk in the world than from Ogmore to Southerndown and
that is the walk from Southerndown to Ogmore. The return
journey is especially good to take at dusk when one can watch
the slow western mobile sunsets below the aeroplane vapour-
trails.

   In the 1930s, when we lived in Cardiff, our car, a Riley,

seemed to know only one route. It would go instinctively to Ogmore-by-Sea. My father only had to sit in the driving seat, turn on the ignition, and off it would go along the A48, up Tumble Down Dick, through Cowbridge, up and down Crack Hill, all of the twenty-three miles to the sea, the sea at Ogmore. Every half sunny Sunday, every holiday, the car knew we wanted to play cricket on the sands of Hardee's Bay while its boss, my father, fished near the mouth of the river for dabs, salmon bass, and ghosts.

Not only my immediate family homed back to Ogmore. Uncles and aunts, fat and thin, cousins short and tall, from Cardiff, Swansea, Ammanford, singing in their closed saloons, 'Stormy Weather' and 'She was a Good Girl until I took her to a Dance' returned to meet and quarrel and take a dip in the unstable Ogmore estuary.

My sister, Huldah, once confided that she had lost her virginity in one of the secret caves of Ogmore while my Uncle Max, unaware, played the violin on the rocks nearby, and cousins and their friends munched gritty tomato sandwiches and stared at the incoming, loosely-chained sea.

Not everybody in the Abse family is stuck on Ogmore. I have an American nephew, Nathan. When he was ten he came to stay with us at Ogmore. His voice was inordinately deep and husky and Virginian. He arrived after nightfall, gave the slate-black emptiness of Ogmore the once over, heard the sheep munching in the dark, then gazing towards the funfair's shimmering lights across the bay of distant Porthcawl, said, 'Hey, man, let's take off for civilization.'

I wish we could stay here longer. I'm fed up with driving up and down the M4, from and to London. But I don't see any solution to that. In the new year we shall still be making the same tedious journeys. No matter, now, as I breathe out the air of London and breathe in the air of Ogmore I know it's all worth it. I walk beside the cutlery-glinting sea, consoled by the sound of the waves' irregularities, by the pitch and tone of them, the 'sssh' of shingle, the way the sea slaps on rocks or shuffles sinking into the sand that sizzles as the tide recedes. And there, quite near really, the steamers pass, slow and hushed, around the breath-holding cliffs on their seamless way to the ports of Barry, Cardiff, Newport and, in dream, further, mysteriously, into 1986.

November–December 1985

This morning (May 4th) an east wind was blowing so vigorously in Ogmore that our wooden gate had been thrust open. From the bedroom window I could see that a ewe with two lambs had trespassed into our garden. They were munching the daffodils and narcissi, a nice, forbidden, wicked breakfast. I rushed downstairs, still in my pyjamas, to shoo them out.

As I closed the gate behind them I thought more of the east wind than the sheep. Probably it was bearing invisible death-seeds from Chernobyl. Perhaps radioactive raindrops were sipped from the daffodil cups by the ewe and lambs. Information, so far, is meagre. In any case, who can believe the complacent, stealthy, reassuring voices of experts and politicians? How much has been covered up before, how much will be told to us now? Will radioactive iodine be taken up by small, thirsty thyroid glands? What about my new granddaughter and all those like her from Ogmore-by-Sea to the Ukraine and beyond where Prometheus is still chained to his rock while the vulture eats his liver?

Last Friday in Cardiff, I visited Llandaff Cathedral. I just happened to be nearby, so popped in as I used to as a boy, passing the yellow celandines beneath the yew tree. Inside soaring places of worship – Jewish, Moslem or Christian – I feel not secular but utterly estranged like one without history or memory. Once more, numb, I observed Epstein's dominating aluminium Lazarus rising. And it was springtime, springtime in the real world and all seemingly dead things were coming alive again though a cancer sailed in from Chernobyl.

Inside the Cathedral, I ambled towards the Lady Chapel reredos where, on either side of the sculpted Madonna, six niches are filled with gold-leafed wreaths of wild flowers. In Welsh, dozens of flowers are named after the Virgin, as is proper in a nation that reveres the Mam of the family. The marigold is called Gold Mair – Mary's Gold; the buttercup, Mary's sweat; the briar rose, Mary's briar; the foxglove, Mary's thimble; the monkshood, Mary's slipper; the cowslip, Mary's primrose; and the snowdrop, Mary's taper (Tapr Mair).

If a man believed in a deity, any deity, goddess, god or God, he would, in that Cathedral, have prayed in English or Welsh or no language at all, for the neutralization of the death wind. And in Ogmore, this morning, as I stood in my pyjamas while

142 the opera-dramatic clouds, grey, cream, or frowning darker,
tracked so visibly westwards, my own lips moved.

May 1986

DANNIE ABSE<br>
Journals from the Antheap (1986)


### Praise of Tenby

This has all the marks of being a *dadolwch*, or poem of reconcili-
ation between a poet and his patron. The patron is a lord of
Dyfed, or Pembrokeshire, called Bleiddudd; but the poem is
remarkable among those of its type in that Bleiddudd is dead,
'gone to the oaken church', and the poet is making peace with
his heir, the new head of Erbin's line, master of the 'little fort' –
Dinbych or Tenby. If the last line of this translation is correct,
which is open to doubt, it looks as though the poem was
intended for recitation at Bleiddudd's funeral feast, at the
November Calends, the festival of the beginning of winter. It is
markedly anti-North Walian: Dyfed and Gwynedd must at this
time have been at one another's throats. I have omitted the
final couplet to God, and also a stray, fragmentary stanza that
follows it in the manuscript.

> I ask for God's favour, saviour of the folk,
> Master of heaven and earth, greatly prudent and wise.
>
> There is a fine fortress stands on the sea,
> The bright headland is gay at the Calends,
> And when the ocean puts forth its might
> Commonly poets are loud over mead-cups.
> The hurrying wave surges against it,
> They abandon the green flood to the Picts.
> And through my prayer, O God, may I find
> As I keep faith, atonement with you.
>
> There is a fine fortress on the broad ocean,
> Unyielding stronghold, sea round its edge.

Enquire, O Britain, who rightly owns it –
Yours, head of Erbin's line, yours be it now!

In this palisade were war-band and throng,
Eagle in cloud on the track of pale faces:
Before that lord and router of enemies,
Prince of wide fame, they drew up their ranks.

There is a fine fortress on the ninth wave.
Finely its populace take their ease.
They do not make merry with taunts and sneers,
It is not their custom to be hard,
Nor shall I traduce their welcome –
Better a slave in Dyfed than yeoman in Deudraeth!
Their throng of free men, keeping a feast,
Would include, two by two, the best men alive!

There is a fine fortress of revel and tumult
A multitude makes, and crying of birds.
Gay was that company met at the Calends
Round a generous lord, splendid and brave.
Before he had gone to the oaken church
From a bowl of glass gave me mead and wine.

There is a fine fortress on the foreshore,
Finely to each is given his share.
I know at Tenby – pure white the seagull –
Companions of Bleiddudd, lord of the court.
The night of the Calends it was my custom
To lie by my king, brilliant in war,
With a cloak coloured purple, having such cheer
I were the tongue to the poets of Britain!

There is a fine fortress resounds with song,
Where every concession I wished for was mine –
I say nothing of rights! I kept good order:
Whoever knows otherwise deserves no feast-gift!
The writings of Britain were my chief care
Where the loud waves broke in tumult.
Let it long remain, that cell I visited!

There is a fine fortress on the height,
Its feasting lavish, its revelry loud.
Lovely about it, that camp of heroes,
Is the wandering spray, long are its wings.
Hoarse sea-birds haunt the crest of the crag.
Let all anger be banished over the hills!
I wish for Bleiddudd the best bliss that may be –
Let these words of remembrance be weighed at his wake!

ANONYMOUS, *c.* 873
trans. Tony Conran
*Welsh Verse* (1986)

Pembrokeshire is divided into two parts by a line cutting across the county separating it sharply into Welsh- and English-speaking districts. Upon the basic Welsh, not to speak of pre-Celtic aborigines, have imposed themselves Scandinavian, Roman, Norman, Saxon, Irish and Flemish elements. The English spoken is good but the Welsh, I am told, is better. Haverfordwest, the centre of the Flemish colonization, was the home of my father's people. Successive bands of mercenary troops, weavers and masons from Flanders at the beginning of the twelfth century, by royal permission, and with a view of keeping the turbulent Welsh in check, were allowed or encouraged to intrude on the then Scandinavian town and district of Haverford (Havrefiord), and ended by dominating more than half the county. The name of a suburb of Haverfordwest, Prendergast, attests the permanence of the colonization, and the neighbouring village of Langum is reputed to be still inhabited by authentic descendants of the 'Flemings', who elsewhere seem to have amalgamated with the Welsh. In view of the mist that hides my origins, mysterious as those of any hero of antiquity, I have sometimes wondered if a strain from Flanders may not have enriched the family bloodstream. Nothing could be likelier.

AUGUSTUS JOHN
*Chiaroscuro* (1952)

*The Mountains of Snowdonia*

I must not fail to tell you about the mountains which are called Eryri by the Welsh and by the English Snowdon, that is the

Snow Mountains. They rise gradually from the land of the sons of Cynan and extend northwards near Degannwy. When looked at from Anglesey, they seem to rear their lofty summits right up to the clouds. They are thought to be so enormous and to extend so far that, as the old saying goes: 'Just as Anglesey can supply all the inhabitants of Wales with corn, so, if all the herds were gathered together, Snowdon could afford sufficient pasture.' To these grazing-grounds Virgil's words can well apply:

And what they crop by day the shorter night renews,
Thus feeding all the flocks thanks to its cooling dews.

At the very top of these mountains two lakes are to be found, each of them remarkable in its own way. One has a floating island, which moves about and is often driven to the opposite side by the force of the winds. Shepherds are amazed to see the flocks which are feeding there carried off to distant parts of the lake. It is possible that a section of the bank was broken off in times long past and that, bound together in a natural way by the roots of the willows and other shrubs which grow there, it has since become larger by alluvial deposits. It is continually driven from one bank to another by the violent winds, which in so elevated a position never cease to blow, and it can never anchor itself firmly to the shore again. The second lake has a remarkable and almost unique property. It abounds in three different kinds of fish, eels, trout and perch, and all of them have only one eye, the right one being there but not the left. If the careful reader asks me the cause of such a remarkable phenomenon, I can only answer that I do not know. It is worth noticing that in Scotland, too, in two different places, one to the east and one to the west, the fish called mullet are found in the sea with only one eye. They lack the left eye but have the right eye.

GERALD OF WALES
*The Journey Through Wales* (1191)
trans. Lewis Thorpe

A horrid spot of hills.

EDMOND HALLEY (1648)

*View from the Summit of Snowdon*

There we stood on the Wyddfa, in a cold bracing atmosphere, though the day was almost stiflingly hot in the regions from which we had ascended. There we stood enjoying a scene inexpressibly grand, comprehending a considerable part of the mainland of Wales, the whole of Anglesey, a faint glimpse of part of Cumberland, the Irish Channel, and what might either be a misty creation or the shadowy outline of the hills of Ireland. Peaks and pinnacles and huge moels stood up here and there, about us and below us, partly in glorious light, partly in deep shade. Manifold were the objects which we saw from the brow of Snowdon, but of all the objects which we saw, those which filled us with most delight and admiration, were numerous lakes and lagoons, which, like sheets of ice or polished silver, lay reflecting the rays of the sun in the deep valleys at his feet.

GEORGE BORROW (1803–81)
*Wild Wales* (1862)

*Penmaenmawr*

. . . instead of bleak and barren mountains there were . . . green and fertile ones and one of the castles in Wales would contain all the Castles that I had seen in Scotland . . . We would have

**148** staid at Conway, if we could have found entertainment, for we were afraid of passing Penmaen Mawr, over which lay our way to Bangor, but by bright daylight, and the delay of our coach made our departure exceedingly late . . . Our coach was at last brought, and we set out with some anxiety, but we came to Penmaen Mawr by daylight; and found a way, lately made, very easy and very safe. It was cut smooth, and enclosed between parallel walls; the outer of which secures the passenger from the precipice, which is deep and dreadful. This wall is here and there broken, by mischievous wantonness. The inner wall preserves the road from the loose stones, which the shattered steep above it would pour down. That side of the mountain seems to have a surface of loose stones, which every accident may crumble. The old road was higher, and must have been very formidable. The sea beats at the bottom of the way.

SAMUEL JOHNSON (1709–84)
*The Diary of a Journey Through North Wales in 1774*

Lo here I sit at Holy head
With muddy ale and mouldy bread;
I'm fastened both by wind and tide,
I see the ships at anchor ride . . .
The Captain swears the sea's too rough –
(He has not passengers enough).
And thus the Dean is forced to stay,
Till others come to help the pay.

When Mrs Welch's Chimney smokes,
'Tis a sign she'll keep her folks,
But, when of smoak the room is clear
It is a sign we shan't stay here.

JONATHAN SWIFT, 1727 (1667–1754)

Brecknockshire is a meer inland county . . . the English jestingly (and I think not very improperly) called it Breakneckshire.

DANIEL DEFOE (1660–1731)
*Tour Through the Whole Island of Britain* (1724)

## Llanthony

*Tuesday, 5 April 1870*

We crossed a field and the fold of a farm house, scrambled down a narrow stony lane and struck the main road again. About a mile above Llanthony we descried the Abbey ruins, the dim grey pile of building in the vale below standing by the little riverside among its brilliant green meadow. What was our horror on entering the enclosure to see two tourists with staves and shoulder belts all complete postured among the ruins in an attitude of admiration, one of them of course discoursing learnedly to his gaping companion and pointing out objects of interest with his stick. If there is one thing more hateful than another it is being told what to admire and having objects pointed out to one with a stick. Of all noxious animals too the most noxious is a tourist. And of all tourists the most vulgar, illbred, offensive and loathsome is the British tourist.

Morrell and I arrived at Clyro 7.50 and dined together comfortably at Cae Mawr sitting up talking afterwards till half past twelve. We were rather tired with our 25 miles walk, but not extraordinarily so.

FRANCIS KILVERT (1840–79)
*Kilvert's Diary 1870–79*
ed. William Plomer (1977)

## Laugharne

It is an old town, and feels it, plentiful with solid pubs and crouching cottages. Rhys ap Gruffydd, of the house of Dinefwr, built the castle in the twelfth century, while the Normans had not yet fully established themselves in this part of South Wales.

The main street, though, stone-built and traditional, tells you little of the real nature of Laugharne, which is that it is on the estuary of the Taf. To get this feeling clearly one has to take that unexpected side road through the quiet, self-effacing cottages, to come out into the lane which tilts down past the Boat House, stuck on that cliff overlooking the streamways and tidal reaches of the zinc mud and silk water. 'My seashaken house On a breakneck of rocks . . .'

> By scummed, starfish sands
> With their fishwife cross
> Gulls, pipers, cockles and sails,
> Out there, crow black, men
> Tackled with clouds, who keep
> To the sunset nets,
> Geese nearly in heaven, boys
> Stabbing, and herons, and shells
> That speak seven seas . . .

Dylan lived in the Boat House during his last years in Wales, and he worked in a shed which he called 'the shack' stuck high over the house by the side of the lane from the village. A window of it looks out over the water, so that the words, above, of the Prologue to his *Collected Poems*, must have been an immediate description of what he saw, and what he often saw, while sitting at the small wooden table which was the shed's only furniture.

MICHAEL SENIOR
*Portrait of South Wales* (1974)

As a whole, the studio was a rat's-nest of chewed, rolled and discarded papers – piles of manuscripts, unanswered (often unopened) letters, empty cigarette packages, small stacks of literary periodicals, tradesmen's bills, and publishers' brochures. Snatches of reworked poetry lay under empty beer bottles. Volumes of poetry mouldered where they had been placed months, years, before. Besides its single table and two straight-backed chairs, the studio contained three or four half-filled cartons of books, and a small black coal-burning stove.

JOHN MALCOLM BRINNIN
*Dylan Thomas in America* (1956)

From this high quarried ledge I see
The place for which the Quakers once
Collected clothes, my father's home,
Our stubborn bankrupt village sprawled
In jaded dusk beneath its nameless hills;
The drab streets strung across the cwm,
Derelict workings, tips of slag
The gospellers and gamblers use
And children scrutting for the coal
That winter dole cannot purvey;
Allotments where the collier digs
While engines hack the coal within his brain;
Grey Hebron in a rigid cramp,
White cheap-jack cinema, the church
Stretched like a sow beside the stream;
And mourners in their Sunday best
Holding a tiny funeral, singing hymns
That drift insidious as the rain
Which rises from the steaming fields
And swathes about the skyline crags
Till all the upland gorse is drenched
And all the creaking mountain gates
Drip brittle tears of crystal peace;
And in a curtained parlour women hug
Huge grief, and anger against God.

But now the dusk, more charitable than Quakers,
Veils the cracked cottages with drifting may
And rubs the hard day off the slate.
The colliers squatting on the ashtip
Listen to one who holds them still with tales,
While that white frock that floats down the dark alley
Looks like Christ; and in the lane
The clink of coins among the gamblers
Suggests the thirty pieces of silver.

I watch the clouded years
Rune the rough foreheads of these moody hills,
This wet evening, in a lost age.

ALUN LEWIS (1915–44)

And now that I am back in Wales, am I the same person, sadly staring over the flat, sad, estuary sands, watching the herons walk like women poets, hearing the gab of gulls, alone and lost in a soft kangaroo pocket of the sad, salt West, who once, so very little time ago, trundled under the blaring lights, to the tune of cabhorns, his beautiful barrow of raspberries . . . I know that I am home again because I feel just as I felt when I was not at home, only more so.

*Living in Wales*
Broadcast by Dylan Thomas, 23 June 1949

from *Shadow of the Trees*

One of the poet Alun Lewis's most famous works is 'The Mountain Over Aberdare'. In this he describes the village of Cwmaman, where he was brought up, ravaged by economic depression of the 'thirties.

Today Cwmaman is similarly depressed, but Lewis would not recognize the steep mountain slopes where he loved to walk. The ancient farms, with their historic Welsh names, have, with one exception, vanished. Although the old Coal Board was responsible for some of this destruction, the cause of much of this change has been the introduction of huge Forestry Commission plantations of fir trees.

These farms, almost all of them Welsh-speaking enclaves in industrial Glamorgan, are now the graveyards of a traditional culture. The open mountainsides have become no-go areas for wildlife and people alike, as the dark, impenetrable fir and spruce plantations have spread over the slopes. In short, in afforesting the 'mountain above Aberdare', the Forestry Commission was effectively bringing to a close a way of life that had existed for many centuries.

Not far away to the north lie the lakes of Llyn Fawr and Llyn Fach. The former, now a reservoir, is famous for the hoard of Bronze Age implements discovered there early in the century. Access to this lake, under the spectacular massif of Craig y Llyn, is not difficult. But Llyn Fach, less than a mile distant, has been completely walled in by the now familiar barricades of the spruce. The lake, a historic and mysterious feature of the landscape, has been effectively sealed off by the Commission.

Further west, in what remains of Welsh-speaking Dyfed, the poet Gwenallt has bitterly protested at the planting 'of the saplings for the Third World War' at Rhydcymerau. Where once small, healthy rural communities flourished, there is now only the shadow of the trees, and the last place for the Welsh language is in the bilingual fire-warning signs.

In opposing the continued afforestation of Welsh uplands and moors, Friends of the Earth Cymru is mindful of the cultural as well as the environmental consequences of turning our country into a timber storage yard for Scandinavian softwoods . . .

ROBERT MINHINNICK
in *Rural Wales* (Summer 1988)

*Llyn Brenig*
(man-made, 1976)

Where grouse rose cackling on the moor
and weasels sloped near farms
a new lake spreads like a water-fan
fringed with anchored fishermen.
Naked as a just-born child
surprised by its own existence
it lies self-consciously
skin wrinkling under the wind.

Birds are confused in migratory tracks.
On high ground, the cuffs of the forest
where uncountable sheep rush in eddies
woolly puppets on invisible wires
controlled by an unseen flockmaster.

The drowned valley knows again
the float of carboniferous seas
swish and hish of water-time
the sculpted art-work of ice.

GLADYS MARY COLES

East of Traeth Bach the hills of Meirionydd rise steeply, with a roll and pitch about Llyn Tecwyn and on and up to the flat tops of Mynydd Ysfarnogod and Clip. It is a lonely stretch with only a narrow coastal strip supporting life, from Harlech to Penrhyndeudraeth. As the ground rises through bracken to bog, rush and sphagnum, even the sheep thin out and a rock-strewn wilderness keeps a walker's pace down. It is a favourite area of mine. Any excuse will serve to take me there. At first the stream beds cut deeply back into a sort of plateau or flat-backed ridge, and the going is hard. But after the first seven or eight hundred feet the flat, broken plateau is reached and a rest is more than welcome. Beyond it the final ridges and folds rise more steeply still, but this long ridge under their shelter has its own separate identity, cut off by bog and stream from the surrounding wilderness and strangely hidden from the sea. This place must once have held importance in the eyes of our early forefathers. Hugging the southern end of this bare, concealed ridge lies the broken detritus of a strange monument. Invisible from the sea and the coastal strip, this monument is nevertheless clearly visible from the tops. Looking down it appears as a delicate circle, like a necklace laid on the flanks of mountain grass. The circular shape is not uncommon – the whole area abounds with circles – but this one is different, more perfect somehow and more delicate in plan. The reason for the relative delicacy is more readily seen as the monument is approached from the Harlech direction, where it suddenly appears against the sky, in profile. It is vaguely like a coronet, though only vaguely because it is made of rough, harsh, granite slabs, natural and undressed, all corrugated by the action of wind and weather. The rocks are long in shape, they point to the sky and, uniquely, they lean outwards, which accounts for the coronet appearance.

It is a wild and solitary place and the only sound, a constant one, is of wind in the grass. Some time, long ago, men foregathered here and worked to a prescribed end – to commemorate and honour some prince or chief. That they chose this place is perhaps not extraordinary. Facing the western sea, these early people must often have suffered invasion and pillage, and this place of honour must have represented comparative safety from the depredations of invading mariners. That they chose to build in this deliberate coronet shape is more obscure. Surely it

denotes deliberation, design if you like, and that denotes hon- **155**
our for the deceased. What sort of man, or woman, was it that
moved men first of all to bear the remains high up into this solitary fastness and then gather quite heavy stones to build his
monument in this way? We cannot know. No clue survives
and indeed the whole monument by now is almost level with
the ground; even the army during the last war dug there. But
the original intention or design is still quite patent. We can
only surmise. The necrophilic cult that engendered it is not
unknown in Wales, and that alone is a feeling shared by that
chief's descendants today. Shared too is a common regard for
the princely virtues, for however ignorant the Welsh may be of
their own ancient history, there nevertheless exists a strong
substratum of nostalgia for the days of the rule of the native
princes, defenders of the heritage of Wales and patrons of its
culture. It may not be explicit, but it is implicit in the way of
life, in the attachment to the language, to communal song, to
certain institutions sacred and secular and specifically Welsh.
And it is implicit in a certain apartness from the English way of
life, the equivocal attitude to tourism and the resentment at certain physical intrusions like reservoirs and army artillery
ranges.

JONAH JONES
*Artists in Wales*, Vol. II
ed. Meic Stephens (1973)

*Climbing Cader Idris*
(for a mountaineer)

You know the mountain with your body,
I with my mind, I suppose.
Each, in our way, describes
the steepening angle of rock.

What differences now as we,
falling into step and conversation,
put to the test our long
thigh muscles and our breath,

turning together to the open view,
a distant plough, a lozenge of field.
We face the slope again, our boots
rough-riding the scree, up, up . . .

. . . past the last ruined hafod, the last flower,
stream falling among boulders,
the mountain ewe and her lamb and at last
Llyn Cau like a secret cupped in hands.

You climb on to the summit
'to test my body further'.
I prefer to stare at shirred water
and the vast face of stone.

I search for words.
While I'm still catching my breath
you describe that dizzy joy
at the sheer page,

'A move so delicate
along a traverse,
just fingertip
between the hold and the fall.'

GILLIAN CLARKE

# VIII

# LEGENDS, FOLKLORE, SUPERSTITIONS

*Three Elders of the World*

Owl of Cwm Cowlwyd,
Eagle of Gwernabwy,
Blackbird of Celli Gadarn.

TRADITIONAL

**158**    And Bendigeid Vran commanded them that they should cut off
his head. 'And take you my head,' said he, 'and bear it even
unto the White Mount, in London, and bury it there, with the
face towards France. And a long time will you be upon the
road. In Harlech you will be feasting seven years, the birds of
Rhiannon singing unto you the while. And all that time the
head will be to you as pleasant company as it ever was when on
my body. And at Gwales in Penvro you will be fourscore years,
and you may remain there, and the head with you uncorrupted,
until you open the door that looks towards Aber Henvelen, and
towards Cornwall. And after you have opened that door, there
you may no longer tarry, set forth then to London to bury the
head, and go straight forward.'

So they cut off his head, and these seven went forward there-
with. And Branwen was the eighth with them, and they came
to land at Aber Alaw, in Talebolyon, and they sat down to rest.
And Branwen looked towards Ireland and towards the Island
of the Mighty, to see if she could descry them. 'Alas,' said she,
'woe is me that I was ever born; two islands have been
destroyed because of me!' Then she uttered a loud groan, and
there broke her heart. And they made her a foursided grave,
and buried her upon the banks of the Alaw.

*The Mabinogion*
trans. Lady Charlotte Guest (1846)

*The Fairies in Wales*

In former times, more than at present, there were frequent
appearances of the Fairies in Wales . . . Abundance of people
saw them, and heard their musick, which everyone said was
low and pleasant, but none could ever learn the tune. Heard
their talking like that of many talking together, but the words
seldom heard. But to those who did hear they seemed to dispute
much about future events, and about what they were to do;
whence it came to a proverb in the parish concerning disagree-
ing persons: *Ni chytunant hwy mwy na bendith y mamau*, i.e. they
will no more agree than the fairies.

They appeared diverse ways, but their most frequent way of
appearing was like dancing companies with musick, and in

the form of funerals. When they appeared like dancing companies, they were desirous to entice persons into their company, and some were drawn among them and remained among them some time; usually a whole year, as did Edmund William Rees, a man whom I well knew, and was a neighbour, who came back at the year's end, and looked very bad. But either they were not able to give much account of themselves or they durst not give it, only said they had been dancing, and that the time was short . . . It was the general opinion in times past, when these things were more frequent, that the fairies knew whatever was spoken in the air without the houses, not so much what was spoken in the houses. I suppose they chiefly knew what was spoken in the air at night. It was also said that they rather appeared to an uneven number of persons to one, three, five, etc. And oftener to men than to women. Thomas William Edmund of Havodavel, an honest pious man, who often saw them, declared, that they appeared with one bigger than the rest going before them in the company . . .

But very often [they] appeared in the form of a funeral before the death of many persons, with a bier, and a black cloth, in the midst of a company about it, on every side, before and after it. The instances of this were so numerous, that it is plain, and past all dispute that they infallibly foreknew the time of man's death . . . We have a constant proof of this in the Corpse Candles, whose appearance is an infallible sign that Death will follow, and they never fail going the way that the Corpse will go to be buried, be the way ever so unlikely that it should go through. But to give some instances in Aberystruth Parish:

It was told me that Mr Howel Prosser, Curate of Aberystruth, seeing a funeral going down the Church lane late in the evening towards the Church, imagined it was the body of a man from the upper end of the parish towards Breconshire, whom he heard before was sick, and thought was now dead and going to be buried. He put on his Band in order to go to perform the burial office, and hastened to go to meet the burial. When he came to it, he saw a people he did not know of, of which he took no notice, as they came from the borders of Breconshire. But putting his hand to the bier to help carry the corpse, in a moment all vanished, and to his very great surprise and astonishment, there was nothing in his hand but the skull of a dead horse . . .

But the following is a more certain instance:

Isaac William Thomas, who lived not far from thence, being at one time at Havodavel, and seeing, as it appeared to him, a Funeral coming down the mountain, as it were to go towards Aberbeeg, or Lanhithel Church. He stood in a field by a wall which was between him and the highway leading to Aberbeeg. When the funeral, which came close to the side of the wall, was come just over against him, he reached his hand and took off the black veil which was over the bier and carried it home with him. It was made of some exceeding fine stuff, so that when folded it was a very little substance, and very light. He told this to several. I knew the man myself, and in my youthful days conversed with him several times. I wish I had spoken with him after this had happened, and had asked many particular questions about it, to have more particular knowledge of this extraordinary supernatural affair . . . but the opportunity for this, in this world, as many others of this nature is lost for ever. But the light of Eternity will shew Myriads of Myriads of things which we cannot know here, nor are fit to know; and which we shall there certainly and infallibly know, without error, as they are, and no otherwise.

EDMUND JONES (1702–93)<br>
An Historical Account of the Parish of Aberystruth (1779)


*Feb.* 7. I asked Miss Jones in my Welsh lesson the Welsh for *fairy*, for we were translating Cinderella. She told me *cïpenăper* (or perhaps *cïpernăper*, *Anglice kippernapper*): the word is nothing but *kidnapper*, moulded, according to their fashion, to give it a Welsh etymology, as she said, from *cïpio* to snatch, to whisk away. However in coming to an understanding between ourselves what fairies (she says *fairess* by the way for a she-fairy) and kippernappers were, on my describing them as little people 'that high', she told me quite simply that she had seen them. It was on or near the Holywell road (she indicated the spot). She was going to her grandfather's farm on the hill, not far from where Justice Williams lived, on the slope of the Rhuallt. It was a busy time, haymaking, I think. She was going up at five o'clock in the morning, when she saw three little boys of about four years old wearing little frock coats and odd little caps running and dancing before her, taking hands and going round, then going further, still dancing and always coming together, she said. She would take no notice of them but went on to the house and there told them what she had seen and wondered that children could be out so early. 'Why, she has seen the kippernappers,' her grandmother said to her son, Susannah Jones's father.

GERARD MANLEY HOPKINS (1844–89)
*The Journal* (1875)

### Pwyll Prince of Dyfed

Pwyll Prince of Dyfed was lord over the seven cantrefs of Dyfed; and once upon a time he was at Arberth, a chief court of his, and it came into his head and heart to go a-hunting. The part of his domain which it pleased him to hunt was Glyn Cuch. And he set out that night from Arberth, and came as far as Pen Llwyn Diarwya, and there he was that night. And on the morrow in the young of the day he arose and came to Glyn Cuch to loose his dogs into the wood. And he sounded his horn and began to muster the hunt, and followed after the dogs and lost his companions; and whilst he was listening to the cry of the pack, he could hear the cry of another pack, but they had not the same cry, and were coming to meet his own pack.

And he could see a clearing in the wood as of a level field, and as his pack reached the edge of the clearing, he could see a stag in front of the other pack. And towards the middle of the clearing, lo, the pack that was pursuing it overtaking it and bringing it to the ground. And then he looked at the colour of the pack, without troubling to look at the stag; and of all the hounds he had seen in the world, he had seen no dogs the same colour as these. The colour that was on them was a brilliant shining white, and their ears red; and as the exceeding whiteness of the dogs glittered, so glittered the exceeding redness of their ears. And with that he came to the dogs, and drove away the pack that had killed the stag, and baited his own pack upon the stag.

And whilst he was baiting his dogs he could see a horseman coming after the pack on a big dapple-grey steed, with a hunting horn round his neck, and a garment of brownish-grey stuff about him by way of a hunting garb. And thereupon the horseman drew near him, and spoke to him thus. 'Chieftain,' said he, 'I know who thou art, but I will not greet thee.' 'Why,' said he, 'perhaps thy dignity is such that it should not do so.' 'Faith,' said he, 'it is not the degree of my dignity that keeps me therefrom.' 'Chieftain,' he replied, 'what else then?' 'Between me and God,' said he, 'thine own ignorance and discourtesy.' 'What discourtesy, chieftain, hast thou seen in me?' 'Greater discourtesy I have not seen in man,' said he, 'than to drive away the pack that had killed the stag and to bait thine own pack upon it. That,' said he, 'was discourtesy, and though I will not take vengeance upon thee, between me and God,' said he, 'I will do thee dishonour to the value of a hundred stags.' 'Chieftain,' said he, 'if I have done thee wrong, I will redeem thy friendship.' 'How,' he replied, 'wilt thou redeem it?' 'According as thy dignity may be; but I know not who thou art.' 'A crowned king am I in the land whence I come.' 'Lord,' he replied, 'good day to thee, and from what land is it thou comest?' 'From Annwn,' answered he; 'Arawn king of Annwn am I.' 'Lord,' said he, 'how shall I win thy friendship?' 'This is how thou shalt,' he replied. 'There is a man whose domain is opposite to mine for ever warring against me. That is king Hafgan, from Annwn; and by ridding me of his oppression, and that thou easily mayest, thou shalt win my friendship.' 'That will I do,' said he, 'gladly. But show me how I may do it.' 'I will,' said he. 'This is how thou mayest. I will make with thee a strong bond of friendship. This is how I will do it: I will set thee in Annwn in my stead, and the fairest lady thou didst ever see I will set to sleep with thee each night, and my form and semblance upon thee, so that there shall be not a chamberlain, nor an officer, nor any other man that has ever followed me shall know that thou art not I. And that,' said he, 'till the end of a year from tomorrow, and our tryst then in this very place.' 'Aye,' he replied, 'though I be there till the end of the year, what guidance shall I have to find the man thou tellest of?' 'A year from tonight,' said he, 'there is a tryst between him and me, at the ford. And be thou there in my likeness,' said he. 'And one blow only thou art to give him; that he will not survive. And though he ask thee to give him another, give it not, however he entreat thee. For despite aught I might give him, as well as before would he fight with me on the morrow.' 'Aye,' said Pwyll, 'what shall I do with my kingdom?' 'I will bring it about,' said Arawn, 'that there shall be neither man nor woman in thy kingdom shall know that I am not thou; and I shall go in thy stead.' 'Gladly,' said Pwyll, 'and I will be on my way.' 'Without let shall be thy path, and nothing shall impede thee till thou arrive in my domain, and I myself will bring thee on thy way.'

He brought him on his way till he saw the court and the dwellings. 'There,' he said, 'the court and the kingdom in thy power. And make for the court. There is none within that will not know thee, and as thou seest the service therein thou wilt know the usage of the court.'

He made for the court. And in the court he could see sleeping-rooms and halls and chambers and the greatest show of buildings anyone had ever seen. And he went into the hall to pull off his boots. There came squires and chamberlains to pull them off him, and all as they came saluted him. Two knights came to rid him of his hunting garb and to apparel him in a robe of gold brocaded silk. And the hall was made ready. Here he could see a war-band and retinues entering in, and the most comely troop and the best equipped anyone had seen, and the queen with them, the fairest woman anyone had ever seen, dressed in a robe of shining gold brocaded silk. And thereupon they went to wash and drew near the tables, and they sat in this wise: the queen one side of him, and the earl, as he supposed, the other side.

And he began to converse with the queen . . .

*The Mabinogion*, late 11th century
trans. Gwyn Jones and Thomas Jones (1974)

The road from Llanfaes to Llandovery flirts with the Usk and is flanked by the moorlands of the Mynydd Epynt northward and the mountainous Fforest Fawr to the south. At Llanspyddyd, where the fourteenth-century church contains a curious canopy above the pulpit, is the grave of Amlwch, the bard. Beyond the medieval bridge and Tudor farmhouse of Aberbran and the yew-trees of Capel Bettws is Penpont. The house has a colonnaded portico and, it is said, memories of Anne Boleyn, whose portrait, *triste* and doe-eyed, graces the rich interior. The pigeon-cote is characteristic of this area, not of the round

**164**   columbarium type but rectangular, with a passage-way cut through the lower storey and crowned with a whimsical conical lantern. The cedars and firs cluster thickly about Scott's neo-Norman chapel. By night it is a dark, lonely spot. There is a reputedly true story of a local man accompanied by his wife, both of them on horseback, returning home from the taverns of Brecon some forty years ago. Approaching this place they saw what appeared to be a white figure hovering beneath the trees. The horses too were alarmed, for they came to a halt and could be urged no farther. He was a timid man, but not without resources. He looked the apparition or whatever it was in the face and said: 'If you are the Lord I know you won't harm me, for my brother is vicar of a parish in Pembrokeshire. And if you be the Devil you surely won't harm me, for I'm living with your sister.'

TUDOR EDWARDS<br>
*The Face of Wales* (1950)

### The Water Horse of St Bride's Bay, Pembrokeshire

The Ceffyl Dwr, or Water Horse, was one of the most firmly believed spectres in rural Wales in the past. It was generally a small but beautiful horse which tempted unwary travellers to

ride but suddenly galloped away throwing the rider to destruction, except ministers who were allowed a peaceful journey.

The Water Horse was often seen on the shore, dappled, grey or like the sand in colour. One was seen in St Bride's Bay after a storm. A farmer caught it and harnessed it to the plough. Everything went well for some weeks. Then, apparently seized with an impulse, the Water Horse dragged both plough and ploughman through the field at a furious pace, down to the shore and into the sea, disappearing in the waves.

TONY ROBERTS
*Myths and Legends of Wales* (1987)


## The Sun of Llanfabon

In the days that are old and golden, Llanwonno church had a silver bell whose tongue splashed chimes of praises all over the land. None had more liking for its luscious jangle than the big-eared men of Llanfabon, and one night an assembly of them trod splay-footed through the river Taff to steal or (as they would prefer to say) to borrow it, knell, shell and clanger. It was necessary to complete the borrowing before sunrise, for at first light they might look to be observed and pursued by their big-eyed neighbours of Llanwonno.

Behold them then, late into the night, descending the stone-spangled slope of the Taff, their fretwork boots going crash-crash on the pebbles and their poles banging fireworks off the rocks. The bell alone was silent, for they had wound the clapper in velvet and straw before enfolding the whole sonorous dome in a cocoon of scarlet flannel nightshirts. However, just as they were crossing the river, the moon bolted out from behind cloud, alarming them greatly, for they mistook it for the sun. Their arms turned to jelly and they let the bell fall slap into a deep pool. It sank gurgling from sight, and not a note has been heard from it since.

But that is why the big-eyed men of Llanwonno call the moon the sun of Llanfabon, and the big-eared, bugle-nosed, barge-footed men of Llanfabon (who tell the whole story backwards) call the sun the moon of Llanwonno.

GWYN JONES
*Welsh Legends and Folk Tales* (1955)

I have wondered that only one legend should be remembered
of those that have been born of all the gloom and the golden
lilies and the plover that glories in its loneliness; for I stand in
need of a legend when I come down to it through rolling
heathery land, through bogs, among blanched and lichened
crags, and the deep sea of heather, with a few flowers and
many withered ones, of red and purple whin, of gorse and
gorse-flower, and (amongst the gorse) a grey curling dead grass,
which all together make the desolate colour of a 'black mountain'; and when I see the water for ever waved except among
the weeds in the centre, and see the water-lily leaves lifted and
resembling a flock of wild-fowl, I cannot always be content to
see it so remote, so entirely inhuman, and like a thing a poet
might make to show a fool what solitude was, and as it remains
with its one poor legend of a man who watered his horse at a
well, and forgot to cover it with the stone, and riding away, saw
the water swelling over the land from the well, and galloped
back to stop it, and saw the lake thus created and bounded
by the track of his horse's hooves; and thus it is a thing from
the beginning of the world that has never exchanged a word
with men, and now never will, since we have forgotten the
language, though on some days the lake seems not to have
forgotten it.

EDWARD THOMAS (1878–1917)<br>
*Wales* (1905)

## The Fairies' Revenge

The farmer of Drws y Coed's son was one misty day engaged as
a shepherd on the side of the mountain, a little below Cwm
Marchnad, and, as he crossed a rushy flat, he saw a wonderfully handsome little woman standing under a clump of
rushes. Her yellow and curly hair hung down in ringed locks,
and her eyes were as blue as the clear sky, while her forehead
was as white as the wavy face of a snowdrift that has nestled on
the side of Snowdon only a single night. Her two plump cheeks
were each like a red rose, and her pretty-lipped mouth might
make an angel eager to kiss her. The youth approached her,

filled with love for her, and, with delicacy and affection, asked
her if he might converse with her. She smiled kindly, and
reaching out her hand, said to him, 'Idol of my hopes, thou hast
come at last!' They began to associate secretly, and to meet one
another daily here and there on the moors around the banks of
Llyn y Gader; at last, their love had waxed so strong that the
young man could not be at peace either day or night, as he was

always thinking of Bella or humming to himself a verse of
poetry about her charms. The yellow-haired youth was now
and then lost for a long while, and nobody could divine his
history. His acquaintances believed that he had been fascinated: at last the secret was found out. There were about Llyn y
Dywarchen shady and concealing copses: it was there he was
wont to go, and the she-elf would always be there awaiting

him, and it was therefore that the place where they used to meet got to be called *Llwyn y Forwyn*, the Maiden's Grove. After fondly loving for a long time, it was resolved to wed; but it was needful to get the leave of the damsel's father.

One moonlight night it was agreed to meet in the wood, and the appointment was duly kept by the young man, but there was no sign of the subterranean folks coming, until the moon disappeared behind the Garn. Then the two arrived, and the old man at once proceeded to say to the suitor: 'Thou shalt have my daughter on the condition that thou do not strike her with iron. If thou ever touch her with iron, she will no longer be thine, but shall return to her own.' The man consented readily, and great was his joy. They were betrothed, and seldom was a handsomer pair seen at the altar. It was rumoured that a vast sum of money had arrived with the pretty lady at Drws y Coed on the evening of her nuptials. Soon after, the mountain shepherd of Cwm Marchnad passed for a very rich and influential man. In the course of time they had children, and no happier people ever lived together than their parents. Everything went on regularly and prosperously for a number of years: they had become exceedingly wealthy, but the sweet is not to be had without the bitter. One day they both went out on horseback, and they happened to go near Llyn y Gader, when the wife's horse got into a bog and sank to his belly. After the husband had got Bella off his back, he succeeded with much trouble in getting the horse out, and then he let him go. Then he lifted her on the back of his own, but, unfortunately, in trying quickly to place her foot in the stirrup, the iron part of the same slipped, and struck her – or, rather, it touched her at the knee-joint. Before they had made good half their way home, several of the diminutive *Tylwyth* began to appear to them, and the sound of sweet singing was heard on the side of the hill. Before the husband reached Drws y Coed his wife had left him, and it is supposed that she fled to Llwyn y Forwyn, and thence to the world below to Faery. She left her dear little ones to the care of her beloved, and no more came near them. Some say, however, that she sometimes contrived to see her beloved one in the following manner. As the law of her country did not permit her to frequent the earth with an earthly being, she and her mother invented a way of avoiding the one thing and of securing the other. A great piece of sod was set to float on the surface of the lake, and on that she used to be for long hours, freely conversing in tenderness with her consort on shore; by means of that plan they managed to live together until he breathed his last. Their descendants owned Drws y Coed for many generations, and they intermarried and mixed with the people of the district. Moreover, many a fierce fight took place in later times at the *Gwyl-fabsant* at Dolbenmaen or at Penmorfa, because the men of Eifionyd had a habit of annoying the people of Pennant by calling them Bellisians.

SIR JOHN RHŶS (1840–1915)
*Celtic Folklore* (1901)

## Llyn y Fan Fach

Two women pick their way down from the lake,
sandals filling with sharp stones
or slithering on the hot grass verge.
'Not far now,' they call. I can see
the black-red cliffs of the farther shore
rearing above knolls ahead. On the left,
far up to the craggy skyline,
parched pasture is stretched like yellow skin
on a fevered body. The sky
is a strident blue; there is no shade here,
no glint of healing water yet.

She has gone back long ago into the lake,
the lady of legend, taking
her mild cows and small snorting calves
and her own dark softness.
A gentleness three times struck with iron
is gone. The harsh track leads at last
to sombre cliffs, shadowed water.
On the shore I feel the breath of a breeze
from who knows what chill corridor.
Later down the track, I call
to those who climb 'not far.'

RUTH BIDGOOD

*Lovers' Well*

At Llanddwyn in Anglesey there was once the well of St Dwynwen, revered by the island's romantics, for St Dwynwen was known as the patron saint of lovers – the Celtic Aphrodite.

Its mysteries derive from an age when Dwynwen, as a beautiful maiden, vowed herself to a life of celibacy, but found that she had fallen in love with a handsome chieftain.

In a dream there came to her a vision. It told of a magic potion which would dispel all thoughts of love. So, from the dells of Newborough Forest she gathered rare herbs and mixed them with a lover's tears and beads of dew from the petals of the snapdragon. Together, she and her lover drank of the potion, and Dwynwen immediately drifted into forgetfulness while Maelon, the young chieftain, turned into a pillar of stone.

A while later the vision returned to Dwynwen and granted her three wishes. She restored Maelon from his granite tomb and wished also to be rescued from the tangles of love. Her third wish was that all faithful lovers should have their dreams fulfilled.

And there, legend has it, on the ground where her transformed lover had stood, a pool of fresh water appeared. In time the soil eroded, and a wall was built around Lovers' Well.

Many years ago there was a young philanderer of Cerig Mawr who admired a fisherman's daughter from Llanddwyn. Often during the summer evenings they would stroll together along the cliff paths and gaze at the sunset over Caernarfon Bay.

Although he was a good-looking young man with a winsome smile, she had heard stories of his philandering from as far north as Llangefni.

One evening when they were out walking they lingered a while at the well of St Dwynwen. There he told her of its mystic powers, and her eyes sparkled with interest.

'Sometimes, when you are alone and all is quiet, you can hear a voice calling from the darkness,' he began.

Then he unfolded one of the mysteries of Lovers' Well. He lowered his voice in reverence, and she tingled all over with excitement.

'If the name of a girl's lover is called into the cavern of the well,' he told her, 'and if his love is true, then, after a while, his name will echo three times from below.' But, he warned, the test of fidelity would have to be performed at the witching hour on mid-summer's eve.

June wore on until, at last, mid-summer's day dawned. Eagerly the fisherman's daughter waited for the sunset. And, as midnight approached, she stole along the paths with a lantern to light her way.

The well of St Dwynwen stood before her, silent as a grave. Her heart was beating fast as she leaned over the low stone wall and looked down into the darkness.

'Gwil . . . ym,' she called into the cavern, for Gwilym was the name of her lover, the woodman of Cerig Mawr.

She listened. Moments passed. Then, from the depths of the well, a voice came back, resonant, haunting.

'Gwil . . . ymmm – Gwil . . . ymmm – Gwil . . . ymmm.'

The girl gasped at the wonder of it all. She called again, and three times the echo drifted back to her. Fascinated, she peered closer into the well, and the glow of her lamp showed someone hiding there. It was Gwilym who clung to the wall in the cavern of the well.

With a startled cry the girl dropped the lantern over the wall and ran off home. As Gwilym looked up he saw a ball of flame come hurtling toward him. He lost his footing and went tumbling into the chill water of St Dwynwen's well.

No one remembers how long he struggled there, or who answered his cries for help. But folk say that his escapade at Lovers' Well brought an end to his days of philandering.

Today the well is choked with sand, and its votaries are few. But sometimes, when hearts are near to breaking, love-lorn girls moon at its ruined walls.

KEN RADFORD
*Tales of North Wales* (1982)

The mine is dark . . . If a light comes in the mine . . . the rivers in the mine will run fast with the voice of many women; the walls will fall in, and it will be the end of the world . . . So the mine is dark . . . But when I walk through the Tan – something – shaft, in the dark, I can touch with my hands the leaves on the trees, and underneath . . . where the corn is green. . . .'

EMLYN WILLIAMS (1905–86)
*The Corn Is Green* (1938)

### 'Knockers' in Mines

People that know very little of arts or sciences or of the powers of Nature . . . will laugh at us Cardiganshire miners that maintain the being of knockers in mines – a kind of good-natured impalpable people but to be seen and heard, and who seem to us to work in the mines . . . However this is, I must speak well of these knockers, for they have actually stood my very good friends, whether they are aerial beings called spirits, or whether they are people made of matter, not to be felt by our gross bodies, as air and fire the like. Before the discovery of Esgair y Mwyn mine, these little people (as we call them here) worked hard there day and night, and there are abundance of honest sober people that have heard them (although there are some people amongst us who have no notion of them or of mines either); but after the discovery of the great ore, they were heard no more. When I began work at Llwynllwyd they worked so fresh there for a considerable time that they even frightened some young workmen out of the work. This was when we were driving levels and before we had got any ore, but when we came to the ore then they gave over and I heard no more talk of them. Our old miners are no more concerned at hearing them blasting, boring holes, landing leads, than if they were some of their own people, and a single miner will stay in the work in the dead of the night without any man near him and never think of any fear or harm that they will do to him, for they have a notion the knockers are of their own tribe and pro-fession and are a harmless people who mean well. Three or four miners together shall hear them sometimes, but if the miners stop to take notice of them the knockers will also stop; but let the miners go on at their own work – suppose it is boring – the knockers will also go on as brisk as can be in landing, blasting or beating down the loose. And they are always heard at a little distance from them, before they come to ore. These are odd assertions, but they are certainly facts, though we cannot and do not pretend to account for them.

LEWIS MORRIS (1701–65)

### Death Flowers and Corpse Candles

In 1890, miners at the Morfa Colliery near Port Talbot reported many eerie manifestations which occurred in the neighbour-hood and in the mine itself. Fierce hounds, known locally as 'the Red Dogs of Morfa', were seen running through the district at night. The colliery was filled with a sweet rose-like perfume emanating from invisible 'death flowers'. Cries for help and sounds of falling earth were heard, and flickering lights, called 'corpse candles', appeared in the tunnels. The ghosts of dead miners and coal trams drawn by phantom white horses were seen, and rats swarmed out of the mine. On March 10, nearly half of the workers on the morning shift stayed at home. Later that day there was an explosion at the colliery, and 87 miners were buried alive and died in the disaster.

Canhwyllau Cyrff or Corpses' Candles, as their name suggests, were always associated with the dead. They appeared in the form of a flame or a ball of fire hovering a few feet above the ground, either stationary or moving.

Corpse candles were usually taken either to be a portent of death or as the soul of the dead. A large yellow flame represented an adult, whereas a small blue one represented a child. Occasionally, more than one flame would appear at the same time, indicating a number of deaths.

One well-known sighting took place in the old county of Carmarthen. Here the housekeeper saw five flames burning at the mansion where she worked. About a week later tragedy struck the mansion. In a room near where the flames were seen five maids all suffocated to death in their sleep. The room had been newly plastered and to hasten its drying a coal fire had been lit. The combined fumes of lime and coal were sufficient to kill the five girls.

In another part of Wales a lady on her way to visit friends had planned to meet their manservant at a certain point on her journey. He was not at the pre-arranged spot, but as she waited a wavering flame appeared floating a few feet above the ground. The light stayed in the same position for about half an hour and only disappeared at the sound of the manservant's horse. Some days later the servant died and owing to an unforeseen mishap his funeral was delayed for half an hour at the very spot the flame had been seen.

Another well-recorded sighting took place as the Llandeilo to Carmarthen coach passed over the river bridge at Golden Grove. As the passengers looked out they saw three ghostly lights hovering over the river. A few days later, three local fishermen were drowned at that place when the coracle from which they were fishing capsized.

RICHARD LEWIS
'Corpse Candles – did they really exist?'
article in *Country Quest*

In an upland homestead just below us, lived an old couple who were widely reputed to be in possession of a small crock of gold – really a basin full of gold. The place always intrigued me as a boy and whenever I visited the farm I could not help thinking of this basin full of sovereigns, and wondered in what corner or hole it was hidden. But like all the hoards of gold I ever heard of, nobody had ever seen it, but all were convinced that it was there, for it was confidently declared that they could never have taken the farm nor stocked it without some such secret aid. There were supposed to be in those days hoards of gold under every stone and cromlech, in every cairn and circle; indeed, the majority of them had been at one time or another interfered with in the hope of finding some.

I was brought up in that widespread and steadfast faith, but I am now an unbeliever. I verily believe that a large number of country people continued to believe in ghosts because the location of these hoards was invariably made known by a visit from some supernatural body. One or two instances, authenticated by responsible people, have found their way into the history of my parish: 'One night, many years ago, a very beautiful lady came up to William, the servant lad at Penpistyll, and stood by his bed in the fern-loft above the cows, where he slept. After standing there for a little while she vanished as if you were to put one hand in another. She came again the following night and stood there in the same manner, but not a word was spoken by either. She came the third night and William now made up his mind to ask her what her mission was. "Will you come with me?" she asked. William could not refuse, and off they went he knew not where, until they came to a huge stone set in the middle of a field. This the lady commanded him to raise, which he did, and to his surprise there was under it a crock of gold, full to the brim. "Take that," she said, "and take care of it." William took the crock with him, and the following morning dug a hole in the Penpistyll wood and buried it there. But, as it chanced, there were some men on the opposite side of the dingle who saw him doing it and who went there after dark and carried the crock of gold away with them. Soon after this they bought a nearby farm and went into the marts and fairs to buy cattle and drive them to England. The farm which they bought was ever afterwards known as *Pantyporthman* – The Drover's Hollow. One member of William's family assured the author that in his childhood this story was firmly believed in by his people.'

'A Mr Bowen, of Llangeler, used to see a ghost night after night at the end of Ghost Lane (*Penlon Bwci*). Upon asking it what its business or mission was, the ghost took him to the window of a nearby farm and showed him a large sum of money hidden there.' Digging for gold was not a pleasant work and not unattended by danger, for almost without exception some supernatural power interfered and brought on storms of thunder and lightning.

The old couple have long gone. Where their reputed minia-ture crock of gold is now no one can say, perhaps watched over by some ghostly guardian ready to protect it with a good supply of thunder and lightning.

D. PARRY JONES
*Welsh Country Characters* (1952)

## Beddgelert

Beth Gelert is situated in a valley surrounded by huge hills, the most remarkable of which are Moel Hebog and Cerrig Llan; the former fences it in on the south, and the latter, which is quite black and nearly perpendicular, on the east. A small stream rushes through the valley, and sallies forth by a pass at its south-eastern end. The valley is said by some to derive its name of Beddgelert, which signifies the grave of Celert, from being the burial-place of Celert, a British saint of the sixth century, to whom Llangeler in Carmarthenshire is believed to have been consecrated, but the popular and most universally received tradition is that it has its name from being the resting-place of a faithful dog called Celert or Gelert killed by his master, the warlike and celebrated Llywelyn ap Iorwerth, from an unlucky apprehension. Though the legend is known to most people I shall take the liberty of relating it.

Llywelyn during his contests with the English had encamped with a few followers in the valley, and one day departed with his men on an expedition, leaving his infant son in a cradle in his tent, under the care of his hound Gelert, after giving the child its fill of goat's milk. Whilst he was absent a wolf from the neighbouring mountains, in quest of prey, found its way into the tent, and was about to devour the child, when the watchful dog interfered, and after a desperate conflict, in which the tent was torn down, succeeded in destroying the monster. Llywelyn, returning at evening, found the tent on the ground, and the dog, covered with blood, sitting beside it. Imagining that the blood with which Gelert was besmeared was that of his own son devoured by the animal to whose care he had confided him, Llywelyn in a paroxysm of natural indignation forthwith transfixed the faithful creature with his spear. Scarcely, however, had he done so when his ears were startled by the cry of a child from beneath the fallen tent, and hastily removing the canvas he found the child in its cradle, quite uninjured, and the body of an enormous wolf frightfully torn and mangled lying near. His breast was now filled with conflicting emotions, joy for the preservation of his son and grief for the fate of his dog, to whom he forthwith hastened. The poor animal was not quite dead, but presently expired, in the act of licking his master's hand. Llywelyn mourned over him as over a brother, buried him with funeral honours in the valley, and erected a tomb over him as over a hero. From that time the valley was called Beth Gelert.

Such is the legend, which, whether true or fictitious, is singularly beautiful and affecting.

GEORGE BORROW (1803–81)
*Wild Wales* (1862)

**178**   **Gelert**, the favourite hound of Llywelyn ap Iorwerth (Llywelyn Fawr). According to the folk-tale associated with the village of Beddgelert, Caerns., the Prince, returning from the hunt, found the animal covered with gore and, assuming that it had attacked his infant son, slew it – only to discover that the dog had killed a marauding wolf and that the child was safe. This version of the story, an early form of which is found in *Chwedlau Saith Ddoethion Rhufain*, was unknown in the village before 1784 for it was the fabrication of one David Prichard, landlord of the local inn, the Royal Goat. The cromlech which is said to be Gelert's grave, like the well-known poem by W. R. Spencer which Joseph Haydn set to music, was based on details supplied by Prichard. A more likely explanation of the village's name is that, in the sixth century, it was the site of a priory dedicated to Celert.

from *The Oxford Companion to the Literature of Wales* (1986)
ed. Meic Stephens

In these parts of Pembroke, in our own times, unclean spirits have been in close communication with human beings. They are not visible, but their presence is felt all the same. First in the home of Stephen Wiriet, then, at a later date, in the house of William Not, they have been in the habit of manifesting themselves, throwing refuse all over the place, more keen perhaps to be a nuisance than to do any real harm. In William's house they were a cause of annoyance to both host and guests alike, ripping up their clothes of linen, and their woollen ones, too, and even cutting holes in them. No matter what precautions were taken, there seemed to be no way of protecting these garments, not even if the doors were kept bolted and barred. In Stephen's home things were even more odd, for the spirit there was in the habit of arguing with humans. When they protested, and this they would often do in sport, he would upbraid them in public for every nasty little act which they had committed from the day of their birth onwards, things which they did not like to hear discussed and which they would have preferred to keep secret.

GERALD OF WALES
*The Journey through Wales* (1191)
trans. Lewis Thorpe

In Wales, however, it is to a woman's milk that one's interest attaches: I submit two references which will explain what I mean. The first of them is to Owen's *Welsh Folk-Lore*, p. 349, where he says that 'traditions of flying snakes were once common in all parts of Wales', and adds as follows: 'The traditional origin of these imaginary creatures was that they were snakes, which by having drunk the milk of a woman, and by having eaten of bread consecrated for the Holy Communion, became transformed into winged serpents or dragons.' The other is to the *Brython* for 1861, p. 190, where one reads in Welsh to the following effect: 'If a snake chances to have an opportunity to drink of a woman's milk it is certain to become a *gwiber*. When a woman happens to be far from her child, and her breasts are full and beginning to give her pain, she sometimes milks them on the ground in order to ease them. To this peasantry in parts of Cardiganshire have a strong objection, lest a snake should come there and drink the milk and so become a *gwiber*.' The word *gwiber* is used in the Welsh Bible for a viper, but the editor of the *Brython* explains that in our folklore it means a huge kind of snake or dragon that has grown wings and has its body cased in hard scales: for a noted instance in point he refers the reader to the first number of the *Brython*, p. 3. It is believed still all over Wales that snakes may, under favourable circumstances, develop wings: in fact, an Anglesey man strongly wished, to my knowledge, to offer to the recent Welsh Land Commission, as evidence of the wild and neglected state of a certain farm, that the gorse had grown so high and the snakes so thriven in it that he had actually seen one of the latter flying right across a wide road which separated two such gorse forests as he described: surprised and hurt to find that this was not accepted, he inferred that the Commissioners knew next to nothing about their business.

SIR JOHN RHŶS (1840–1915)
*Celtic Folklore* (1901)

The dragon of our dreams roared in the hills
That ring the sunlit land of children's songs.
Red with the lacquer of a fairy-tale,
His fiery breath fried all besieging knights.
Whole seasons could he lay the land in waste
By puffing once upon the standing corn!

He was our dragon dressed in red, who kept
Sly ghosts from lurking underneath the thatch,
And made the hen lay dark-brown eggs for tea.
One word to him, just as you went to bed,
Made Twm, the postman, call next afternoon:
'Ho, Bachgen,' that is what he'd say, 'just look,
A fine blue postal-order from your Mam!
Twm gets a pint for bringing that, I bet!'

The dragon cured us when the measles came,
And let the mare drop me a coal-black foal.
He taught us where nests lay, and found us fish,
Then thawed the snow to save the winter lamb.

Ho Ddraig Goch, my pretty, pretty friend!
We were his children, knowing all his ways;
We laid out nightly gifts beneath the hedge,
Five linnet's eggs, a cup, a broken whip,
And heard his gracious sighs sweep through the trees.
But tears for all the fools who called him false!
One lad who sniggered fell down Parry's well;
The English Parson had a plague of warts;
Old Mrs Hughes was bitten by a cat;
The school roof fell in when the teacher smiled!

Ho, Ddraig Goch, they tell me you are dead;
They say they heard you weeping in the hills
For all your children gone to London Town.
They say your tears set Tawe in a flood.
I'm older now, but still I like to think
Of your great glass-green eyes fixed on the Fferm,
Guarding the children, keeping them from harm.

Don't die, old dragon, wait a few years more,
I shall come back and bring you boys to love.

HENRY TREECE (1912–66)

*The Strata: to Llywelyn Siôn*

Llywelyn, jackhammers ring in unison
At the gate. The ribs of monastery
    And fulling mill must collapse through thorn.
    It's an open grave, this house where you were born.

And shameful, the discoveries of time.
Sunlight pours into the privy-slot
    Black as the century that laid your faith.
    Llywelyn, this cloister smells of death.

Yet I know I have seen in faint rushlight
A man grow hunchbacked over a poem
    Before stretching into sleep's luxury,
    His pool of ink unblinking, a dark eye

That follows me six hundred years later
Through the thin woods of Llangewydd.
    Poet, you will understand my body's thirst
    As from this ground I watch unearthed

A cross like a cloverleaf incised in granite,
A markstone, a boundary of fear
    And belief. And clearly at once I see
    The strata, the separate rings of the tree

Of time, each growing from the last.
Llywelyn, living man, this is my history lesson,
    An instant's shocked discovery
    That I am able to claim what is mine,

To fashion with blunt words my own design
Of the cross. All we need is the courage
    To look around and we will find our own
    Mythology. Here, on native ground.

ROBERT MINHINNICK

# IX

# LATER HISTORY, INDUSTRY, STRIKES

Revolutionary and riotous; religious and musical; sporting and artistic, coal-bearing Rhondda. The starting-point of hunger marches, religious festivals, and Communist miners' delegations to Russia. Place of origin of champion boxers, noted preachers, talented musicians and composers, famous choir conductors, operatic stars and novelists.

JACK JONES (1884–1970)
*Rhondda Roundabout* (1934)

*Morning Comes Again*

Morning comes again to wake the valleys
And hooters shriek and waggons move again,
And on the hills the heavy clouds hang low,
And warm unwilling thighs crawl slowly
Out of half a million ruffled beds.

Mrs Jones' little shop will soon be open
To catch the kiddies on the way to school,
And the cemetery gates will chuckle to the cemetery-keeper,
And the Labour Exchange will meet the servant with a frown.

Morning comes again, the inevitable morning
Full of the threadbare jokes, the conventional crimes,
Morning comes again, a grey-eyed enemy of glamour,
With the sparrows twittering and gossips full of malice,
With the colourless backyards and the morning papers,
The unemployed scratching for coal on the tips,
The fat little grocer and his praise for Mr Chamberlain,
The vicar and his sharp short cough for Bernard Shaw,
And the colliery-manager's wife behind her pet geranium
Snubbing the whole damn lot!

IDRIS DAVIES (1905-53)


from *Gwalia Deserta*

VII

There are countless tons of rock above his head,
And gases wait in secret corners for a spark;
And his lamp shows dimly in the dust.
His leather belt is warm and moist with sweat,
And he crouches against the hanging coal,
And the pick swings to and fro,
And many beads of salty sweat play about his lips
And trickle down the blackened skin
To the hairy tangle on the chest.
The rats squeak and scamper among the unused props,
And the fungus waxes strong.

And Dai pauses and wipes his sticky brow,
And suddenly wonders if his baby
Shall grow up to crawl in the local Hell,
And if tomorrow's ticket will buy enough food for six days,
And for the Sabbath created for pulpits and bowler hats,
When the under-manager cleans a dirty tongue
And walks with the curate's maiden aunt to church . . .

Again the pick resumes the swing of toil,
And Dai forgets the world where merchants walk in morning
    streets,
And where the great sun smiles on pithead and pub and
    church-steeple.

IDRIS DAVIES (1905–53)


## The Rhondda

The inhabited parts of the Rhondda are more interesting as
revelations of ugliness than as the usual pleasant prospects
pointed out to travellers. Nevertheless, though the actual valley
is depressingly industrial, the surrounding hills are magnificent in a not too overwhelming style. I have done my best to
suggest the beauty of this hill landscape in my novels, particularly in *The Red Hills* and *The Withered Root*, and in some of my
short stories. But it seems to me that even the inhabited parts of
the Rhondda, and the similar valleys near by, are worthy of the
intelligent visitor's interest, if only to show him how a certain
section of apparently civilized mankind lives.

In *Honey and Bread* I have tried to show such a valley as the
Rhondda before it was industrialized – period about 1840. In
those days it was supposed to be one of the loveliest valleys in
Wales, full of trees, though now, of course, a tree, at least a fat
and healthy one, is a rarity.

RHYS DAVIES (1903–78)
*Print of a Hare's Foot, Autobiography* (1969)


The first thing I saw was the slag heap.

Big it had grown, and long, and black, without life or sign,
lying along the bottom of the Valley on both sides of the river.
The green grass, and the reeds and the flowers, all had gone,
crushed beneath it. And every minute the burden grew, as cage
after cage screeched along the cables from the pit, bumped to a
stop at the tipping pier, and emptied dusty loads on to the
ridged, black, dirty back.

On our side of the Valley the heap reached to the front garden
walls of the bottom row of houses, and children from them
were playing up and down the black slopes, screaming and

shouting, laughing in fun. On the other side of the river the chimney-pots of the first row of houses could only just be seen above the sharp curving back of the far heap, and all the time I was watching, the cable screeched and the cages tipped. From the Britannia pit came a call on the hooter as the cages came up, as though to remind the Valley to be ready for more filth as the work went on and on, year in and year out.

'Is the pit allowed to do this to us, Mr Gruffydd?' I asked him.

'Do what, my son?' Mr Gruffydd asked.

'Put slag by here,' I said.

'Nowhere else to put it, my son,' he said. 'Look up by there at the top of the mountain, by the Glas Fryn. There are the daffodils, see.'

And indeed, there they were, with their green leaves a darker sharpness in the grass about them, and the yellow blooms belling in the wind, up by the Glas Fryn and all along the Valley, as far as I could turn my head to see.

Gold may be found again, and men may know its madness again, but no one shall know how I felt to see the goldness of daffodils growing up there that morning. The Glas Fryn was the nearest place to our house where they grew. It was later that I pulled bulbs to grow in our garden, but the garden was so small and the earth so blind with dust from the slag that they gave up trying and died.

But that morning Mr Gruffydd put me down among them all, close to them, where I could take them in my hands to breathe the cool breath of them and give thanks to God.

RICHARD LLEWELYN (1906–83)
from *How Green Was My Valley* (1939)


*Boy:* Dear Mother,
When I go to work tomorrow
I shall be a man
And my lamp number will be 364.
If you were here you would see
My size 8 boots and my helmet.
I shall be working under the Black Mountain
Where the bare trees
Circle the Preacher's Rock.

The stream still runs down Park Avenue
And the river is still black.
The old poet still lives
In his house of books by the river
And he's still going to the devil.
Every Sunday he sits by the river water
Looking for fish and a sign.
I asked where he got his poems
From and he said from the shadows
On the black water, the blind
Flies in the Cynon Pit
And silica men with Bibles
In the cemetery pockets.
The boy from the corner house
Has gone away to England.
He'll be unhappy more than once.
Mary Moon's got a baby
Without a father, and Idris
Is ill from religion.
The George Pit is haunted,
Islwyn has silicosis, and Rhys
Jones robbed a meter.
Blind Ted still plays
The piano in pubs
And Maggie May joined the Salvation Army.
The Cynon Pit is closing
And Dan Davies has retired.
John Rees was buried by rock
And is gone for ever . . .

ROBERT MORGAN
from *Rainbow Valley*

from *Nightgown*

She had married Walt after a summer courtship during which
they had walked together in a silence like aversion.

Coming of a family of colliers, too, the smell of the hulking
young man tramping to her when she stepped out of an evening was the sole smell of men. He would have the faintly

scowling look which presently she, too, acquired. He half resented having to go about this business, but still his feet impelled him to her street corner and made him wait until, close-faced and glancing sideways threateningly, she came out of her father's house. They walked wordless on the grit beside the railway track, his mouth open as though in a perpetual yawn. For courting she had always worn a new lilac dress out of a proper draper's shop. This dress was her last fling in that line.

She got married in it, and they took one of the seven-and-sixpenny slices of the long blocks of concreted stone whipping round a slope and called Bryn Hyfryd – that is, Pleasant Hill. Like her father, Walt was a pub collier, not chapel.

The big sons had arrived with unchanged regularity, each of the same heavy poundage. When the sex of the fifth was told her, she turned her face sullenly to the wall and did not look at him for some time. And he was her last. She was to have no companionable daughter after all, to dote on when the men were in the pit. As the sons grew, the house became so obstreperously male that she began to lose nearly all feminine attributes and was apt to wear a man's cap and her sons' shoes, socks, and mufflers to run out to the shop. Her expression became tight as a fist, her jaw jutted out like her men's, and like them she only used her voice when it was necessary, though sometimes she would clang out at them with a criticism they did not understand. They would only scowl the family scowl.

For a while she had turned in her shut-up way to Trevor, her last-born. She wanted him to be small and delicate – she had imagined he was of different mould from his brothers – and she had dim ideas of his putting his hand to something more elegant than a pick in the pits. He grew into the tall, gruff image of his brothers. Yet still, when the time came for him to leave school at fourteen, she had bestirred herself, cornering him and speaking in her sullen way:

'Trevor, you don't want to go to that dirty pit, do you? Plenty of other things to do. One white face let me have coming home to me now.'

He had set up a hostile bellow at once. 'I'm going to the pit. Dad's going to ask his haulier for me.' He stared at her in fear. 'To the pits I'm going. You let me alone.' He dreaded her hard but seeking approaches; his brothers would poke jeering fun at him, asking him if his napkins were pinned on right, it was as if they tried to destroy her need of him, snatching him away.

She had even attempted to wring help from her husband: 'Walt, why can't Trevor be something else? What do I want with six men in the pit? One collier's more work in the house than four clean-job men.'

'Give me a shilling, 'ooman,' he said, crossing his red-spotted white muffler, 'and don't talk daft.' And off he went to the Miskin Arms.

So one bitter January morning she had seen her last-born leave the house with her other men, pit trousers on his lengthening legs and a gleaming new jack and food tin under his arm. From that day he had ranged inextricably with his brothers, sitting down with them at four o'clock to bacon and potatoes, even the same quantity of everything, and never derided by them again. She accepted his loss, as she was bound to do, though her jutting jaw seemed more bony, thrust out like a lonely hand into the world's air.

They were all on the day shift in the pits, and in a way she had good luck, for not one met with any accidents to speak of, they worked regular, and had no fancies to stay at home because of a pain in big toe or ear lobe, like some lazybones. So there ought to have been good money in the house. But there wasn't.

They ate most of it, with the rest for drinking. Bacon was their chief passion, and it must be of the best cut. In the shop, where she was never free of debt, nearly every day she would ask for three pounds of thick rashers when others would ask for one, and if Mr Griffiths would drop a hint, looking significantly at his thick ledger, saying: 'Three pounds, Mrs Rees, *again?*' her reply was always: 'I've got big men to feed.' As if that was sufficient explanation for all debt and she could do nothing about it; there were big, strapping men in the world and they had to be fed.

Except with one neighbour, she made no kind of real contact with anyone outside her home. And not much inside it. Of the middle height and bonily skimped of body, she seemed extinguished by the assembly of big males she had put into the world off her big husband. Peering out surly from under the poke of her man's cap, she never went beyond the main street of the vale, though as a child she had been once to the seaside, in a buff straw hat ringed with daisies.

Gathered in their pit-dirt for the important four o'clock meal, with bath pans and hot foods steaming in the fireplace, the little kitchen was crowded as the Black Hole of Calcutta. None of the sons, not even the eldest, looked like marrying, though sometimes, like a shoving parent bird, she would try to push them out of the nest. One or two of them set up brief associations with girls which never seemed to come properly to anything. They were of the kind that never marry until the entertainments of youth, such as football, whippet-racing, and beer, have palled at last. She would complain to her next-door-up neighbour that she had no room to put down even a thimble.

This neighbour, Mrs Lewis – the other neighbours set her bristling – was her only friend in the place, though the two never entered each other's house. In low voices they conversed over the back wall, exchanging all the eternal woes of women in words of cold, knowledgeable judgment that God Himself could have learnt from. To Mrs Lewis's remark that Trevor, her last, going to work in the pits ought to set her on her feet now, she said automatically, but sighing for once: 'I've got big men to feed.' That fact was the core of her world. Trevor's money, even when he began to earn a man's wage, was of no advantage. Still she was in debt in the shop. The six men were profitless; the demands of their insides made them white elephants.

So now, at fifty, still she could not sit down soft for an hour and dream of a day by the seaside with herself in a clean new dress at last and a draper's shop hat fresh as a rose.

But often in the morning she skulked to London House, the draper's on the corner of the main road, and stopped for a moment to peer sideways into the window where two wax women, one fair and one dark, stood dressed in all the latest and smiling a pink, healthy smile. Looking beautiful beyond compare, these two ladies were now more living to her than her old dream of a loving daughter. They had no big men to feed and, poised in their eternal shade, smiled leisurely above their furs and silk blouses. It was her treat to see them, as she stood glancing out from under Enoch's thrown-away cap, her toe-sprouting shoes unlaced and her skirt of drab flannel hanging scarecrow. Every other week they wore something new. The days when Mr Roberts the draper changed their outfits, the sight of the new wonders remained in her eyes until the men arrived home from the pit.

Then one morning she was startled to find the fair wax lady attired in a wonderful white silk nightgown, flowing down over the legs most richly trimmed with lace at bosom and cuffs. That anyone could wear such luxuriance in bed struck her at first like a blow in the face. Besides, it was a shock to see the grand lady standing there undressed, as you might say, in public. But, staring into the window, she was suddenly thrilled.

She went home feeling this new luxury round her like a sweet, clean silence. Where no men were . . .

RHYS DAVIES (1903–78)
in *The Collected Stories of Rhys Davies* (1955)


In the train Wiliam sat with his hand under his chin. The train went past houses and he could see lights flickering in their windows. He could imagine the wife cutting bread-and-butter, and filling the food-tin and tea-bottle. The man would be discarding the dirty handkerchief from his pocket and taking up a clean one. His boots would be warming on the fender, black for today, a Monday, and made supple by the grease that had not dried out yet in the lace-holes, and sweating in the heat of the fire. The man would put his head out of the door and call out, 'No, it isn't raining. I won't take a sack today.' He'd throw an old coat over his shoulders, fastening it with a safety-pin.

'Oh God!' groaned Wiliam, 'why couldn't I be setting off in the same way?'

And then his hatred of the quarry came back to him. He pictured it, black on the mountainside with a grey cap of cloud on its head, like an old witch making fun of him, and he groping his way towards it on a dark morning like this, and no work for him to start on when he arrived there in the cold of the morning, only going about with his hands in his pockets, begging. That's what it was, and nothing else. Going from one table to the next and standing there like a mute. One or two would give him an unsplit stone to work with, but most would refuse. Being courteously refused by some because of the real shortage of stones, being coldly refused by others, and being hypocritically refused by some of the meaner ones. There was nothing better than being a casual worker for getting to know people.

There was the old Wil Evans (Wiliam seethed to think of him now) refusing in his cunning way to give him a stone one summer afternoon. Dead on knocking-off time that afternoon, a load of stones from the quarry face came for Wil and Wiliam decided to ask him first thing the following morning. That night in bed he had some kind of intuition and he went to work half an hour earlier than usual. As he expected, who should be there already but old Wil Evans, having split a large number of stones and with a big pile of untrimmed slates on his bench. He could not stomach asking him for a stone then, but he made sure that everybody in the quarry knew about it.

And then at the end of the month how difficult it was to put up with the frowns of the overseer if he hadn't split enough slates, and then to have to beg for more stones.

He thought of his father having agreed to terms at the beginning of the month, and very often they were very bad terms, and not knowing whether he would be paid for his labour at the end of the month. A quarryman's wage was like a lucky dip. And then there was the rash of minor strikes which had broken out in the last few years. Not a halfpenny coming in from anywhere and everybody eating more than his ration through being home all day. His mother had to pluck up courage to face the shopkeeper, and the shopkeeper had to be patient.

In his opinion the quarrymen were blind not to see the advantages of joining the Union and fighting for a minimum wage and standard working agreements. Many more had joined recently, but not enough. What was the point of kicking up a fuss and coming out on strike if they did not have the strength of the Union behind them? Well, perhaps they were content to have their feet in chains.

Those were Wiliam's thoughts as the train moved slowly along, puffing like a man going up a steep hill. Sometimes it would stop at a dreary little station, quiet as the grave, the silence punctuated only by the snorts of steam from the engine. In the darkness the porter would hold his lamp aloft and its beams would form a circle of light in the morning mist. Then he would turn the lamp again and the train would slowly pull away, leaving the porter and his lamp buried in the darkness. Soon Wiliam became tired of thinking and fell asleep.

Once more during the journey the scenes at the quarry came

alive into his mind. He was nearing the end of his journey and night was drawing in again. He could see the men in the shed, their caps pulled down over their eyes, cold and miserable, waiting by the doors of the shed for the hooter to sound. Like grey rats in their holes they would peer around the doorposts. Then, when the hooter blew, they rushed headlong like a pack of hounds down the tramline towards the mountain. He remembered those faces now, hard-looking but hiding much geniality. They managed to laugh when things were at their blackest and made fun even of low wages. Many of them were dying of consumption.

Once more, thinking about the quarry, he began to boil with indignation. He would like to kill Morus Ifan, the Little Steward. He knew he had something personal against his father and would like to sack him, but his father could control his temper, something Wiliam could never do. He re-lived the scene when he was given notice. He had gone to see Buckley, the Steward, to ask for something better than casual labour, but he was not to be found, so he asked Morus Ifan instead. He remembered the look of contempt on his face. That was enough, but when he began reproaching him for his association with the Labour Party and his work for the Union, Wiliam could not restrain himself and went for his throat. It was luck for the Little Steward that somebody happened to come by at that moment. Hatred for him welled up inside, and he faced the coal-pit ahead of him with strength and determination.

KATE ROBERTS (1891–1985)
*Feet in Chains* (*Traed Mewn Cyffion*, 1971)
trans. Idwal Walters and John Idris Jones (1977)

## The Perils of Slate Quarrying

It was like a subterranean world! Above the blasted walls of slate scarcely enough of the blue heaven was visible for me to distinguish midday from twilight. The perpendicular sides were hung with men. But on a sudden the whole mountain seemed to totter, loud cries of warning re-echoed from various points – the mine was sprung. A large mass of rock loosened itself slowly and majestically from above, fell down with a mighty plunge and the thunder ran around in wild echoes.

These operations which are of daily necessity are so dangerous
that, according to the statement of the overseer himself, they
calculate on an average of 150 wounded and seven or eight
killed in a year.

The slate invariably splits in sharp-edged flakes so that an
inconsiderable piece thrown a great distance is often sufficient
to cut a man's hand or even head clean off.

PRINCE VON PUCKLER MUSKAU
following a visit to the Penrhyn Slate Quarry, Bethesda (1928)


*The Mason's Law*

Though the slate
where his hand slipped
could not stand
    worthy of a name,
at least it could lie
in his living room,
set in the floor.

*Er Cof* unfinished,
under our feet, recalls
the mason and his law:
    Honour the dead
with your craft;
waste nothing; leave
no botched memorial.

JEREMY HOOKER


*Port Talbot*

The breakers' jumbled yard: valley,
hills, strewn plain, reflect back
undulations of the sea.

Where steel and tidal waters meet,
not turbulance and steam
but rust, what's left of heat,

in breaking down crisp ore
almost to the heart, the heart's
still beating core.

Mist's rolling-mills in sheets
send rain. There's sun. But night
alone here alters what it meets –

even when, silent, a furnace-flare
will flatter the sleeping sky
like a dream of what was here,

three glimmering decades outstared
now by a ghost – and only
rust is eager and red-haired

in no-man's land, this town,
my town, whose thunder's the sound
of thunder running down.

JOHN DAVIES

### The Scotch Cattle

. . . the most spectacular movement of all and possibly the most
widespread and massive single action to convulse South Wales
in the nineteenth century was the great strike of 1816. Once
again, the origin was 'classic', rising food prices coinciding
with a heavy reduction in wages. Beginning in Merthyr, the
strike, spread by marching gangs throughout Monmouthshire,
proved persistent, well organized and violent . . .

The Cattle were a highly organized secret society which
might have originated in the Luddite troubles of the late war
years (Ned Ludd was credited with their formation). They
enforced solidarity through terror, by means of a developed
system of warning notes, night meetings, signals by horn.
Blacklegs and other offenders were visited by a Herd dressed in
animal clothes, women's dresses, turncoats, led by a horned
Bull. Property was attacked, the window-sashes of the overly

ambitious being a favourite target; there was some physical
assault. The movement persisted into the 1830s.

GWYN A. WILLIAMS
*The Merthyr Rising of 1831* (1988)

*Transportation to Van Diemen's Land*

Llangarfon's the parish that had my life's morn,
Tregud, in that parish, is where I was born.
And now, as I am going to quit your bright shore,
I'll give you my name, for I'll see you no more;
My name's David Davies, I bid adieu,
May God give long life and protection to you.

DAI CANTWR
trans. Evan Williams

*Riots at Merthyr*

We regret to learn that a serious riot broke out at Merthyr
Tydfil, yesterday. A letter we have just seen, says – 'After the
Riot Act had been read last night, the populace gutted two or
three houses – broke all the windows at Mr Coffin's house,
which they entered, and burnt his furniture in the street. The
magistrates sent expresses to the Lord Lieutenant of the
County, to the Commanding Officer of the troops stationed at
Brecon, and to the Staff of the Glamorgan Militia at Cardiff.'
The riotous proceedings we are informed have been confined
to the attacks on Mr Coffin's house and the houses of the Officers of the Court of Requests, from which it is conjectured that
the unlawful tumults originated from the unpopular character
of that Court.

*The Cambrian*, 4 June 1831

On Saturday last the awful sentence of the law was carried into
effect, at Cardiff, on Richard Lewis alias Dick Penderin . . .
   On arriving in the court yard, the executioner put a cap on

**196**    Richard Lewis's head and pinioned his arms, as usual; the prisoner being all the while engaged in fervent ejaculations, accompanied by uniform protestations of his innocence. He ascended the platform with a firm step . . . declaring, as he walked up the ladder, 'I am going to suffer unjustly. God, who knows all things, knows it is so.'

Lewis Lewis: 'Richard is innocent! for I know him not to have been there. I was by the soldier. If I had been sharing the same fate, I would have disclosed it on the scaffold.'

*The Cambrian*
20 August 1831

from *Dic Penderyn*

*Singer:*    As I walked out one summer morning
Along the streets of Cardiff town,
I heard the sound of shipwrights working,
The stroke of hammers beating down.

Oh tell me now what ship you're building
Upon the cobbles of this square,
What kind of mast is that you're raising
With such a blunt and heavy spar.

No ship we build this August morning,
No mast we raise upon this street,
But a gallows-tree for Dic Penderyn,
A trap to fall beneath his feet.

JOHN STUART WILLIAMS

*To all Colliers Traitors, Turncoats and others*

We hereby warn you the second and last time: We are determined to draw the hearts out of all the men above named, and fix two of the hearts upon the horns of the Bull; so that

everyone may see what is the fate of every traitor – and we
know them all.

So we testify with our blood.

x, Hoar Frost Castle, April 19th 1832.
Letter written in red ink (blood)
put out during strike of 1832.

## The Rebecca Riots

. . . the destructive spirit of Rebeccaism has now spread itself
over the whole of the Three Commotes District, a great number
of gates and bars having been demolished this week in that
part of the country. Amongst others Pontyates, Meinciau,
Pontyberem and both the gates at Kidwelly have been
destroyed.

On Friday night [30th June] a visit was paid by Rebecca and
her children to the village of Llanddarog, about six miles from
Carmarthen. They mustered about five hundred, armed with
guns, swords and pickaxes. Notice had previously been given
that Rebecca intended paying a visit to the above gate and
accordingly, about midnight, this renowned lady and her
daughters fulfilled their promise. When they arrived at the gate
they enquired of the toll collector what was to be paid, to which
the frightened gentleman instantly replied *'Nothing for you
ma'am.'* Rebecca having acknowledged the politeness of the
collector desired him to go into his dwelling and shut himself
in, which he immediately did and her orders were given for the
destruction of the gate. In a short time it was levelled with the
ground amid the exultation of the 'family' and the firing of
guns.

They then proceeded to Troedyrhiw gate, which met the
same fate.

*Carmarthen Journal*
7 July 1843

## The Chartist Movement

Hundreds were standing there in the wind: men from the valleys of Gwent, their faces still black from shift; women,

shawled and shivering, with babies on their backs, and little barefooted children crying on the tips.

For the first time I saw the Chartist, Zephaniah Williams; the man of destiny standing high on a rock, wonderful in oratory, ominous in silence. So will I remember him all the days of my life, then, in the greatness of his power, not chained in the working gang under a pitiless sun and with an overseer's lash to drive him. Fine he looked on that rock with his arms outstretched.

'Look,' whispered Mo. 'There is Henry Vincent, and William Jones Watchmaker beside him,' and he pointed.

'To the sword, then!' Williams cried in Welsh. 'To powder and shot, then, if it is forced upon us, for how else can we negotiate if they will not come to table? And even if we got them to table can mere words sway the likes of Guest of Dowlais and Crawshay of Cyfarthfa, these dogs of masters? Has Parliament any interest in petition when it is run by these aristocrats of wealth who rule our lives? What kind of freedom is it when we are driven to the polls to vote for Whig or Tory under threat of the blacklist? Where is a recognized anti-Truck Bill or a Bill for stabilized prices? You have none, and you will never have one, for Parliament is run by men who own the Shops and fix the prices that starve us – not by the will of the people, mark me, but by the law of birth and wealth, and so it will be until we dislodge them!'

The crowd howled at this and showed their fists.

'We are men of peace and threaten nobody!' shouted Zephaniah. 'But if it is blood they are after they shall have it, for the time is past when they can ride roughshod and break up meetings with crops. So if Crawshay Bailey has ideas about breaking this one let him come with his Volunteers and try it, for we will meet him with muskets.'

'Damned near sedition,' whispered Afel Hughes to me. 'Soon he will be baiting Victoria.'

'Aye!' roared Zephaniah, as if he had heard. 'The Gentlemen Cavalry, booted and spurred, straight from the hunt to flog the Unwashed. Do you want the truth of them – these men of idleness who sit in their Company Parks and make profit from your misery and watch your children die – protected by the laws they alter to suit their pockets, hiding under the skirt of the Queen they use as a puppet, God bless her,' and he winked

while the crowd yelled. 'To hell with them and to hell with Parliament, and God help our Virgin Queen, I say, for if words cannot shift the iniquitous laws of England that bind her hands,
then the cannon of the people must, and blow into oblivion her
enemies, the parasites of her crown and the wanglers of the
Pension List!'

ALEXANDER CORDELL
*Rape of the Fair Country* (1959)

### The Treachery of the Blue Books

In March 1846 William Williams, MP for Coventry, moved a
resolution in the House of Commons demanding that a commission be set up to inquire into 'the state of Education in the
Principality of Wales, especially into the means afforded to the
labouring classes of acquiring a knowledge of the English
tongue' . . . In the course of his speech he made a memorable
appeal to balance-sheet pragmatism which won approval on
all sides of the House.

> It should be borne in mind, that an ill-educated and
> undisciplined population, like that existing among the
> mines in South Wales, is one that may be found most dan-
> gerous to the neighbourhood in which it dwells, and that a
> band of efficient schoolmasters is kept up at a much less
> expense than a body of police or soldiery.

The government reaction was swift. A commission was created
and came down to Wales . . . The report of the Blue Books, as
they were called, drew a dark picture of ignorance and, what
was much worse, immorality . . .

The underlying assumption of the report was that 'ignorance' and 'ignorance of the English language' were synony-
mous . . . the Welsh could not stomach, on any account, the
equating of this state of ignorance with immorality . . . By this
stage in their development the Welsh were extremely articulate and literate people, and all their papers and magazines
bristled with prolonged and elaborate refutations to disprove
the shameful accusations made by the commissioners.
National reputations were made by the men who made the
most effective replies, and a new form of nationalism came

into existence, based not so much upon any consistent philosophy as on the touchy pride that Shakespeare portrayed so well in its Tudor form in the character of the Welsh soldier Fluellen. The English public of course understood nothing of this . . .

Welsh journalism gave currency to a phrase *Brad y Llyfrau Gleision* (The Treachery of the Blue Books) which is still in general use to describe this crucial turning point in modern Welsh history. The terminology is significant. It refers back to *Brad y Cyllyll Hirion* (The Treachery of the Long Knives), a dramatic episode in Theophilus Evans's *Drych y Prifoesoedd* (A Mirror of Past Ages) which describes how the Anglo-Saxon villain, Hengist, instructed his deputation to a peace conference and friendly feast with the Britons to carry knives hidden in their boots to kill off the best leaders in Vortigern's army. This mythical incident in the ancient struggle between the Saxons and the British was still alive in the folk-memory of the Welsh. This latest insult gave it a fresh currency.

In 1850, thanks to industrialism and the expansion of chapels, there were far more Welsh-speaking Welsh than had existed in 1800 and they represented a far higher percentage of the existing population of Wales than had been the case in 1800. Furthermore they had spread abroad and taken their language and their religion with them. They had the capacity to become a formidable political force in their own right without necessarily making any fundamental change in their own nature. They became a force. But they also changed and the main agent of change was the kind of educational system that sprang from a total but unspoken acceptance of the policies recommended by the Blue Books. In the controversy which raged between the most respected nonconformist leaders and the few people who dared to defend the Report, it would seem, in Cardiff Arms Park parlance, that the English were hammered into the ground, and that the Welsh leaders like Henry Richard and Dr Lewis Edwards and Ieuan Gwynedd deserved to be carried shoulder-high off the field by their triumphant supporters. The subsequent history of Wales shows clearly enough that it was the commission that had won the day.

EMYR HUMPHREYS
*The Taliesin Tradition* (1983)

. . . one of the worst tithe disturbances [was] that at Mochdre in June 1887. On that occasion eighty-four people, thirty-four of them policemen, were injured, and the Riot Act had to be read. A public inquiry was set up to investigate the incident, under the chairmanship of a London stipendiary magistrate, John Bridge.

Bridge decided that neither side could shoulder the blame; the steepness of the narrow lane had been the most likely cause of the crowd getting out of hand, although he did criticize those people responsible for encouraging crowds to gather at sales. Among his other conclusions, Bridge made the important suggestion that if in future the landlords rather than the tenants were to be liable for payment of tithes, the tenant farmer need have no cause to complain, and similar riots should not recur. In March 1891 an Act was passed which implemented this proposal, and it was this reform that was largely responsible for the absence of trouble after 1891. Henceforward, even if the landlord raised the rent to compensate for the extra payment of tithe, the tenant could hardly refuse to pay the tithe without also refusing to pay the rent and thus face eviction.

Cattle were still distrained and sold, but no attempts were made to interfere with the bailiffs and auctioneers. There is a long and amusing account in *Y Faner* in 1894 of the distraint of a cow belonging to James Davies of Nant-y-Merddyn, Llansannan. When the bailiff arrived to take the cow to Denbigh to be sold he found the animal decked in red ribbons, with cards on its horns; a typical one, in the form of an obituary card, read:

*In loving memory*
*of the*
*BELOVED COW*
*of Mr James Davies, Nant-y-Merddyn Uchaf,*
*Llansannan*
*Who went a prey to the insatiable greed*
*of the Ecclesiastical Commissioners*
*April 25th, 1894*

from *The Tithe War*
(Clwyd Record Office Publication, 1978)

The people of Tonypandy retaliated as the Celts had against the
Romans; they went up the mountains to find the huge stones
left behind by the Ice Age and rolled them down the slopes to
keep the police away.

GEORGE THOMAS
*Mr Speaker* (1985)

Cloistered in Park Place, Cardiff, the Jews had shielded me
from the hard facts of life, the General Strike had barely disturbed the even tenor of their days, but here in Swansea we
were in what had been the metallurgic centre of the world.
Landore, just up the road from Hafod, had thrived on sweated
labour, men working their guts out at great furnaces for too
long for too little.

Nickel, tin, steel, coal, copper, spelter. It was all in our little
valley. It had belched grit and dust and fumes, and everywhere
was drab to the eye. Everything you touched was coated in grit,
but I was a child who, as Mother put it, had been shoved from
pillar to post, and adaptation to the environment was uncon-
sciously done. I went down to the Cwm on Saturday afternoons
to call for Davy, and we toddled off to pick coal for his mother.
We went through the park that wasn't a park at all in those
days, but a slice of derelict land. Hordes of big girls bullied and
shrieked and commandeered all there was.

They stood on the swings whooping higher and higher, their
skirts lifting and flapping, their knees jerking with the effort to
rise.

'Bella Bowen went right over the top.'

'Look at those! Two on one swing. They'll break it.'

The chains on the swings creaked, the girls jeered, 'Yah!'
They sang bawdily, 'Chase me Charlie, chase me Charlie, up
the leg of me drawers – whoop!'

We dodged away, clutching the bags his Mother had given us
to fill, and on past the row of whitewashed cottages that
seemed to be stopping the tip from creeping away.

'They're vulgar,' I announced about the girls.

'My mother says they're common – especially Bella Bowen,'
agreed Davy.

The tip was very loose, the big red cinders and slag were brought from the works in drams that crawled along like giant insects, always working, and we climbed happily.

At the top we sat and looked around, not down at the black and grey, or at the girls on the swings, but out and beyond, beyond the roofs and the works and the industrialists' dreams. We looked to where there was the faintest promise of grass on hills to the north, or back to the south where the docks sent up spindly cranes and the sea glittered on the horizon. We must have been at least fifty feet up, and it was like heaven, just Davy and me and the cold cold air.

'I've been over there,' I said, gesturing to Kilvey Hill that was, to me, still a mountain.

'What for?' Sniff. Sniff.

'My Mother took me collecting.' Sniff. Sniff.

We watched an old woman toiling her way up the Tip towards us, weaving across and back to make her climb easier, bending, picking up the right-sized cinders and dropping them into her bag.

'She's as strong as a bull,' Davy said. 'My Pa says so. She'll outlive us.'

'She sells that coal,' I said. 'She makes a fortune.'

We laboured down again, like men with wooden legs descending Everest, filling our bags, delighted if we found a Big 'un, our lungs hurting with the cold, waiting for the spring that was kind and came early.

EDITH COURTNEY
*A Mouse Ran Up My Nightie* (1974)

## *Private Jones*

Dafis the post came down the lane to Siencyn's cottage earlier today than usual. He walked his bicycle through the stony muddy ruts, ringing his bell to call them out. Siencyn was still in bed, but Marged, his wife, had been up a couple of hours, feeding the wild chickens that nested in the apple trees and gorse bushes and mixing some swill for Granny the sow.

'It's come, Marged *fach*, it's come,' Dafis shouted, his excitement at a gleeful pitch. 'Siencyn's notice is come.'

He brandished a small brown envelope.

Marged straightened her heavy body, wiped her wet hands in her sack apron, showed nothing.

'*Diw mawr*,' she said to herself, thinking that something important was happening inside her.

'Siencyn!' Dafis called, leaning his bicycle with its tied-on parcels against the crumbled wall of the cottage. 'Your calling-up notice I got for you. Look alive, boy.'

Siencyn poked his long head out of the tiny bedroom window, his hair the colour of swedes. He was in his flannel nightshirt.

'Coming now, Dafis,' he said cheerily and withdrew. He pulled his trousers and clogs on, and came downstairs buckling his leather belt across a handful of trousers, very excited.

Dafis opened the letter, Marged looking over his shoulder. She was twice his size.

'Printed matter,' Dafis said. 'There for you. Instructions, look. Railway travel voucher. Free trip, see?'

'In the train?' Siencyn asked.

'Third class,' Dafis said. 'From Cardigan station, Great Western Railway, to Talcen station, ditto. East Wales Fusiliers it is for you, Siencyn *bach*, poor dab. Plenty of VCs they got already. Watch out, you.'

'East Wales Fusiliers, is it?' Siencyn repeated. 'Well, well. Third class?'

'When is it?' Marged asked.

'Friday next, 21st inst.,' Dafis said. 'Take your identity card, Siencyn *bach*, don't forget that, now. Or it's CB you'll be right from the word go.'

'*Jawch*,' said Siencyn, 'there's a lot to remember, Dafis. Where's my identity card, Marged? In the poe in the spare room, is it?'

'And your birth certificate is there,' she said, knowing where to put her hands on things. 'You'll have to find somewhere else to keep your things from now on, Siencyn *bach*.'

'Aye, that's true,' he said, rubbing his tangled hair. 'Well, I better go round and tell everybody.'

'Don't trouble,' said Dafis. 'I'll tell them on my round. Stay you, my boy. I'll come down tonight and give you a bit of wisdom, see? Four years of it in the last war I had, and no more for me thank you.' He looked at his right hand, from which three fingers were missing. 'German sniper did that,' he said proudly, and then screwed up his red bunioned face into a wink. 'Held it up above the parapet, see, Siencyn, and got a nice little blighty. But there, you don't know what a parapet is yet, I don't doubt.'

'I'll learn,' Siencyn said, with all the good will in the world.

'You will,' Dafis said, speaking with the sardonic finality of experience. 'Solong both.'

'Solong Dafis, thank you,' Siencyn said.

Dafis pushed his bicycle off, the cycle clips pulling his small trousers up nearly to his knees. He wore a straw boater all the year round, Dafis did.

The third winter of the war was just relaxing its grip on this closed corner of Cardiganshire; six weeks of frost had held up the winter ploughing and the spring sowing, and Siencyn had been having a soft time of it, lying in bed in the mornings, chopping a bit of firewood, mending a few broken scythes and shafts, patching up the cowsheds of his employer, cutting enough hay for the dray-horses, and a pint or two some nights. He had been medically examined and registered a whole year back, but his call-up was deferred for the summer harvest and the autumn trapping – Siencyn was the official trapper of the parish and sent four hundred and thirty-seven rabbits to Cardigan station, Great Western, in five weeks – and then the winter ploughing. He had got tired of waiting, restless and unable to merge himself in his work and the weather and the requirements of the horses and of Marged. He was a good-natured man, but out of patience with things. He had quarrelled with Marged a lot this winter, beating her once, leaping out of bed on a Sunday morning when the cracked church bell was tolling, and beating her for calling him an idle heathen.

ALUN LEWIS (1915–44)
from *Private Jones*
in *Selected Poetry and Prose of Alun Lewis*, ed. Ian Hamilton (1966)

*Gwalia Deserta XV*

O what can you give me?
Say the sad bells of Rhymney.

Is there hope for the future?
Cry the brown bells of Merthyr.

Who made the mineowner?
Say the black bells of Rhondda.

And who robbed the miner?
Cry the grim bells of Blaina.

They will plunder willy-nilly,
Say the bells of Caerphilly.

They have fangs, they have teeth!
Shout the loud bells of Neath.

To the south, things are sullen,
Say the pink bells of Brecon.

Even God is uneasy,
Say the moist bells of Swansea.

Put the vandals in court!
Cry the bells of Newport.

All would be well if – if – if –
Say the green bells of Cardiff.

Why so worried, sisters, why?
Sing the silver bells of Wye.

IDRIS DAVIES (1905–53)

Wales has also had a toilsome march. It has traversed many a mountain and marsh: it has been attacked by innumerable foes: and the national existence of this brave little army of patriots appeared many a time to have been blotted out. But it has surmounted every obstacle; it has crossed every steep hill and morass; it has vanquished the efforts of every enemy by the indomitable vitality of its patriotism. It has a few more battles to fight, but Wales will not turn back, for beneath lie the fruit-laden valleys of the future and the golden gates of Cymru Fydd.

RT HON. DAVID LLOYD GEORGE (1863–1945)
from a speech at Liverpool, 20 November 1891

*The First World War*

Wales must continue doing her duty. I should like to see a Welsh army in the field. I should like to see the race who faced the Normans for hundreds of years in their struggle for freedom, the race that helped to win the battle of Crecy, the race that fought for a generation under Glendower against the greatest captain in Europe – I should like to see that race give a good taste of its quality in this struggle in Europe, and they are going to do it.

May I tell you, in a simple parable, what I think this war is doing for us? I know a valley in North Wales, between the mountains and the sea, a beautiful valley, snug, comfortable, sheltered by the mountains from all the bitter blasts. It was very enervating, and I remember how the boys were in the habit of climbing the hills above the village to have a glimpse of the great mountains in the distance and to be stimulated and

**208**    freshened by the breezes which came from the hill-tops and by
the great spectacle of that great valley. We have been living in a
sheltered valley for generations. We have been too comfortable, too indulgent, many perhaps too selfish. And the stern
hand of fate has scourged us to an elevation where we can see
the great everlasting things that matter for a nation, the great
peaks of honour we had forgotten, duty and patriotism, and,
clad in glittering white, the great pinnacle of sacrifice pointing
like a rugged finger to heaven. We shall descend into the valleys again, but as long as the men and women of this generation last they will carry in their hearts the image of these great
mountain peaks whose foundations are unshaken though
Europe rock and sway in the convulsions of a great war.

RT HON. DAVID LLOYD GEORGE (1863–1945)
quoted in *The Land of My Fathers* (1915)


*Aneurin Bevan*

. . . had to leave [school] at thirteen to work in the mines to sup-
plement the meagre wages of my father. Shortly thereafter his
father died in Aneurin's arms of pneumoconiosis, a coal dust
disease to which miners' lungs are subject. In an autobiograph-
ical sketch Bevan bitterly comments that no compensation was
paid to his family because the illness was not, at that time, considered an industrial disease.

MARK M. KRUG
*Aneurin Bevan* (1961)

# X

# CUSTOMS, TRADITIONS, LAW

*Early Welsh Precepts*

The THREE who are first in point of precedence according to politeness:- the most infirm; the poorest; and he who does not know the language.

THREE things, which according to politeness should be prepared for guests:- a kind and affectionate reception; a ready and handsome provision; and a friendly conversation.

THREE things, which according to politeness should not be asked of a guest: where he came from; his worldly condition; and the place of his destination.

THREE things which are indecorous over meat:- gossiping; coquetting; and praising or blaming the meat, since it should be received as God sends it.

### Captain Fluellen and Henry V

*King Henry:* Then call we this the field of Agincourt,
Fought on the day of Crispin Crispianus.

*Fluellen:* Your grandfather of famous memory, an't please your majesty, and your great-uncle Edward the Black Prince of Wales, as I have read in the chronicles, fought a most prave pattle here in France.

*King Henry:* They did, Fluellen.

*Fluellen:* Your majesty says very true; if your majesties is remembered of it, the Welshmen did goot service in a garden where leeks did grow, wearing leeks in their Monmouth caps; which, your majesty knows, to this hour is an honourable padge of the service; and I do pelieve your majesty takes no scorn to wear the leek upon St Tavy's day.

*King Henry:* I wear it for a memorable honour; For I am Welsh, you know, good countryman.

*Fluellen:* All the water in Wye cannot wash your majesty's Welsh plood out of your pody, I can tell you that: God pless it and preserve it as long as it pleases his grace and majesty too!

*King Henry:* Thanks, my good countryman.

*Fluellen:* By Cheshu, I am your majesty's countryman, I care not who know it; I will confess it to all the 'orld: I need not be ashamed of your majesty, praised be got, so long as your majesty is an honest man.

*King Henry:* God keep me so!

(Act IV, Scene VII)

***

### Captain Fluellen and the Leek

*Gower:* . . . but why wear you your leek today? St Davy's day is past.

*Fluellen:* There is occasions and causes why and wherefore in all things: I will tell you, as my friend, Captain Gower; – the rascally, scald, peggarly, lousy, pragging knave, Pistol . . . he is come to me, and prings me pread and salt yesterday, look you, and pid me eat my leek . . .

ENTER PISTOL

| | |
|---|---|
| *Fluellen:* | I peseech you heartily, scurvy, lousy knave . . . to |
| | eat, look you, this leek. . . . |
| *Pistol:* | Not for Cadwallader and all his goats. . . . Must I |
| | bite? |
| *Fluellen:* | . . . if you can mock a leek you can eat a leek . . . Pite, |
| | I pray you; it is goot for your green wound and your |
| | ploody coxcomb. |
| *Pistol:* | Must I bite? |

(Act V, Scene I)

SHAKESPEARE (1564–1616)
*Henry V*

. . . Yesterday, being St David's Day, the King, according to custom, wore a leek in honour of the Ancient Britons, the same
being presented to him by the sergeant-porter, whose place it is,
and for which he claims the clothes His Majesty wore on that
day; the courtiers in imitation of his Majesty wore leeks also.

*The Flying Post* (1699)

from *The Praise of St David's Day. Shewing the reason why the
Welch-men Honour the Leeke on that day*

Who list to reade the deeds
   by valiant Welch-men done,
Shall find them worthy men of Armes,
   as breathes beneath the sunne;
They are of valiant hearts,
   of nature kind and meeke,
An Honour on St David's Day,
   it is to wear a Leeke.

And now if you would know,
   why they the Leeke do weare,
In honour of St David's day,
   it plainly shall appeare.
Upon St David's day,
   And first of March that weeke,
The Welch-men with their foes did joyne,
   then honoured be the Leeke.

And being in the field,
    their valour they did try;
Where thousands on both sides being slaine,
    within their bloods did lye.
And they not knowing how
    their friends from foes to seeke,
Into a Garden they did go,
    where each one pull'd a Leeke:

And wore it in his hat,
    their Countreymen to know;
And then most valiantly they did,
    o'ercome their warlike foe.
Then were noe colours knowne,
    or any feathers eeke;
The featheres first originall,
    it was the Welch-mans Leeke.

And ever since that time,
    the Leeke they use to weare.
In honour of St David's day,
    They doe that Trophy beare.
A Reverend Bishop was
    St David mild and meeke,
And 'tis an honour that same day,
    for them to wear a Leeke.

ANONYMOUS, 18th century
from *This World of Wales* (1968)
ed. Gerald Morgan

Another custom, which is now in many places relinquished, was that of the Plygain, or service in the church, about three o'clock in the morning on Christmas-day; when, according to Mr Pennant, 'most of the parishioners assembled in church, and after prayers and a sermon, continued there singing psalms and hymns with great devotion till broad day; and if, through age or infirmity, any were disabled from attending, they never failed having prayers at home, and carols on our Saviour's nativity.'

PETER ROBERTS
*Cambrian Popular Antiquities* (1815)

The *Mari Lwyd* custom has been described as 'a pre-Christian horse ceremony which may be associated with similar customs spread over many parts of the world'. Although it survives to our day in parts of Glamorgan and Carmarthenshire, there is evidence that it was formerly widely found throughout Wales, often in conjunction with wassail-singing. It is known by other names besides *Mari Lwyd* (grey Mary) in different districts; these include 'Horse's Head' in Gower, *Pen Ceffyl* (Horse's Head) and *Y Warsel* (The Wassail) in parts of Carmarthenshire, *Y March* (The Horse) or *Y Gynfas-farch* (The Canvas Horse) in Pembrokeshire. In addition the actual period during which the custom was carried on varied in different parts of the country. An account published in 1852 states that in Glamorgan and Monmouthshire the ceremony 'began on Christmas Night and was continued for a fortnight, three weeks or a month', but in the same counties it was also specifically associated with the New Year and Twelfth Night. In Brecknock and Pembrokeshire it was associated with the New Year and in north Wales and Carmarthenshire with both Christmas and the New Year. It is likely however that visits by the *Mari Lwyd* party were made over a period of several days in each case, and that the association with any particular day during the Christmas Season had become exceedingly tenuous. By the nineteenth century the ritual significance of the *Mari Lwyd* had been almost completely forgotten and the religious custom had become a diversion which was felt in a vague way to be an essential part of the prolonged celebration of Christmastide. If the rival claims of Christmas and New Year's Day and the confusion brought about by the New Style of reckoning the days of the Calendar in the eighteenth century are borne in mind, the local differences in the dating of the *Mari Lwyd* and similar customs are readily understandable.

The *Mari Lwyd* itself consisted of a horse's skull which had been prepared by burying it in fresh lime or which had been kept buried in the ground after the previous year's festivities. Sometimes a wooden block was used instead of a horse's head. The lower jaw was fixed with a spring which caused the mouth to shut with a loud snap when operated by the person carrying the *Mari*. A pole about five feet long was inserted into the horse's skull, and a white sheet draped over it. Coloured ribbons were used to decorate the skull, and bottle glass used to represent the eyes; pieces of black cloth were sewn on to the sheet to serve as ears. The man carrying the *Mari* stood underneath the sheet, holding the pole and operating the lower jaw with a short wooden handle. Reins with bells attached were placed on the *Mari*'s head and held by the 'Leader' who also carried a stick for knocking doors.

The decoration of the *Mari Lwyd* or *Cynfas-farch* as practised in the St Davids district of Pembrokeshire was somewhat different. A canvas sheet a couple of yards square such as was 'used for carrying odds and ends of corn chaff etc. or the *brethyn rhawn* (horse-hair sheet) used over the kiln for drying corn . . . was sewn at one of the corners for about a yard to form a snout and head of an Ichthyosaurus or any other animal of such beauty! The eyes were represented by large buttons and two brown harvest gloves tacked on for ears, the head tightly stuffed with straw. The man stood underneath the canvas and a long pitchfork stuck into the straw enabled him to turn the head about in every direction. It was then carried about and the first intimation often received was the sight of this prowling monster peeping around into the room, or sometimes shewing his head by pushing it through an upstairs window. One case was recorded, by my mother, of a sudden death through fright of this. It almost always created a collapse of some and the scamper of others.'

No details are available of the composition of the party which accompanied the Pembrokeshire *Mari Lwyd*. In Glamorgan, however, the party was made up of the *Mari Lwyd*, the 'Leader', 'Sergeant', 'Merryman' and 'Punch and Judy'. Merryman would sometimes play the fiddle, while Punch and Judy would be dressed in tattered clothes and had blackened faces. All the other members of the party (according to *Nefydd*) would be decorated with numerous ribbons and sometimes with a wide sash about their waists. When the procession approached a house which it was intended to visit, the leader tapped the door while the party sang the traditional rhymes. A number of different versions of the words and music sung by the *Mari Lwyd* party have been recorded . . . The party outside engaged in a battle of wits with the householders and sang

*extempore* verses to which those indoors were obliged to reply in
a similar manner.

TREFOR M. OWEN
*Welsh Folk Customs* (1959)

## Souling

The custom of souling was known by several different names
in Welsh. In north Wales *hel bwyd cennad y meirw* (collecting the
food of the messenger of the dead) was the most common form,
although *hel solod* (collecting souls or soul-cakes) was also
known, as, for example in Corwen, Merioneth. In another part
of Merioneth, Dinas Mawddwy, the term *bara-a-chawsa* (bread-
and-cheesing) was used. The word 'sowling' was used in south
Pembrokeshire but in Carmarthenshire the phrases *diwrnod
rhanna* (doling day) *pice rhanna* (dole cakes) and *bara rhan* (dole
bread) were found; the latter is also given by Iolo Morganwg in
his list of Glamorgan customs. The custom, under one name or
another, was widespread in Wales and was particularly popular in the English border counties of Cheshire and Shropshire.

The one statement which can be made with certainty about
soul-cakes is that their gift was in some way acceptable to the
dead. Wright and Lones suggest that the giving of soul-cakes to
relatives and acquaintances probably represents the custom in
its older and purer form, in which case it is presumably the
dead kin of the giver who are concerned in some mysterious
way. Another interpretation claims that the poor on All Souls'
Day collected gifts for the priests, in pre-Reformation times, for
them to pray for the release of their poor relatives from purga-
tory. In view of the significance of the festival to the medieval
church this explanation is quite plausible, but it is important to
note that it is the dead relatives of the collector and not those of
the giver who are concerned if this viewpoint is correct. A further complication is introduced by the association with the
harvest which is implied by the form of the custom in certain
districts. According to Pennant, the poor, on receiving the soul-
cakes, prayed to God to bless the next crop of wheat, while in
Kidwelly, Carmarthenshire, only those who helped, or the

children of those who helped, at the harvest got the *pice rhanna*, the local name for the soul-cakes.

Details of the ingredients used in the preparation of soul-cakes have been recorded in different parts of Wales. In Cerrigydrudion, Denbighshire, about 1830, a small cake of barley meal was made, using so much salt that it was barely edible; it was called *cacen gŵyl y meirw* (cake of the feast of the dead). The symbolical significance of salt as a purifying and preserving agent is probably to be seen here as in the old practice of placing salt in or on a coffin. By 1893 the custom had altered somewhat, small coins, apples and pieces of bread and butter being given in Llangwm, and Llanfihangel Glyn Myfyr as well as Cerrigydrudion. In the Edeirnion district of Merioneth small cakes were made for children, and larger ones for the old people who came round. In Laugharne a large sack of flour was used on this occasion at each farm and the maids would be up all night making the barley bread which was given together with cheese to the poor. In Cardiganshire the custom was to make big muffins and give them to one's friends and acquaintances, a practice similar to that recorded by Wright and Lones. The Kidwelly farmwife baked 'large flat cakes' for the occasion, while *bara can a miod* (white-bread and little cakes) have also been mentioned in a dictionary published in 1826. In Corwen, Merioneth, 'the cake was generally made of barley-flour, without any addition of more appetizing ingredients than salt and water; it was about one inch thick and four inches in diameter'. The fact that 'apples bread and cheese or any other article of diet were given at those houses where cake had not been prepared, or had been distributed' suggests a degenerate form of the custom which had in fact become more usual than the earlier bread-gift in the border areas. In those districts bordering on Cheshire and Shropshire, in particular, the verses sung show the influence of wassailing, the receipt of apples and nuts likewise show traces of a Winter's Eve custom of collecting fruit for use in divination and celebration rather than in commemoration of the dead.

As to the manner in which the custom was conducted, we are told that in Edeirnion the callers were labourers' children, poor women and occasionally old men. The door was knocked and whether there was an answer or not, the caller asked *'Welwch chi'n dda gai damed o fwyd cennad y meirw?'* (Please may I

have a little of the food of the messenger of the dead?) In  **217**
Corwen a similar request was made with the addition of an
*Amen* at the end. In Dinas Mawddwy the doggerel used was:

> *Bara a chaws, bara a chaws*
> *Os ca'i beth, mi neidia',*
> *Os na cha'i ddim, mi beidia'.*

(Bread and cheese, bread and cheese; if I get some I'll jump;
If I don't I won't.)

Another piece of doggerel was used in Bryneglwys, Denbighshire in the late nineteenth century:

> *Dega Dega, dowch i'r drws.*
> *A rhowch i gennad y meirw.*

(*Dega, dega,* come to the door, and give to the messenger of
the dead.)

If the request was refused the following verse was repeated:

> *Deca, deca* (?sic) *o dan y drws,*
> *A phen y wraig yn siwtrws*

(*Deca, deca* under the door, and the wife's head in smither-
eens.)

The Carmarthenshire and Cardiganshire forms recorded were
similar:

> *Rhanna! rhanna! Dydd gwyl eneidie,*
> *Rhan i 'nhad am gywiro sgidie,*
> *Rhan i mam am gywiro sane,*
> *Rhan i'r plant sy'n aros gartre.*

(Share! Share! All Souls' Day, a share to my father for mending the shoes, a share to my mother for mending stockings, a
share to the children who stay at home.)

*Dydd Gŵyl eneidiau* had become *dwgwl aneidie*, a dialect pronunciation which later gave the meaningless form *Dwbwl dameidie*
(double pieces). Like collecting *calennig* (for which a similar
type of the verse was used) or collecting *crempogau* (pancakes)
the children gathered for their living relatives rather than for
the dead, to such a degree had the custom lost its true purpose.

In Merioneth the children carried a little bag or basket and began collecting at dawn continuing until noon, as in *calennig*-collecting, and in contradistinction to the evening visits of the border country souling parties who chanted 'wissel wassel' and called for 'bread and possal, apple or a pear, plum or a cherry' as well as a 'sol cake'.

TREFOR M. OWEN
*Welsh Folk Customs* (1959)


### Sin-Eating

'In the County of Hereford was an old Custome at funeralls to (hire) have poor people, who were to take upon them all the sinnes of the party deceased. One of them I remember lived in a cottage on Rosse high-way. (He was long, leane, ugly, lamentable poor raskel.) The manner was that when the Corps was brought out of the house and layd on the Biere, a Loafe of bread was brought out, and delivered to the Sinne-eater over the corps, as also a Mazer-bowle of maple (Gossips bowle) full of beer, w$^{ch}$ he was to drinke up, and sixpence in money, in consideration whereof he tooke upon him (*ipso facto*) all the Sinnes of the Defunct, and freed him (or her) from walking after they were dead. This custome alludes (methinkes) something to the Scapegoate in y$^e$ old Lawe.

Leviticus, chap. xvi. verse 21. 22. . . . This Custome (though rarely used in our dayes) yet by some people was (observed) continued even in the strictest time of y$^e$ Presbyterian government: as at Dynder, volens nolens the Parson of y$^e$ Parish, the (kinred) relations of a woman deceased there had this ceremonie punctually performed according to her Will: and also the like was donne at y$^e$ City of Hereford in these times, when a woman kept many yeares before her death a Mazard-bowle for the Sinne-eater; and the like in other places in this Countie; as also in Brecon, e. g. at Llangors, where Mr. Gwin the minister about 1640 could not hinder y$^e$ performing of this ancient custumme. I believe this custumme was heretofore used over all Wales.

'See Juvenal Satyr. VI. (519–521), where he speakes of throwing purple thread into y$^e$ river to carry away ones sinne. In North Wales, the sinne eaters are frequently made use of; but

there, insted of a Bowle of Beere, they have a bowle of Milke.
Methinkes, Doles to Poore people with money at Funeralls
have some resemblance of that of y^e Sinne-eater. Doles at
Funeralls were continued at Gentlemens funeralls in the West
of England till the Civil-warre. And so in Germany at rich
mens funeralls Doles are in use, and to every one a quart of
strong and good Beer.—Cramer.'

JOHN AUBREY (1626–97)
*Remains of Gentilisme and Judaisme* (Folk Lore Society 1880)

### Shovel money

At all funerals which take place at Llangurig, when the coffin
has been lowered into the grave, the parish clerk holds a shovel
over the open grave upon which he receives the contributions
from the relatives and friends of the deceased. The custom is a
relic of the times when the Roman Catholic religion prevailed
in the principality and it was customary to pay money to the
priest for offering masses for the souls of the dead. The money
placed on the shovel is called *arian-y-rhaw* (shovel money) and
is the clerk's fee. As it is regarded as a mark of respect and
esteem towards the deceased to contribute, and as nothing but
silver or gold is received, it frequently happens that the clerk
receives a large sum. If in adding up the money an odd
sixpence occurred it was formerly deemed an omen that
another funeral would take place shortly.

A Parochial Account of Llangurig, 1870

### Epitaph of Hugh Lloyd of Powys

A talent rare by him possessed
T'adjust the bones of the distressed;
When ever called he ne'er refused
But cheerfully his talent used.
But now he lies beneath this tomb,
Till Jesus comes to adjust his own.

(in the church, Michaelchurch-on-Arrow)

An attempt to revive the old Welsh form of lynching called *cludo ar ysgol* (to carry the ladder) in which the victim is seized, strapped lengthways on a ladder and carried or jolted through the place was made last weekend at Talysarn, a village near Caernarfon. It appears that an Englishman named Joseph Preston had taken legal proceedings against a Welshman in his employ but the verdict was in favour of the latter. When Preston arrived at Talysarn he was met at the station by a crowd. A ladder could not be found so a wheelbarrow and ropes were in readiness to lynch the Englishman. Preston, fortunately, managed to escape, but not without being roughly treated. At Caernarfon on Saturday nine men were charged with rioting and committing an assault upon Preston, and were remanded.

*Oswestry Advertizer*, 1880

*Jan 4 [1797]:* Mary Prenold, for embezzling bread, beef and candles, to be publicly whipped in the hall before dinner next Wednesday. A frame for whipping persons is to be immediately made on the plan of that at the House of Correction at Montgomery.

*Feb 8:* Eliz Jones to be flogged the first day after Mr Baxter (the surgeon) reports her fit for the operation for absenting the House without leave.

*Nov 22:* That Hannah Thomas be punished with 18 lashes, Mary Owens with 12, and Susannah Gouty, Eliz Thomas, Sarah Hotchins, Cadwalader Lewis, Mary Price and Eliz Williams, with 6 each for being idle and not spinning as much in the last fortnight as they ought. Several others for the same cause confined in the crib.

*February 26 [1800]:* That the schoolmaster, having got one of the paupers in the House with child, be discharged, it being in the opinion of the Board, an offence which cannot be overlooked in any officer. At the same time the Directors think it right to express their satisfaction with the good conduct of the schoolmaster in other respects.

*Records of the Forden House of Industry*

Just as at a 'maiden assize', the judge is presented with a pair of white gloves, so this white banner symbolizes the joyful fact that the gaol is empty. Such was the case the other day at Beamaris, the capital of the county of Anglesey, where, with a population of 52,000, there had been only one prisoner within the gaol for a fortnight. On his discharge the gates were thrown open and the white flag hoisted. Such a phenomenon is rarely, if ever, witnessed in the densely-populated haunts of trade and manufacture.

*The Graphic,* 1873

# XI

# RELIGION, HYMNS, PREACHERS

In the evening I preached in the large hall at Mr Mathews' in Llandaf. And will the rich also hear the words of eternal life? *With God all things are possible.*

JOHN WESLEY (1703–91)
26 August 1779

I knot their praises, for long centuries mute.
The core of all faith is one, it is splendid to meet
With souls one with the quick at Being's root.

Over my head they are there, they are one with the light
Where through the expanse peace gathers. When night
Veils the sky, each is a shining gap to my sight.

John Roberts of Trawsfynydd, priest to the needy,
In the dread plague shared out the bread of the journey,
Knowing the powers of the dark had come, and would break
   his body.

John Owen the joiner, that many a servant concealed,
For the old communion his hand an unwearying shield,
Lest the plait be unravelled, and the beams of the great house
   yield.

Richard Gwyn smiled in their face at what they were at:
'I have sixpence towards your fine' – for he'd not
In the cause of his Master, price his life more than that.

They that ran light, I cannot reckon them all,
A company gathered together beyond the pits of hell:
Surely nothing can scatter them who paid the selfsame toll.

The last, quiet payment. World for world giving then,
For the Spirit to guide them giving that ultimate pain,
Giving a flower for his root, for his cradle a grain.

Torture did rack them, disembowelling rend,
Ere the sight where a ladder was given their souls to ascend
To the broad next morning of Golgotha, their blest Lord's world
   without end.

Welshmen, were you a nation, great would be the glory
These would have in your story.

WALDO WILLIAMS (1904–71)
(trans. Tony Conran)

John Wesley, the founder of English Methodism, never came to Ebbw Vale, though he knew and preached at Brecon and Abergavenny. He wrote in his Journal for Monday 15 October 1739: 'Upon a pressing invitation, some time since received, I set out for Wales ... came to Abergavenny ... I felt a strong aversion to preaching here. However I went to the person in whose ground Mr Whitfield preached, to desire the use of it. He said, "with all his heart". About a thousand people stood patiently (though the frost was sharp, it being after sunset), while, from Acts xxviii 22, I simply described the plain, old religion of the Church of England, which is now almost everywhere spoken against, under the new name of Methodism.'

Wesley had met and talked with Howell Harris of Trevecca and the other leaders of the earlier Welsh Revival and was assured that their work in the principality was of God. You could say, that Wesleyan Methodism came to the valleys with the influx of workers from south-west England to the mines and ironworks, just as almost a century later, Primitive Methodism came in the wake of the arrival of iron workers from Shropshire.

The Methodists, or Wesleyans, were earnest folk who met regularly for preaching services and gathered in their class meeting to share what God was doing in them and through them, in order that they might grow in Christian grace and in the likeness to Jesus Christ, but they continued to attend the parish churches for their sacramental life. There were real similarities between the Methodist Societies of the Church of England in the previous century.

For various reasons the nineteenth century saw Wesleyan Methodism being split into a number of different branches such as the Wesleyan Reform, the Primitive, the New Connexion and the United Methodists, with Kilhamites and the Bible Christians.

In 1932 the smaller unions of these groups culminated in all, except the Wesleyan Reform movement, becoming the Methodist Church of Great Britain and Ireland.

While Wesley was beginning his mission of evangelism in England, Howell Harris was preaching and converting in Wales and by 1739 was joined by George Whitfield.

Howell Harris was an ardent Welshman. Most of the Methodist Societies he formed were Welsh speaking. Howell Harris wrote, after meeting Wesley, that they agreed on almost everything except the Calvin doctrine of Predestination. As they failed to agree on this point, they remained a separate denomination, and were known as Calvinistic Methodists.

The small groups of worshippers in the farms and isolated cottages in the valleys of northern Monmouthshire did not belong to a particular sect but, agreed on the Gospel of Jesus Christ and worshipped together in their own homes.

In good weather they visited the parish churches at Bedwellty, Blaenau Gwent (Blaina), Llanhilleth, Llanelli, and Llangynidr, the Independents went to Croes Penmain (Oakdale). Baptists had a meeting place at Gelli Crug (Abertillery). One of the first Independent ministers in the area was Rev. Edmund Jones, affectionately known as 'The Old Prophet', (*Yr Hen Profwydd*) and he held services at the larger farms as a part of his pastoral work. The chief meeting place at Pen-y-Cae (Ebbw Vale) was at Ty-Yn-Y-Llwyn farm where Tyllwyn is now situated.

John Wesley made the journey from Cardiff to Aberdare and Brecon several times, and also visited Merthyr, but Methodism came to Ebbw Vale with the Guests and Homfrays from the Wakefield area of Yorkshire, and the Guests and Homfrays from Shropshire.

In 1795 the first Methodist minister was appointed to Merthyr, which was a part of the Brecon circuit.

Thomas Guest took an avid interest in the new chapel at Merthyr which was opened on 18 June 1797. He was a lay preacher himself, and was supported by the Browns who were later to play an active part in the formation of the chapels and churches in Blaina and Ebbw Vale. A poem originally in Welsh, in praise of Thomas Brown said

> *I'r Saeson Wesleyaidd ym ddygan haelionus,*
> *Y mae ei haelfrydedd fel llanw heb drai.*

(To the English Wesleyans he acts generously, His generosity is a flow without ebb.)

KEITH THOMAS
from *James Street Methodist Church:*
*A History of Methodism* (1987)

*Friday, 19.* I preached near the market-place, and afterwards rode over to Trefeca. Howell Harris' house is one of the most elegant places which I have ever seen in Wales. The little chapel and all things round about it are finished in an uncommon taste, and the gardens, orchards, fish-ponds and mount adjoining make the place a little paradise. He thanks God for these things and looks through them. About six-score persons are now in the Family – all diligent, all constantly employed, all fearing God and working righteousness. I preached at ten to a crowded audience, and in the evening at Brecon again, but to the poor only, the rich (a very few excepted) were otherwise employed.

\*

Before I talked with him myself I wondered H. Harris did not go out and preach as usual. But he now informed me he preached till he could preach no longer, his constitution being entirely broken. While he was thus confined he was pressed in spirit to build a large house, though he knew not why or for whom. But as soon as it was built men, women and children without his seeking came to it from all parts of Wales. And except in the case of the Orphan House at Halle, I never heard of so many signal interpositions of Divine Providence . . .

\*

*Thursday, 26.* I preached at five and again at eleven. I think this was the happiest time of all. The poor and the rich seemed to be equally affected. Oh how are the times changed at Cowbridge since the people compassed the house where I was and poured in stones from every quarter! But my strength was then according to my day and (blessed by God) so it is still.

JOHN WESLEY, 1779 (1703–91)
*Journal* ed. N. Curnock (8 vols. 1909–16)

Huw Maurice, Glan y Gors, Sierlyn (Edward Charles) etc., are talked of here as being three of the rankest infidels of all the Gwyneddigion, who are all of them considered as ten thousand times worse than Tom Paine, and all this on the word of Ginshop Jones, who was at the Methodistical association at

South Wales, and South Wales as Hell.

IOLO MORGANWG (1747–1826)

### Sunday Schools and the Teaching of Welsh

. . . about the year 1807–8, Thomas Charles started the large gatherings called *Cymanfaoed Ysgolion*, or School Associations.

Sunday Schools continue to be conducted on the same lines in Wales, and they retain the peculiarity that they are attended by men and women of all ages. Moreover, they form an institution recognized and encouraged by all Protestant denominations alike. Their importance from the point of view of Welsh and its literature consists in the fact that the Welsh are taught in these schools to read in their own tongue. The work done in them, it is true, extends further, namely, to the exposition of the words of Scripture, the only text read in them; but it does not come within the scope of that work to do anything directly to teach the people to write their language or to compose in it . . .

The work of the Sunday School covers the whole extent to which the bulk of Welsh people are taught Welsh at all outside their hearths and homes . . . the style of the authorized version of the Welsh Bible is the ideal of those who try to write and speak good Welsh. The fact that the Bible forms the earliest prose reading of the youth of Wales, and that they commit a great deal to memory under the direction of the Sunday School, makes that result unavoidable; and this is not to be deplored, as the style of the Welsh Bible is on the whole excellent.

SIR JOHN RHŶS and DAVID BRYNMOR-JONES
*The Welsh People* (1900)

The revival of religion has put an end to all the merry meetings for dancing, singing with the harp, and every kind of sinful mirth, which used to be so prevalent amongst young people here. And at a large fair, kept here a few days ago, the usual revelling, the sound of music, and vain singing, was not to be heard in any part of the town; a decency in the conduct, and sobriety in the countenances, of our country people, appeared the whole of that fair, which I never observed before.

D. E. JENKINS
*The Life of Thomas Charles, BA, of Bala* (1908)

The sudden decline of the national minstrelsy, and customs of Wales, is in a great degree to be attributed to the fanatick impostors, or illiterate plebeian preachers, who have too often been suffered to over-run the country, misleading the greater part of the common people from their lawful church; and dissuading them from their innocent amusements, such as singing, dancing, and other rural sports, and games, which heretofore they had been accustomed to delight in, from the earliest time. In the course of my excursions through the Principality, I have met with several harpers and songsters, who actually had been prevailed upon by those erratic strollers to relinquish their profession, from the idea that it was sinful. The consequence is, Wales, which was formerly one of the merriest and happiest countries in the world, is now become one of the dullest.

JONES
*The Bardic Museum* (1802)

Behind me here on the other side of the moor there lived and laboured one of the best known and one of the most quaint Welsh preachers of the last century – The Reverend Dafydd Evans, Ffynnon Henry . . .

Before I give his sermon on the prophet Jonah I must stress again, if the reader is to understand Dafydd Evans or his sermon, that these men understood the Bible only in terms with which they were familiar, and reasoned on the analogy of life, its facts and relationships as known to them, and experienced by them – that is, life as lived within the simple framework of their own agricultural society, patriarchal in its atmosphere and ways. Its two fundamental and abiding relationships were those of father and son and master and servant. Dafydd therefore could not conceive of any relationship between God and man except that of master and servant unless it was that of father and son, which in reality meant the same thing, for the patriarchal power of the father over his sons remained as long as he lived. William Addison in his book *The English Country Parson* says: 'The gospel abounds in rural imagery that must make it even more real to the countryman on the six days of his week than on the Lord's Day. God is not an intellectual abstraction to him. Man and God have the simple relationship of man and master, and in the country man and master are still often found to be son and father.'

In the story of Jonah, God, the farmer-boss, is calling him to undertake at once a particular job which was distasteful to Jonah, who though he had very many good points was by nature stubborn and intractable. The dialogue therefore is perfectly natural, and as he was giving it to the hill farmers of Ffynnon Henry he clothed it in their own dialect as well, picturing it as something that takes place on a farm very often, where a farmer has to call suddenly on one of his servants to go at once on a certain errand or to turn to another job without delay. Whether the Almighty speaks in dialect, I don't know, but if He does I think He will find that of north Carmarthenshire as rich and adequate as any.

To get the full effect of the dialogue, that between a masterful boss who will stand no nonsense and a stubborn, somewhat defiant servant, it has to be read quickly:

'God: Jonah, I want you to go to Nineveh.

'Jonah: What for?

'God: To preach.

'Jonah: I haven't got a sermon.

'God: I'll give you a sermon. Forty days and Nineveh shall fall.

'Jonah: No, I won't; go yourself.

'God: I'll make you go.

'Jonah: I bet you won't; and off he went . . . down towards Joppa somewhere; there he found a ship bound for Tarsus and agreed to go with it. He didn't haggle with the captain at all about the fare, but paid at once, and in he went to the ship, and she sailed away. "I am all right now," said Jonah; "I am sure I shall win the wager now." But God sent His big servant, the wind, like a policeman, after him to get him to go to Nineveh, but how to get him out of the ship? Then the big servant began to lay the whip on the second servant, the water, which began to jump and to open its mouth, threatening to swallow the whole ship. The sailors began to get alarmed and each one calling on his god ... They cast lots which fell on Jonah, and he had to give an account of himself. "What shall we do?" said the men. "Throw me into the sea," replied Jonah. Here is gameness for you: he would rather go to the bottom than go to Nineveh; he would rather lose his life than lose his wager with God. Yet the sailors, fine chaps they were, didn't like the idea of giving him up, so they had another try: "Now, boys, all hands on deck," but it would not do. The big servant was roaring like a she-bear ... and was pressing the ship between his arms until it creaked: "Throw that old man into the sea, throw that old man overboard or I will drown every one of you right now." They decided in the end to do so. A clergyman was called to read the service so that he might be buried with religion at any rate, and he was lowered gently into the sea. So the two servants have got him from the ship, but now to get him to Nineveh! They had there a huge whale ready to receive him. "*Hawff*," said the whale and swallowed him without ceremony like swallowing a fly. But if he did so, he soon repented, for Jonah was a tough one wherever he was. After swallowing him the old whale made off like a mad thing through the sea, and the fish shouted after him, "Hei, Hei, what's the matter with you, what's happened today?" "Oh, I have swallowed a man," said the old fish. "Tut, tut, you've swallowed a man many a time before, and a bigger one than that, I warrant." "Yes, yes, I know it is a small one, but the little devil (*filein*) is alive in my stomach." And away he galloped through the depth of the sea like cattle in the heat, colliding with this fish and that, swelling up all the time, moaning and repeating, "*Ach-y-fi*, if I can get rid of this I will never swallow a man again." (Yes, you will, the first chance you'll get!) And he, the old stubborn preacher, he could not understand what was happening or where he was going ... The fish felt all the time as if he had labouring pains. In three days and three nights he had relief and he threw the old preacher on the beach without ceremony (*yn rhondyn*). Up he jumped on his feet: "Good-bye to you," he said; "good riddance after you." "Good riddance after you, too," said the whale.'

God comes on the scene again 'and tells him the second time "Go to Nineveh." Jonah did not speak this time, but went quietly enough. Ah, that had taken the starch out of him. You lost your wager, Jonah, there's nothing for it now but to preach. On entering the town he runs over his sermon and then shouts as loud as he can, "Forty days and Nineveh shall be overthrown." Children and grown-ups crowd round him in their hundreds and follow him through the streets. A band of sailors stand at one corner: "Hei, Jack," shouts one of them, "this is the old chap we threw into the sea the other day between Joppa and Tarsus . . . Look, he is full of herring scales every bit."' Jonah takes no notice, but goes on preaching. He stands before a shoemaker's shop; the poor shoemaker in alarm and fear repents instantly in tears and sorrow, declaring that he will never put alder bark instead of leather under shoes again.

He stands before a grocer's shop and shouts his message. The grocer follows the example of the shoemaker, declaring that he will never give short weight again, nor put sand in the sugar. Similarly before the draper, wringing from him the avowal that never again will he give short measure or cheat with the trimmings. Fitting the act to the word, he calls on his servants to ransack the place for sacks, to repent in. Next he takes up his stand before a brothel. Here he gets cheek. Last of all he declares his message before the King's Palace, standing 'with his long stick in his hand, his eyes aflame with the fire of judgement, the noise of the destruction and of the fall of the city in his voice. "Forty days and Nineveh shall be overthrown." The King comes down from his throne, snatches off his crown, drops the sceptre, takes off the royal robes, puts on sacking and there he is rolling in the ashes like an old horse in a ploughed field, commanding everybody to do the same.' The outcome of their repentance was that God forgave them.

Jonah, in high dudgeon, went outside the city and had it out with God: 'See what a pickle I am in now. I knew how it would be before I started. I said the whole thing was a lie. I knew that if they showed the least semblance of penitence you would forgive them. I know you of old. You think more of these foreigners than you think of me – sending me here to preach a lie. You and I are not going to be friends again. I wish I had drowned in the sea.'

D. PARRY JONES
*Welsh Country Characters* (1952)

Priscilla Edwards was a woman of some consequence in the village of Morfa. A Christian soul and deeply religious, she possessed a prosperous farm and was rich from a family inheritance. She remained single (after rejecting many suitors), she worked and governed her farm with an energy and art equal to any male's, she owned many of the village cottages, employed many men and girls, and at Christmas gave everyone a pair of boots – nailed for the men and buttoned at the sides for the women.

At the time of this tale Priscilla was gone forty and had a tall and tight body whose members never ailed or tired, and a lean face with plainly defined features. She was a woman with a Will and a Way, and she contributed largely to the expenses of Soar, the little Methodist chapel of Morfa. There, however, she had lately come into conflict with the new minister.

Mr Vincent Thomas-Thomas was not admired in Morfa. He was not a native of the district and his sermons were of a cold and calculating kind, quite unlike those of his deceased predecessor, the fiery and native Noah Williams. His nature, too, was bossy, and he thought Priscilla interfered too much in the chapel affairs. But because of her contributions to Soar, he was obliged to allow her much licence. It was only when Priscilla desired to bring her pet cow, Alice, to chapel for the Sunday-evening service that their enmity became active.

RHYS DAVIES (1903–78)
in *The Collected Stories of Rhys Davies* (1955)


*The Chapel*

A little aside from the main road,
becalmed in a last-century greyness,
there is the chapel, ugly, without the appeal
to the tourist to stop his car
and visit it. The traffic goes by,
and the river goes by, and quick shadows
of clouds, too, and the chapel settles
a little deeper into the grass.

But here once on an evening like this,
in the darkness that was about
his hearers, a preacher caught fire
and burned steadily before them
with a strange light, so that they saw
the splendour of the barren mountains
about them and sang their amens
fiercely, narrow but saved
in a way that men are not now.

R. S. THOMAS

### Mr Rowlands

When he reads a lesson, it is plain to see that above all other
Gods he loves 'the Lord that smiteth'. He opens his mouth and
rejoices in the rich and massy Welsh. He makes no attempt at
mere clear reading, which would be of no use to an imagina-
tive audience, that is familiar with the Bible; but, raising and
lowering his voice, now hurrying as if to a precipice where all
will be overthrown, now creeping as if he feared what is to
come, he makes the chapter anew, creating it as if he were
sculptor or musician. I suppose he uses nearly as many musical
notes as if he sang; but the result differs from singing, as prose
from poetry; and so noble is the prose that it suggests only one
possible answer to the question which, like a school-man, he
once asked. Whether the music of the spheres be verse or prose?
Yet, if the note of the lesson is melancholy, full of the dreariness
of moving over the void and creating, the note of the sermon is
triumphant, or if not triumphant it is minatory, or if not minatory it is scornful, and at times a listener expects to see him
wrapped in a cloud and carried away from an undeserving and
purblind race.

The medium of what English people would call his rhetoric
is the '*hwyl*', an exuberant, impassioned, musical modulation
of the voice, and, to compare great things with small, compara-
ble to the very finest intoning to which has been added (if we
can suppose it) a lyrical, egotistical indulgence in all moods of
pity, scorn, tenderness, anger, sorrow, joy, anxiety and hope. It
can be familiar or lofty. It is as powerful as harp and song

together; and the force of it often arises from the fact that what is heard is rather the musical accompaniment of the man's thought than the thought itself. Hence its terrible and lovely purposes, and the many sentiments with which it is shot, and the dubiousness of the loftier passages . . . At other times his words rise up and circle and make fantastic architecture, as real as dreams, for the terror of the soul that for the time is forced to dwell therein. And though the substance of his sermon is but anecdote, biblical reference, exhortation, warning, picturesque logic built upon some simple religious theme, men and women weep under this divine bullying.

EDWARD THOMAS (1878–1917)
*Wales* (1905)

### Sabbath Labour

It would take a very great deal to persuade him to work on the Sabbath, and he would not expect his labours to be blessed if he did. But he saw no harm in spending many hours every Sabbath, standing with his pipe in his mouth watching the pig eating, and calculating when it would be ready for the knife, how much it would weigh, and after slaughter whether he would make black pudding or brawn, whether it would pay to keep or to sell the offal, to whom among his neighbours he was under obligation to send a piece of spare-rib and so on. Thomas did not think there was any harm in spending the Sabbath discussing such matters with Barbara; but he would not be induced, even by the offer of a large sum of money, to put on his leather apron for one single hour on the Lord's Day.

DANIEL OWEN (1836–95)
*Rhys Lewis*
trans. D. M. Lloyd (1885)

### from *The Boy in the Bucket*

*Dockery-crick . . . dockery-crick*, went the clock in the silence. Outside the chapel windows the Sabbath-silent sun deluged morning over the valley. Only a few clouds, woolly puffs of sunlit

willow-herb, floated by on the blue. On the opposite side of the *cwm* a great whale-browed mountain rose bedecked and glittering into the sunlight. It had the fascination for Ceri of a vast velvet monster risen green from the lumber room of sea bottom, bearing upon its brow grove-growths and out-cropping rocks and rows of cottages. Sunday after Sunday, morning and evening, he watched it from his seat, in silence as now, or with the shameless shouting of the rooks in his ears, but today he was not able to pay so much attention to it as usual. He was afraid P.C. Roderick was going to call at the house with a Blue Paper.

The service was bound to start soon now. The six black-clad daughters of Penffordd were already in, they had swept up the aisle in their silk-swishing mourning and, like one man, stuck their foreheads to the hymnbook ledge. Richards the Stoning in the side seats was getting restless. He was an old man with white hair and beard, but the thick hairs in his ears were brown as though he had been smoking through them. He stretched his legs in impatience and the splitting timber of his pew-back crack-cracked sharp as pistol-shots in the silence. Mrs Rees the Bank in her fox-furs was worried by a fly. From the little gallery behind came a loud cackle like trucks shunting and Ceri knew without looking back that the Bara-chaws was up there, clearing the metallic phlegm out of his throat for the singing.

Ceri always loved the sunlight to fill up the chapel. The walls, washed in a buttercup light, looked so clean, and the bright green paint on the gas brackets glistened with such freshness that they appeared wet. On the wall behind the pulpit a large curved ribbon with *Duw cariad yw* on it was painted in salmon-tin gold – 'God is love'. And as Ceri was admiring the gleam of it the door beside the pulpit opened and Jones the schoolteacher led the deacons into the Big Seat. Jones was Ceri's dayschool teacher, he had scabs in his hair and he used to go behind the blackboard to pick them off. The preacher, a very narrow man in black and glasses, entered and went up into the pulpit. His hairless head was lacquered a heavy brown, it always took the reflection of the chapel lights on its polish, and now there was a nice ring of windows gleaming all around it. He gave out the hymn, the harmonium started and all the people stood on their feet to sing.

Ceri's mother used to sit in the front of the chapel to see that the little children gathered together there behaved themselves during the service. Because of that Ceri felt it was safe to look around a bit. Right in front of him was Hughes the Vulcan, old dome-head, the back of his neck glowing like a ploughed sunset. You could always rely on old Hughes to sigh out loud, bored, if the sermon was poor, and this helped Ceri to know what to tell his mother about it when she questioned him. Across the aisle Mair Morgans was wearing a new lot of best clothes. Her straw hat had juicy cherries all around it and on her crimson coat were large wooden buttons, round and yellow, with plaited edges like tartlets. The pew door hid the rest of her but most likely she had new shoes on too, because every now and then she would stop singing, move her book sideways and have a good peep down at her feet.

But one thought kept on worrying Ceri; what would his mother say when Roderick the policeman knocked at the front door with the Blue Paper in his hand? It drove him desperate to think of it. She made everything out to be so serious, such as being kept in after school, or swearing by accident, or breaking down in the psalm he was supposed to have learnt for the *gymanfa.* He didn't mean any harm but she always made him feel that whatever he did was wicked. Only the other day when they all had their heads bowed over their potatoes and she was asking a blessing he and his little sister couldn't stop giggling and his mother said that was an *insult* to *Iesu Grist.* What would she say when she knew he had been playing with the O'Driscolls and had broken the street lamp throwing stones? He felt a sultry flush soaking his face and just then he caught her large varnished eye full upon him; she had turned it back over her shoulder in a frown because Ceri was dreaming and had forgotten he was supposed to be singing the hymn.

GLYN JONES
in *Selected Short Stories of Glyn Jones* (1971)

*Capel Calvin*

There's holy holy people
They are in capel bach –
They don't like surpliced choirs,
They don't like Sospan Fach,

They don't like Sunday concerts,
Or women playing ball,
They don't like Williams Parry much
Or Shakespeare at all.

They don't like beer or bishops,
Or pictures without texts,
They don't like any other
Of the nonconformist sects.

And when they go to Heaven,
They won't like that too well,
For the music will be sweeter
Than the music played in Hell.

IDRIS DAVIES (1905–53)

Grandfather, then, was in great good humour over his thatch-
ing. Cadwaladr and Tom were spinning straw ropes, and Jack
and we boys assisting. The stories of last night were referred to
and re-discussed in all sorts of ways. Tom Roberts looked at
them in the Methodist aspect, Jack in the jocular, Cadwaladr in
the cynical view, but all believed in them without reserve. One
might expect Tom, at least, to be sceptical from his Methodist
and Radical leanings, but it was far otherwise: he was of all by
far the most credulous. Neither did his Methodist training tend
to check superstition in him; it rather enhanced it. Methodist
books of that date swarmed with marvels; supernatural
appearances, warnings, singing in the air, sudden judgements
on rulers and persecutors; God's miracles and the devil's miracles abounded everywhere. The *Lives of the Saints* is not more full
of such wonders than the *Mirror of the Times*, the Methodist
Church History. And for people who read the Old Testament
histories so much, what more natural than to expect miracles
everywhere? The witch Esther had her parallel in the witch of
Endor: the magic of Ellis was the legitimate successor of that of
Egypt. Scepticism on these subjects is more prevalent now, but
thirty years ago it was rare indeed in the Welsh *cwms*. To dis-
believe supernaturalism was then thought utter infidelity; it
was flying in the face of Providence – an obstinate hardening of
the mind against all evidence.

ROBERT ROBERTS (1834–85)
*The Life and Opinions of R.R., a wandering scholar . . .* (1923)

The attitude of the Chapel towards those of its communicants
who had loved not wisely but too well, was pompous, hypocritical and rather ridiculous. I recall a case being dealt with in the
Gyfeillach of our Baptist Chapel when a girl who had given
birth to a fine baby some time previously came to plead for her
place back, i.e. to be restored to the status of a full communicating member again. The minister reviewed the details of 'our
sister who has transgressed and fallen, etc., etc., and who is
now conscious of her great sin, etc., and who has now come in
all humility, etc., etc., to beg to be accepted again as one of the
community of God, etc. Did it accord with the wishes of the
Gyfeillach for her to be re-admitted?' She was re-admitted *nem*

*con* – and everybody congratulated her, while secretly a few
envied her recent experience. Never once did I attend these
degrading meetings without a feeling of spiritual nausea. I
thought then it was a lot of hypocritical nonsense – and I still
think so. Of course, there were the dauntless exceptions – those
who defiantly bore the fruits of their love and said outright, 'I
shall never beg for my place back.' I saw such a grand old girl
last year, when she was over ninety years of age – her memory
of the last thirty years very dim, but she could tell me all about
my childhood years, so I suspect she remembered well the days
when Love was triumphant in her life.

JAMES WILLIAMS
*Give me Yesterday* (1971)


There was John Elias, who, when preaching to a great gathering in the open air, described how God let fly an arrow from His
bow. So great was his emotional power that as he spoke the
gathering parted to allow passage for the shaft.

H. V. MORTON
*In Search of Wales* (1932)


from *The Glory that was Sion's*

Twm Tybach was abhorred of Capel Sion. In all acts he was
evil. He was born out of sin, and he walked in the company of
loose men. His features were fair, and he had a rakish eye,
before which the heart of Madlen utterly melted. Now Madlen
owned two pigs, a cow and a heifer, several heads of poultry,
and Tybach, the stone-walled cottage that is beyond the
Schoolhouse. In his fortieth year Twm coveted Madlen's possessions; and inasmuch as Madlen was on the borderline of her
womanhood she received Twm's advances with joy. So Twm
hired Old Shemmi's horse-car and drove Madlen to
Castellybryn, where the two were married in the house of the
registrar. The occasion is memorable to Madlen because that
night she slept in a virgin's bed, her husband having gone into
the bed of Old Mari who sold sweet loshins in the market place.

Thereon Twm lived on Madlen. He poached a little, but he

was credited with more rabbits and hares than he would risk his liberty to trap; in season he pretended to help his neighbours in the hayfield, but nearly always succeeded in getting under covert with a woman.

He was as irreligious as an irreligious Welshman can be. He defied the Big Man openly; never except on market and fair days did he wear his best clothes; in passing the Respected Josiah Bryn-Bevan and Mistress Bryn-Bevan he kept his cap on his head and whistled, and once he made Mistress Bryn-Bevan sick by spitting loudly on the ground; he frequented the inn which is kept by Mistress Shames, where he consorted with the disreputable Shon the Pig Drover – one without honour in the land.

Six weeks after his wedding Twm was stricken by illness. The Respected Josiah Bryn-Bevan, then Judge to Capel Sion, declared that the Lord was smiting His enemy, a just fate for all that offendeth Him. The third day of his illness Twm crept into the four-poster bed in the kitchen, and he ordered Madlen to bake a loaf of leavened bread and to place it on his belly; and a stubby beard grew on his chin.

The evening of that day Dr Morgan came by Tybach; Madlen stopped him, saying, 'Indeed, now, doctor *bach*, come him in and give me small counsel about Twm.'

The doctor examined Twm and he said to him; 'Well-well, Twm, you will perish in a few days.'

When Madlen heard this she placed a kettle of water on the fire and brought down her husband's razor from the highest shelf of the dresser.

Twm's face turned very white, for the man was afraid of Death.

'There's no chance for you, little Twm,' the doctor said. 'You are a hundred times worse than the boy in the Bible who took up his old bed and walked.'

The account of how the days of the evil-favoured Twm Tybach were rounding on him was carried from mouth to mouth, and none was sorry. It was told to the Respected Josiah Bryn-Bevan in Shop Rhys. The teller of it was Bertha Daviss. This is what she said:

'Dear me! Dear me! The old calf of Twm Tybach is passing.'

'Madlen will want mourning,' said Rhys quickly. 'She has not had a death for many years.'

The Respected Josiah Bryn-Bevan was a religious man, and aware of Twm's evil reputation.

'Indeed to goodness,' he said, with much solemnity. 'And you do say so now, Miss Daviss?'

'Iss, iss,' said Bertha, addressing the minister. 'Man, man, why for he does not know that Twm Tybach is a Congregationalist? Was not old Eva his mother cut out of the Seiet when Twm was born? For sure me, that was so.'

'What iobish do you spout, Bertha!' said Rhys. 'What credit is the scamp unto Sion?'

'Be you merciful, little Rhys,' returned the minister. 'Do you forgive others as you need forgiveness.'

'Maybe Twm is no credit,' observed Bertha, 'but we will have to bury him. Is not our graveyard the fullest in all the land?'

'You say wisely, Bertha Daviss,' said the minister. 'You say wisely, Bertha *fach*. Iss not the grave our last home then? We must begrudge it to no man. O little ones, there is largish space in the Big Man's acre.'

'No, no, Respected *bach*,' cried Bertha. 'For why? The grave-yard is full. Father was the last to be laid there. And in comfort did he go up when he knew of that glory.'

Rhys Shop looked upon the minister. The minister looked upon Bertha: his gaze travelled from her clogs, her torn stockings and her turned-over petticoat to the yellow skin of her face and the narrow eyes which looked out damply over her bridgeless nose.

'Woman,' he cried at last, 'dost thou speak what thou

knowest to be true, or dost thou repeat unto me – yea, unto me
thy Judge – that which is idle gossip?'

'The truth, Bryn-Bevan *bach*. The truth.'

The minister was confounded. The muscles of his cheeks moved nervously under his red beard. Then he arose and saying, 'Fair day, boys *bach*,' buttoned his frock-coat and grasped his varnished stick, and left the shop. Rhys and Bertha stood by, and when he was gone they stood in the way of the door and watched the high, thin, tall-hatted figure treading heavily down the road towards Capel Sion; and at the week-night Meeting for Prayer everyone there knew that though the Respected Bryn-Bevan was blessed with much wisdom, understanding, and knowledge, the Big Man had loaded him with a burden heavy to bear.

Never within Capel Sion, nor within the boundaries of the parish, has been heard such a plea as that which was spoken by Bryn-Bevan that night. In the language of Adam and Eve he petitioned that his brother Twm Tybach would find repentance in the fullness of time, so that Death would find his putrid body cleansed and worthy of burial in the bosom of the new graveyard.

With the minister's amen, Abel Shones, the officer for poor relief, rose and suggested a deputation to wait upon the vicar seeing permission to inter Twm's body in the church graveyard.

'Very mad is Abel Shones, males *bach*,' said Old Shemmi. 'When Twm's sins are forgotten, the Church will claim him as her own.'

'And possession, dear me, counts for much in the law,' said Sadrach Danyrefail.

Lloyd the Schoolin' was for compromise.

'At the entrance to Capel Sion,' he said, 'we will put up an old stone on which is written these words: "Tomos Tomos, Tybach, lieth not here. Tomos lieth in the parish church. Why, dear people? Because the graveyard of Capel Sion was so full that there was no room for further burials."'

'What's the use of a tombstone,' asked Old Shemmi, 'if there is nothing under it? Does a landless man go to Castellybryn to buy a plough?' ...

CARADOC EVANS (1878–1945)
in *My People* (1915)

[Haymaking] was a very difficult time for him, days of great anxiety, for his welfare and the winter needs of his cattle depended upon getting his hay and corn in in good condition. He felt at times that he had not got all the personal attention and favour that he merited as a hard-working, decent man. To mix things up still more, there seems to be little doubt that in his mind there had survived, unawares to him, some age-long, pre-Christian way of regarding 'The One Above'. It surged up into consciousness at harvest times and brought with it a lot of difficulties, so that he was quite at a loss how to relate one thing to another. This old, old way of looking at things may have influenced him also at other times, for his mind was far fuller of ancient beliefs, ways and lore than of things picked up in his own lifetime: for example, he would not start sowing except on a certain day of the week, nor would he kill his pig or put eggs under a broody hen except when the moon was waxing.

In order to leave no doubt on a major and a most important point, let it be said at once that the God he believed in, and Whom he worshipped on Sundays, was the Almighty God, Whose existence, nature, will, love and demands are revealed to us in the Bible. Him alone he knew and trusted; to Him he belonged, because his immortal soul had been ransomed by Him at such a terrible price.

Here, however, we are dealing with survivals, of whose origin and age he was entirely ignorant: habits of thought, ways of looking at things that, since they are not strictly biblical, may be regarded as pre-Christian, or may indeed be inevitably common to all countrymen and to all times. I do not say that every farmer felt puzzled by these primitive survivals, but some curious expressions escaped many in harvest time.

What the countryman's pre-Christian conception of his god was I am not quite sure, but if some of the expressions used, and the attitude adopted towards him, are anything to go by, 'The One Above' was not regarded as altogether unfriendly, but he seems to have been thought of as a bit of a wag and a rogue – young, mischievous, standing for no moral principle, nor guided by any just code; he was not above playing tricks with 'those down below', and against whose wiles the farmer often pitted his own cunning. He went by different names: *Y Bachgen*

*Fry* (the young fellow above); *Y Bachgen Mawr* (the big fellow); *Y Gwr Bonheddig* (the gentleman); *Bachgen Pert yw e'* ('He is a great lad he is', uttered in a back-patting sort of attitude and not without some hopes that it might be overheard).

These and similar expressions escaped the Welsh country-man at times, especially when in the fields. But he would be shocked if he heard them in the Sunday worship: it would be considered levity and blasphemy of the most offensive charac-ter. But they tripped out on the lips of many in the hayfield.

Was he a kind of demi-god or under-god, that may have been given dominion over the fields and crops only, but no share or say in the control of any living creature? It is difficult to esti-mate his position and power, or trace his origin. I have heard, and read, of farmers trying to dodge, mislead and put this *bachgen pert* completely off the scent, whether he was regarded as altogether unfriendly or whether it was that he could never refrain from playing some mischievous trick if he saw a chance. In haymaking time a farmer might be seen going towards the turnip field with his hoe, apparently intending to spend the day at thinning, or taking with him some other tool, or tools, leading one to think that he and his men were going to cut a trench, and then slip over the hedge quietly, and begin to turn the hay. The work would commence in some sheltered corner and not a word would be said until, perhaps, they had almost finished turning it, when the farmer would say, as he felt the first few drops of rain on his face: 'It is no use, lads, he has seen us (*Mae e' wedi 'n gweld ni*).

It may be nothing more than a way of speaking. Christian believers do and say a lot of things that contradict their creed, and this may be nothing more than our addiction, harmless enough, to putting mascots on our cars, refusing to walk under a ladder, avoiding the number thirteen and touching wood. We know very well that these things have not in the least the power to affect our life or destiny, and yet we do them.

Doctor T. Gwynn Jones in his book *Welsh Folk-lore and Folk Custom* says, 'A small farmer known to me in my youth, then well over seventy years of age, illiterate and of great simplicity of mind, would invariably pretend to prepare for some other task when he intended to do something requiring fine weather.'

In a Pembrokeshire case, during a very wet summer, a

farmer, to the great astonishment of his neighbours, decided to carry his hay on Sunday. Before they had been at it for an hour or two, distinct thunder was heard, and some of the workmen suggested giving it up. The farmer laughed and said he was not superstitious. From two to three o'clock the storm drew nearer, the lightning flashes were very vivid and the thunderings almost incessant, though unaccompanied by rain. The men were afraid, and the farmer's will at last gave way. *'Rhown y gore iddi, fechgyn,'* he said, *'Mae Hi wedi 'n gweld ni'* ('Give it up, boys, she has seen us').

An old farmer of Flintshire, sometime in the last century, seeing his hay carried away one morning by a flood during a very wet summer, cried out, *'Yna dôs ag e ir diawl a thâl y rhent, ar degwn hefyd'* ('There, take it to the devil and pay the rent, and the tithe as well'). This mixture of apprehension and levity in regard to the weather especially is not uncommon among farmers and other members of the agricultural community.

In regard to the weather, one had to be careful what one said; if one happened to say, 'I think it's going to clear up,' another would utter a cautionary reply, 'Be careful in case you are overheard.'

D. PARRY JONES
*Welsh Country Characters* (1952)

# XII

# BARDS, CHOIRS, EISTEDDFODAU

*Hen Wlad fy Nhadau*
*(The Land of My Fathers)*

Mae hen wlad fy nhadau yn annwyl i mi,
Gwlad beirdd a chantorion, enwogion o fri;
Ei gwrol ryfelwyr, gwladgarwyr tra mâd,
Tros ryddid collasant eu gwaed.

Hen Gymru fynyddig, paradwys y bardd,
Pob dyffryn, pob clogwyn i'm golwg sydd hardd;
Trwy deimlad gwladgarol, mor swynol yw si
Ei nentydd, afonydd, i mi.

Os treisiodd y gelyn fy ngwlad tan ei droed,
Mae hen iaith y Cymry mor fyw ag erioed;
Ni luddiwyd yr awen gan erchyll law brad,
Na thelyn berseiniol fy ngwlad.

*Chorus:*
*Gwlad, gwlad, pleidiol wyf i'm gwlad,*
*Tra môr yn fur i'r bur hoff bau,*
*O bydded i'r heniaith barhau.*

The poetical history of Wales before the modern period, which is considered to begin *c.* 1600, is traditionally divided into three periods: the Cynfeirdd, the Early Poets, from the beginnings to *c.* 1100; and the Gogynfeirdd, the Next to the Early Poets, *c.* 1100–*c.* 1350; and the Cywyddwyr, the masters of the *cywydd* metre, *c.* 1350–*c.* 1600. The Gogynfeirdd are also called the Poets of the Princes and their work Court Poetry. The Cywyddwyr and their work are also called the Poets and the Poetry of the Nobility.

The work of the early poets, the Cynfeirdd, already exhibits a notable characteristic of Welsh poetry throughout the ages: the poet is accountable to society, and is its spokesman. He is recorder, instructor, and celebrant. *Beirdd byd barnant wŷr o galon*, says the *Gododdin*-poet: 'The bards of the world pass judgement on men of valour.'

GWYN JONES
*The Oxford Book of Welsh Verse in English* (1977)

The millennium from the year 600 to 1600 saw the development and decline of poetry in the strict Welsh metres and the perfection and classification of the sound-echoing devices known as *cynghanedd*. Technically the peak came with Dafydd ab Edmwnd in the middle of the fifteenth century. The twenty-four measures, already classified in the fourteenth century, were by him tightened up and made more difficult in order to discourage the half-trained practitioner in verse. But a high degree of metrical and phonetic skill is to be observed in the very earliest Welsh verse and one remembers Julius Caesar's statement that the Druids used verse as a pedagogical device. According to pre-Christian Greek travellers to Britain, the word *bardd*, still the Welsh word for a poet, was in use at the beginning of the first century BC. And when I refer to the decline of poetry in the strict metres with the outburst of verse in the new stanza forms at the end of the sixteenth century, let it not be thought that the twenty-four measures have since fallen into desuetude or become merely museum pieces. They have been in continuous use, and a knowledge of them is essential to anyone who hopes to win the chair at the National Eisteddfod.

And at least two of the old measures, the *englyn* and the *cywydd*,
are in regular use by a very large number of writers today.

GWYN WILLIAMS
Introduction, *Welsh Poems, Sixth Century to 1600* (1973)

## An Early Eisteddfod

[1176] At Christmastide in that year, the Lord Rhys ap Gruffudd held a court with great splendour in Cardigan Castle, and arranged two kinds of contests there, one for bards and poets, and the other for harpists and crowthers and pipers and other musicians. He had two chairs placed for the winners, and honoured them with lavish gifts. Among the harpists, a youth of Rhys's own court was successful, and of the poets, those of Gwynedd were supreme. All seekers of largesse obtained from Rhys all that they asked for, and no one met with refusal. That feast, before it was held, had been proclaimed a year in advance throughout Wales, and England, Ireland, and the other islands.

*The Chronicle of the Princes*
in *A Book of Wales*, ed. D. M. and E. M. Lloyd (1953)
trans. D. M. Lloyd

It is wonderful how . . . with so skilled and so rapid an execution of the fingers, the proportions of music are kept and the skill with which concord is produced and the tune preserved intact through tremulant notes and intricate organa of many voices, now with agreeable rapidity, now bringing equality from inequality, now concord from discord. Be it the chord of the fourth or of the fifth which is sounded, both alike have B flat as their root and return to it; and so all reaches its final with sweetness of joyful sound. So subtly do they strike and cease their notes; and so, under cover of the blunt sounds of fuller chords, by their thin tinklings they play about more fully, give more pleasure, and soothe more playfully.

GERALD OF WALES
*The Description of Wales (1194)*
trans. Lewis Thorpe

While thus from theme to theme the Historian passed,
The words he uttered, and the scene that lay
Before our eyes, awakened in my mind
Vivid remembrance of those long-past hours;
When, in the hollow of some shadowy vale,
(What time the splendour of the setting sun
Lay beautiful on Snowdon's sovereign brow,
On Cader Idris, or huge Penmaenmawr)
A wandering Youth, I listened with delight
To pastoral melody or warlike air,
Drawn from the chords of the ancient British harp
By some accomplished Master, while he sate
Amid the quiet of the green recess,
And there did inexhaustibly dispense
An interchange of soft or solemn tunes,
Tender or blithe; now, as the varying mood
Of his own spirit urged, – now as a voice
From youth or maiden, or some honoured chief
Of his compatriot villagers (that hung
Around him, drinking in the impassioned notes
Of the time-hallowed minstrelsy) required
For their heart's ease or pleasure.

WILLIAM WORDSWORTH (1770–1850)
from *The Excursion* (1814)

*Penillion-Singing*

Besides the single songs, there were songs in dialogue,
approaching very nearly to the character of dramatic poetry;
and penillion, or unconnected stanzas, sung in series by different singers, the stanzas being complete in themselves, simple
as Greek epigrams, and presenting in succession moral precepts, pictures of natural scenery, images of war or of festival,
the lamentations of absence or captivity, and the complaints or
triumphs of love. This penillion-singing long survived among
the Welsh peasantry almost every other vestige of bardic customs, and may still be heard among them on the few occasions

on which rack-renting, tax-collecting, common-enclosing, methodist-preaching, and similar developments of the light of the age, have left them either the means or inclination of making merry.

THOMAS LOVE PEACOCK (1785–1866)
*The Misfortunes of Elphin* (1829)

> *Hardd yw Conwy, hardd yw Nefyn,*
> *Hardd yw brigau coedydd Mostyn,*
> *Harddaf lle'r wy'n allu 'nabod*
> *Yn y byd yw dyffryn Meifod.*

(Conway is fair, Nevin is fair, the tips of the Mostyn trees are fair, the fairest place I can ever know in the world is Meivod Valley.)

> *Cleddwch fi, pan fyddwyf farw,*
> *Yn y coed dan ddail y derw;*
> *Chwi gewch weled llanc penfelyn*
> *Ar fy medd yn canu'r delyn.*

(Bury me, when I am dead, in the trees under the oak leaves; you shall see a yellow-haired youth on my grave playing the harp.)

> *Mae dwy galon yn fy mynwes,*
> *Un yn oer a'r llall yn gynnes;*
> *Un yn gynnes am ei charu,*
> *A'r llall yn oer rhag ofn ei cholli.*

(There are two hearts in my bosom, one is cold and the other warm; one is warm through love of her, and the other is cold through fear of losing her.)

in *A Book of Wales*
ed. D. M. and E. M. Lloyd (1953)

Looking at the Sunday-school teaching of Welsh as a whole, one may say that the edifice is in a manner made complete by the rôle played by literary societies, and literary competitions in which prizes are given for singing, for writing Welsh, both prose and verse, and for translating from English into Welsh, and vice versa. These competitions do not occur more than once a year even in the neighbourhoods where they are the rule; and, speaking generally, they are sporadic and depend for their origination on individuals who feel interested in Welsh and Welsh music. They are altogether a very indefinite quantity, but literary societies have been of late becoming more

general and somewhat more permanent. They all serve, however, as feeders to the Eisteddfod, and they have in recent years
exercised great influence on the cultivation of Welsh and
Welsh literature.

SIR JOHN RHŶS and DAVID BRYNMOR-JONES
*The Welsh People* (1900)

*At the Eisteddfod*

The close-ranked faces rise,
With their watching, eager eyes,
And the banners and the mottoes blaze above;
And without, on either hand,
The eternal mountains stand,
And the salt sea river ebbs and flows again,
And through the thin-drawn bridge the wandering winds
  complain.

Here is the Congress met,
The bardic senate set,
And the young hearts flutter at the voice of fate;
All the fair August day
Song echoes, harpers play,
And on the unaccustomed ear the strange
Penillion rise and fall through change and counterchange.

Oh Mona, land of song!
Oh mother of Wales! how long
From thy dear shores an exile have I been!
Still from thy lonely plains,
Ascend the old sweet strains,
And at the mine, or plough, or humble home,
The dreaming peasant hears diviner music come.

This innocent, peaceful strife,
This struggle to fuller life,
Is still the one delight of Cymric souls –
Swell, blended rhythms! still
The gay pavilions fill.
Soar, oh young voices, resonant and fair;
Still let the sheathed sword gleam above the bardic chair.

**254**     The Menai ebbs and flows,
And the song-tide wanes and goes,
And the singers and the harp-players are dumb;
The eternal mountains rise
Like the cloud upon the skies,
And my heart is full of joy for the songs that are still,
The deep sea and the soaring hills, and the steadfast
    Omnipotent Will.

SIR LEWIS MORRIS (1833–1907)

## An Eisteddfod Confrontation

I remember a big *eisteddfod* in the Workman's Hall one year. My father's choir, the Handel Glee Party, were running the competition and it went on throughout the day.

In the evening they had the Champion Solo competition, where the tenor and the contralto and the soprano and the bass would compete against each other and be given the medal for the winner – the Champion of that day. I was only a small boy, and because I was the son of the conductor I had to present the medal to the winner.

The person the audience thought should have had the prize – indeed, *she* thought she should have had the prize, wasn't given it. It was given to the contralto, and while I was beginning to place the medal on this lovely ribbon around her neck, the soprano came barging in.

She was like an Italian; she was big, she had black black hair with a bun at the back, and a fantastic voice, there's no question about it. But the adjudicators were judging her on musicality, on interpretation.

As I was presenting the medal to the contralto, this soprano came in and she pushed me on one side, medal as well, and she pointed to the gallery where the adjudicators were and said: 'If I'd a gun I'd shoot the bloody lot of you,' and walked off.

I was terrified. *Cythrel Canu* – the Devil in Song.

SIR GERAINT EVANS
from *Wales on the Wireless* (1988)
ed. Patrick Hannan

I do not think it is possible to approach the National Eisteddfod as it stands today and make a fair judgement. If you have been exposed in childhood and youth to the enchantment and the fanatical compulsions of this type of festival, you just go through life in bemused addiction and that's that. Whatever one might think of the forbidding parochialists who wield the all-Welsh rule like a tomahawk and grin as they point at the number of lacerated scalps they've left in the valleys of Glamorgan and Monmouthshire, this still remains the most fascinating and cordial cultural phenomenon on earth.

Yes, despite all the curious suggestions of vestry intrigue, the proudly vaunted inadequacy of the catering (no beer tent), it still wears the old slogan: *'Calon wrth galon'* like a crown. That motto, 'Heart with Heart' – to be seen on the ancient Eisteddfod chair of Powys – still puts its finger on the enduring appeal of this great tribal conjunction of song, verse, craft, hiraeth and gossip.

That is one thing about a small nation which is capable of such a relatively vast concourse of its artistically active citizens; the whole social, domestic anatomy of the land can be gone over inch by inch. At intervals in the glorious volleys of vocalism and bardry, the sly, twisting mouths of an eloquent and witty people pool the diverting aberrations of every hamlet from Anglesey to Aberthaw. At the end of Eisteddfod week a bard has been crowned and a million closets aired.

If a layman is dismayed by what he might think an astonishing preponderance of ministers of religion in the crowds that ambulate between the marquees and booths, then he must remember that for a couple of centuries the chapel has been a characteristic part of our idiom, and that no nation has come nearer to being a theocracy, a people in vassalage to its preachers. It is part of the protective restraint of a people naturally over-passionate. In Scotland, in ancient times, the pagan rapture inherent in most poets and most poetry was given its head, and the authorities were driven to classing the bards of their land as 'a class of frenzied vagabonds'. Not so in Wales; take a look at the Gorsedd members as they shuffle to the crowning. An impeccably tidy lot. All passion, if not spent, tightly on the lead.

The great dynasty of preachers shaped our soul and established the rules of our not inconsiderable rhetoric. And behind the preacher has always stood the image of the powerfully literate ploughman and miner who have given to our working people an impressive and articulate dignity. That is why the Eisteddfod cuts so deep into our social earth. There is not a single artist in Wales today who, in his earliest years, was not made more aware and communicative by the cult of self-expression developed by the teeming vestries of our valleys. That is why, in certain phases of the Eisteddfod, one detects a certain yearning for a return to the chapel's day of dominance. Behind it there is a good deal of historic justice.

There are few Welshmen over the age of thirty-five whose childhood was not a shell-burst of eisteddfodic activity, sparked off by the great legion of musical *aficionados* who supervised our Sunday schools. Each and every one of us, from the time he got the shawl out of his mouth and could shout *'Yma!'* ('Here!') when the Eisteddfod conductor called out the name under which he had entered, was an Eisteddfodwr, a real gone guy behind the banner of the festival.

In the earliest Penny Readings our artistic limbs were massaged for a lifetime of cultural jousting and tuft-hunting. The training was Spartan and you had to be pretty sharp to hold your own around the vestry bends. In a tiny way I did fairly well as a prizewinner. I must, in my best stretches, have been one of the few really healthy units in the economic life of my part of the Rhondda.

The adjudicators in our small contests were nearly always the same; two very pensive deacons judging the recitations and two voters of a more Bohemian sort on the singing. One of the recitation judges was a man of stern and anti-democratic bent, convinced that humanity would blow its top and go off on some long, gross Saturday night of miscellaneous debauchery if ever released from its great restraining trusses of dogma and intimidation. His face always lit up when I bounded up the pulpit steps and made the tiles bounce with a rendering of Coriolanus's famous skin-stripping assessments of the plebs. I also had a piece from the Book of Job that made him purr like a cat in cream.

These were legitimate tactics. In the Eisteddfod world a close study of the temperament and taste of the adjudicator was as important as the timbre of voice or the dramatic angle at which one held one's sheet music. At those same Penny Readings one of the vocal adjudicators was a man of desperately sentimental sadness. He had been washed up on more or less permanent duty at the Penny Readings after the bumpiest emotional life since Hosea, whom he often quoted. A dozen jiltings and a certain jocose liking for being looted by every girl he met, made him an easy target for the sadder, soggier type of lyric.

If at the beginning of the bouts I saw his mood was particularly shadowed, I would choose with care from my quiver of deathbed chants and quick-action mid-Victorian weepies. 'We'll kiss away our tears when we cross the Great Divide', or one of the most neurasthenic songs ever written and which never failed to send my father racing for the ear-plugs and a shillelagh, 'Do not dally on hearing the call, In the grave is an answer to all.'

When my rivals saw the tears gather in the adjudicator's eye, and watched him roll his head in helpless abandon under the downpour of suggested sorrow, they would stuff their copies back in their pockets and wonder if it would be too grave an infringement of vestry-law if they arranged to have me jumped and sandbagged in the shadows of the porch on the following Tuesday.

The prizes at these early and radiant Eisteddfods were not lavish, but they struck us as having the splendour of the chairs now made with deep and loving craft for the winning bards at the National Eisteddfods. They were small satin bags attached to ribbons that went around the neck, and it was the convention to wear these articles rather like a mayor's chain on the way home, showing off and tempting footpads, for in the bag would be a threepenny or sixpenny bit.

By the time puberty came along and loosened the tight grip I had had on the Penny Readings for many years, I had won so many of these satin bags they had furnished the fabric to provide fancy blouses for the whole front row of a dance band organized by one of my brothers and called The Gitanos, an outfit which, under the protective tactic of looking frenzied and exotic, managed to work off a record number of wrong notes on to the public. The threepences and sixpences, which might have meant my beginning as a tycoon, I spent on so much toffee I was denounced by a senior deacon as licentious and a potential diabetic.

The excitement of leaving the valley for a major Eisteddfod in some adjoining *cwm* was unforgettable. For young male reciters dark velvet trousers seemed to be regarded as a kind of obligatory court wear, and indeed they seemed to bring a fine sensual edge to certain vowels. This could lead to tense moments, for a bit of traditional chicane was to keep entering a boy for an age-group that he had long left. One often saw a boy, heavily adolescent, wearing velvet trousers that had been a fair fit when he had worn them for the under-ten competition. And when we were marshalled outside the bus his mother would be on hand to see that this youth had the seat by the driver with plenty of leg room so that he would not subject the fabric to too many stresses. The boy had also been instructed to keep his gestures on the stage to a minimum and to make his whole posture as recessive as possible.

For the mothers generally the Eisteddfod meant days of painful solicitude. I remember being in a bus bound for Maesteg, then, as now, an eisteddfodic hub. I was tidily dressed, in a dark sort of way, for I had been entered to compete under the *nom de chant* of Janus in the Junior Open Solo to sing a piece called 'The Promised Land', a defeatist lyric, strongly in favour of the grave, against the drink and scored for a deep, plangent alto.

I was champing at a very crumbly type of cracker. This had been recommended to me as a means of relaxing pre-Eisteddfod nerves by my teacher, a keen competitor himself. He had never won any prizes but he could carry a waistcoatful of cracker crumbs with more aplomb than any man I have seen. I was leaning forward talking to a friend in the seat in front, when a mother's hand grasped my wrist. 'Stop that,' she said. 'You are dropping those crumbs deliberately down our Meirion's neck. You know he's ticklish, our Meirion. You know he never sings his best when he's itching on the stage.'

Minor eisteddfods are commonly held in marquees. The 'National' of course exists mainly in the vast pavilion which makes its way annually north and south, inflated for the great week and then deflated for its eleven months' rest, like a massive lung, which is just what it is.

I can recall some very picturesque marquees. They could add a lot of tension to the event. Often erected in too great haste by amateurs they could be notoriously fissile. In a high wind one could be torpedoed right off the stage by a loose flap. One often saw members of a male voice group, lashed back from a dozen cosy hostelries by devout and dour committee men, chundering around the marquee looking for the correct entrance and sent hurtling by the innumerable guy-ropes and asking the conductor when at last they formed their crescent on the stage, for five minutes' grace for the removal of clods.

I was once a member of a group entered in a mid-Glamorgan eisteddfod for the Action Song for the Under Twelves. The song was 'Ye Mariners of England'. We had been fitted out by our families with what they thought a rough version of naval uniform. This rig, as you would expect from so essentially landlocked an area as Porth, was inaccurate, and our gestures as we did an impression of a rapid horn-pipe brought many frowns from the more Calvinistic adjudicators.

It had rained for days. The canvas flap above the stage bulged and darkened with water in a fashion that brought offers from the Liverpool council. On our last thundering note the flap burst and we took rank as the first action-song team to stick together as a group while being actively washed through the main entrance of the marquee. One adjudicator gave us extra points for realism, but he was dripping and giddy with shock at the time.

These are scraps of recollection, but multiplied a million times they explain the wonderful glow of that first week in August when the Gorsedd trumpeters bring the National Eisteddfod once again to life. No faction fight between the Welsh-speaking folk of Wales and those from whom the language has been taken can impair the toughness of this festival. It has ridden bravely on some of the highest and most treacherous waves of national mischance. It was at a time of intense doubt, danger and division that the bards and the following multitudes came together to hold the first Eisteddfod. The Romans were departing from Britain. The void they left was full of howlings from the bitter east. To say the good word for warmth, hope and harmony, the newly elected chief of the Welsh, the man with the curious cocktail of a name, Owain ap Macsen Wledig, convened the first great tribal salutation to art and peace.

The present period is also one of doubt and division. The splendid emotional and intellectual qualities that go to make up Welshness are likely to be dissipated in a squalid dispute about the sounds clacked by the tongue to express ideas. You might be pleasing the bones of Hywel Dda by writing *'cwcw'* instead of 'cuckoo' but there are many of us who do not see that it matters greatly.

And time, which erodes beaches, faces, faiths, will do as much for even so venerable a language as the Welsh. As the hierarchy of the new industries linked intimately with London, ousts the old dominance of the manse in our Establishment, the glow will die away from behind the neo-chauvinists. Simple electronics will do the rest. The most banal of television culture will break the back of the most vigorous village culture. Out of the gloom comes Merlin urging a more tolerant assessment by the Gorsedd Circle of the need to keep the non-Welsh-speaking Celts within the racial fold.

GWYN THOMAS (1913–81)
*A Welsh Eye* (1964)

from *Adjudication*

For the first time that afternoon he felt an involuntary tremor passing through his whole body, a kind of hot trembling in the pit of his stomach, a quick, almost imperceptible jerk of his legs and shoulders. The palms of his hands and the hollows under his eyes were moist too. *Diawch*, better watch his hands or he'd be marking his collar.

The hall was filling up. It was getting warmer there now; the choirs and the parties were arriving, that's what it was. It would be packed out in half an hour. Still, it would suit him to have the air warm and moist and to have the place full: he was always at his best with a large audience.

That bloomin' G again! Funny how it was bothering him today. He didn't know what was the matter with him lately. Still, he had got it beautifully last night; he'd got it, smack in the middle, a full, round, absolutely *steady* note that had made old Edwards sit up with a vengeance. But he hadn't been absolutely confident about it lately, that was the trouble. Well, indeed, it was coming to something, worrying about a little G; him, of all people. But there, it would be all right; he was always at his best when he was a little nervous.

Here it was at last, thank goodness.

They were announcing the tenor solo competition. To be taken after the adjudication on the three lyrics. Would they answer? Ron? T.J.? Danny Boy? Iorwerth? Up to the stage in readiness, please.

He gingerly fingered his black bow tie; must get it straight and quite flat against the collar. Fancy T.J. saying that the bow was supposed to be *outside* the wings. Swank, pure swank, just because he knew Walter Glynne. Over the wings, indeed! Good, he looked and felt all right. Hair tidy, cuffs showing just a little bit, only the middle button, and a crease like a razor, fair play to Lizzie Hannah. Now, take it easy. Keep cool, that was the ticket. Dignified, like.

He slipped a Vocalzube into his mouth and walked slowly along the aisle towards the stage.

'All the best, Dan *bach*!' Evans the Ironmonger as usual. What an enthusiast he was. *He* knew what singing was, if anybody did. Damn, he must get that G! People expected it of him. He mustn't let them down, and that's what would happen if he made a mess of the thing. Damn it all, he was shivering again. There's draughty bloomin' places these wings in the Welfare Hall were!

He adjusted his white scarf carefully over his collar again, and buttoned up his overcoat.

'Hullo, Ron boy? How are things with you, T.J.?' Easy, quiet confidence, that was the ticket. He nodded affably to Iorwerth; didn't know him – from down the valley somewhere, Llangyfelach way. Soft collar, brown suit, these youngsters didn't care a button how they looked. Yes indeed, T.J. did have his bow over the wings. Well, if that was the right way, it looked rotten. All bunched up like a cabbage and the stud showing. And his parting wasn't straight either. Never any style about T.J., and a face like a clock: fancy asking him to his face why he'd changed his stage name from 'Dan' to 'Danny Boy'. So insensitive, somehow. 'Calling for you, Ron. All the best, boy.'

Not a bad voice, Ron's. Nice quality, but his intonation had never been good; always sharpening – there, he was at it now:

'and thy gra-a-a-a-cious mien' – bad, bad, very bad. Just that litttle bit off the note, but fatal, fatal. Yes, Pughe-Thomas had noticed it too. Trust him. Writing like mad . . .

The G. Yes, he'd do it all right; he was feeling fine again now. In the bag, Dan *bach*. He was going to be on top of his form after all. In good voice as they say. What a fool he'd been! He'd pull the place down with it. There was Ron coming to it now . . . now . . . *there*! Poor, very poor. He got there, true, but it was thin, reedy, closing in instead of opening out . . .

'Well done, Ron boy. Good going . . .

ISLWYN WILLIAMS (1903–57)
in *Twenty-five Welsh Short Stories* selected by Gwyn Jones and
Islwyn Ffowc Elis (1971), trans. Islwyn Williams

### Capel Hebron

In Capel Hebron the choirs are singing,
And Martha and Jane and Hywel and Emrys
Are lost in the rapture of anthem and chorus
And the walls of the chapel are shaking with song,
And wave after wave of music crashes
Over the maddened multitude.
Chorus of Handel, mighty and glorious
Rolls and reverberates again and again,
Tearing the barriers and bastions asunder,
Shaking the heart and the depths of the soul.
O spirit of music and wonder and passion
Flood with thy rapture our derelict valleys,
And give unto men the motion to action,
The impulse to build what is worthy of man.

IDRIS DAVIES (1905–53)

### Uncle Johnnie

My Uncle lived on the Moel,
a cottage with a garden behind and a rock above;
he was a collier, Pentre Pit, Annibynwr, Labour and a bard;
at his elbow, the *Tyst* and *Faner*,

a chunk of *cywydd* and a chunk of cheese
side by side on his table day after day.
On the slopes of the Moel,
a mixed society, taste and tradition;
ministers, lawyers, shopkeepers, colliers, teachers . . .

My uncle never mixed . . . He just rose at dawn,
breakfast in the small kitchen with Sarann and the cats,
before he was off over the Moel, past the incline and feeder,
into the hurly-burly and perils of the pit.
And then, at the end of the shift, back the same way and
    same manner,
throwing his block into the *cwtch*, feeding the chickens, bath,
    and a basin of broth,
settling for the night with a book or poem.
Nantlle his origin, accent and vocabulary,
making one think Welsh the only language;
chapel, eisteddfodau, preachers, poets his world,
and outside this narrow Welsh way
nothing really made sense . . .
People on the mountain had their interests –
keeping pigs or whippets,
blowing a trombone, playing quoits, rearing pigeons,
and when the Depression came, hours unbearable and
    boring,
some would display a genius for hand-ball or the gazooka!
But my uncle went through all the ravages of the valley –
Evan Roberts' Revival and the '26 Strike,
the dark days of 1914 and the dark days of 1941,
nothing distracting him from the patient craft of his poem,
a good book, and the miracle of his mother-tongue.

RHYDWEN WILLIAMS


If I were asked where English poetry got these three things, its
turn for style, its turn for melancholy, and its turn for natural
magic, for catching and rendering the charm of nature in a
wonderfully near and vivid way, – I should answer, with some
doubt, that it got much of its turn for style from a Celtic source;
with less doubt, that it got much of its melancholy from a Celtic

source; with no doubt at all, that from a Celtic source it got nearly all its natural magic.

The Celt's quick feeling for what is noble and distinguished gave his poetry style; his indomitable personality gave it pride and passion; his sensibility and nervous exaltation gave it a better gift still, the gift of rendering with wonderful felicity the magical charm of nature. The forest solitude, the bubbling spring, the wild flowers, are everywhere in romance. They have a mysterious life and grace there; they are Nature's own children, and utter her secret in a way which makes them something quite different from the woods, waters, and plants of Greek and Latin poetry. Now of this delicate magic, Celtic romance is so pre-eminent a mistress, that it seems impossible to believe the power did not come into romance from the Celts. Magic is just the word for it, – the magic of nature; nor merely the beauty of nature, – that the Greeks and Latins had; not merely an honest smack of the soil, a faithful realism, – that the Germans had; but the intimate life of Nature, her weird power and her fairy charm. As the Saxon names of places, with the pleasant wholesome smack of the soil in them, – Weathersfield, Thaxted, Shalford, – are to the Celtic names of places, with their penetrating, lofty beauty, – Velindra, Tyntagel, Caernarvon, – so is the homely realism of German and Norse nature to the fairy-like loveliness of Celtic nature. Gwydion wants a wife for his pupil: '"Well," says Math, "we will seek, I and thou, by charms and illusions, to form a wife for him out of flowers." So they took the blossoms of the oak, and the blossoms of the broom, and the blossoms of the meadow-sweet, and produced from them a maiden, the fairest and most graceful that man ever saw. And they baptized her, and gave her the name of Flower-Aspect.' Celtic romance is full of exquisite touches like that, showing the delicacy of the Celt's feeling in these matters, and how deeply Nature lets him come into her secrets. The quick dropping of blood is called 'faster than the fall of the dewdrop from the blade of reed-grass upon the earth, when the dew of June is at the heaviest'. And thus is Olwen described: 'More yellow was her hair than the flower of the broom, and her skin was whiter than the foam of the wave, and fairer were her hands and her fingers than the blossoms of the wood-anemony amidst the spray of the meadow fountain.' For loveliness it would be hard to beat that; and for magical clearness and nearness take the following:

'And in the evening Peredur entered a valley, and at the head of the valley he came to a hermit's cell, and the hermit welcomed him gladly, and there he spent the night. And in the morning he arose, and when he went forth, behold, a shower of snow had fallen the night before, and a hawk had killed a wild-fowl in front of the cell. And the noise of the horse scared the hawk away, and a raven alighted upon the bird. And Peredur stood and compared the blackness of the raven, and the whiteness of the snow, and the redness of the blood, to the hair of the lady whom best he loved, which was blacker than the raven, and to her skin, which was whiter than the snow, and to her two cheeks, which were redder than the blood upon the snow appeared to be.'

And this, which is perhaps less striking, is not less beautiful:

'And early in the day Geraint and Enid left the wood, and they came to an open country, with meadows on one hand and mowers mowing the meadows. And there was a river before them, and the horses bent down and drank the water. And they went up out of the river by a steep bank, and there they met a slender stripling with a satchel about his neck; and he had a small blue pitcher in his hand, and a bowl on the mouth of the pitcher.'

And here the landscape, up to this point so Greek in its clear beauty, is suddenly magicalized by the romance touch:

'And they saw a tall tree by the side of the river, one-half of which was in flames from the root to the top, and the other half was green and in full leaf.'

Magic is the word to insist upon, – a magically vivid and near interpretation of nature; since it is this which constitutes the special charm and power of the effect I am calling attention to, and it is for this that the Celt's sensibility gives him a peculiar aptitude . . .

Style is the most striking quality of their poetry. Celtic poetry seems to make up to itself for being unable to master the world and give an adequate interpretation of it, by throwing all its force into style, by bending language at any rate to its will, and expressing the ideas it has with unsurpassable intensity, elevation, and effect. It has all through it a sort of intoxication of style, – a *Pindarism*, to use a word formed from the name of the

poet, on whom, above all other poets, the power of style seems
to have exercised an inspiring and intoxicating effect; and not
in its great poets only, in Taliesin, or Llywarch Hen, or Ossian,
does the Celtic genius show this Pindarism, but in all its pro-
ductions:

> 'The grave of March is this, and this the grave of Gwythyr;
> Here is the grave of Gwgawn Gleddyfrudd;
> But unknown is the grave of Arthur.'

That comes from the Welsh *Memorials of the Graves of the
Warriors* . . .

Take the well-known Welsh prophecy about the fate of the
Britons:

> 'Their Lord they will praise,
> Their speech they will keep,
> Their land they will lose,
> Except wild Wales.'

To however late an epoch that prophecy belongs, what feeling
for style, at any rate, it manifests! And the same thing may be
said of the famous Welsh triads. We may put aside all the vexed
questions as to their greater or less antiquity, and still what
important witness they bear to the genius for literary style of
the people who produced them!

MATTHEW ARNOLD (1822–88)
*On the Study of Celtic Literature* (1867)

*A Prescription*

> Sweet-tempered, pestering
> young man of Oxford
> juggling with ghazals,
> tercets, haikus, tankas,
> not to mention villanelles,
> terzanelles and rondelets;
> conversant with the phonetic
> kinships of rhyme, assonance
> and consonance; the four

nuances of stress, the three
junctions; forget now
the skeletonic couplet,
the heroic couplet, the split
couplet, the poulter's measure;
speak not of englyn
penfyr, englyn milwr;
but Westward hasten
to that rising, lonely ground
between the evening rivers,
the alder-gazing rivers,
Mawddach and Dysynni.

Let it be dark when, alone,
you climb the awful mountain
so that you can count the stars.
Ignore the giant shufflings
behind you – put out that torch! –
the far intermittent cries
of the nocturnal birds
– if birds they are –
their small screams of torture.
Instead, scholar as you are,
remark the old proverb
how the one who ascends
Cadair Idris at night
comes back in dawn's light
lately mad or a great poet.
Meanwhile, I'll wait here
in this dull room of urine-
flask, weighing-machine,
examination-couch, X-ray screen,
for your return (triumphant
or bizarre) patiently.

DANNIE ABSE

'And now, Caersalem.' Fingers gloved
Against the itch of love flick through
The hymn-books. Throats are cleared. And then
The harmonies surge out across the bay.
It is the Castle Choir, replete
With righteousness and love of minor keys.
They sing here every Sunday in the summer,
And the tourists stop, their fancy
Tickled by the natives' curious ways.

I used to hate the sound of them.
They made me feel like death. Those hymns,
Admonishing the hedonistic prom.
So we hurried past, derisive
Boyos with an eye for grosser curves
Than those the educated baton traced.

They crucified the sun, those dismal hymns,
And yet they had a relevance.
It wasn't long ago, but then the Welsh
Still had a Sunday. Now
The beaches are transistorized, and joy
Is straining on a less attentive leash.

And Pantycelyn's proud reproaches sound
Like distant music in our alien ears.

HERBERT WILLIAMS

*Apologia*

Your Wales was never mine, I know.
The towering shadows the dead throw
lie like elegies over your day.
I usually face the other way.
For you the present is the last
dying moment of the past.

For me the present is the first
leaf-green bud from which will burst
the future, like an un-named rose
for my children's hands to close
themselves around, bend to and breathe:
the flowering Wales that you bequeath.

RAYMOND GARLICK

# ACKNOWLEDGEMENTS

We are grateful to the following authors, owners of copyright, publishers and literary agents who have kindly given permission for poems and passages of prose to appear in this anthology.

Dannie Abse for 'A Prescription'; and Century Hutchinson & Co. Ltd for the extracts from *Journals from the Antheap* (1986); and Anthony Sheil Associates Ltd for the extract from *A Poet in the Family* (1974).

John Barnie and Dangaroo Press for 'The Sheep Say Nothing' and 'Cwm Bryn-Arw' from *Lightning Country* (1987).

Idris Christopher Bell for the translations by Sir H. Idris Bell and the extracts from *The Development of Welsh Poetry* (1925).

Ruth Bidgood and Poetry Wales Press for 'At Strata Florida' from *Lighting Candles* (1982) and 'Llyn y Fan Fach' from *Kindred* (1986).

John Malcolm Brinnin and Laurence Pollinger Ltd and J. M. Dent & Sons Ltd for the extract from *Dylan Thomas in America* (1956).

D. Brown & Sons for the extracts from *Talk Tidy* by John Edwards (1985) and Julius Rodenberg's *An Autumn in Wales*, transl. William Linnard (1985).

Michael Burn and David Bolt Associates and Chatto & Windus Ltd for 'Welsh Love Letter' from *Open Day and Night* (1978).

Jonathan Cape Ltd for the extract from *Chiaroscuro* by Augustus John (1952); and Mrs Sheila Hooper Ltd for the extracts from *Kilvert's Diary 1870–79*, ed. and sel. William Plomer (1977).

Century Hutchinson Ltd for the extract from *A Welsh Eye* by Gwyn Thomas (1964).

Joseph P. Clancy for 'S4C' from Poetry Wales, vol. 21, no. 1 (1985); and Macmillan Publishers Ltd for the translation of 'Winter and Warfare' from *The Earliest Welsh Poetry* (1970).

Gillian Clarke and Carcanet Press Ltd for 'Climbing Cader Idris' from *Selected Poems* (1985).

Gladys Mary Coles and Duckworth & Co. Ltd for 'Llyn Brenig' from *Leafburners: New and Selected Poems* (1986).

William Collins Sons & Co. Ltd for the extract from the translation by D. M. Lloyd from *A Book of Wales* (1953).

Tony Conran and Christopher Davies Ltd for 'On Translating Welsh Poetry' from *Spirit Level* (1974); and Poetry Wales Press for the translations of 'Song to a Child', 'Praise of Tenby', 'From Exile' by Dafydd Benfras, 'The Battle of Argoed Llwyfain' by Taliesin and 'The Catholic Martyrs' by Waldo Williams from *Welsh Verse* (1986).

Alexander Cordell and Victor Gollancz Ltd for the extract from *Rape of the Fair Country* (1959).

*Country Quest* for the extract from 'The Drovers' Cattle' by R. B. Jones from vol. 24, Nov. 1983, and for the extract from 'Corpse Candles – Did They Really Exist?' by Richard Lewis from vol. 24, March 1984.

Tony Curtis and Poetry Wales Press for 'Jack Watts' from *Selected Poems* (1986).

Christopher Davies Ltd for 'Split' by John Tripp from *Collected Poems* (1978).

John Davies and Gomer Press for 'Port Talbot' from *At the Edge of Town* (1981).

Duckworth & Co. Ltd for the extract from 'Beneath the Barley' from *The Collected Arthur Machen*, ed. Christopher Palmer (1988).

Gareth Edwards for the extract from *Most Memorable Matches*, pub. Stanley Pane (1984).

Tudor Edwards and Batsford Ltd for the extract from *The Face of Wales* (1950).

Islwyn Ffowc Elis and Penguin Books Ltd for the extract from 'Black Barren' from *The Penguin Book of Welsh Short Stories*, ed. Alun Richards (1976).

Ffynnon Press for the extracts from *Welsh Country Characters* by David Parry Jones (1973).

Peter Finch and Poetry Wales Press for 'A Welsh Wordscape' from *Selected Poems* (1987).

Bobby Freeman and Image Imprint for the extracts from *First Catch Your Peacock* (1980).

Raymond Garlick and Gomer Press for 'Directions for Visitors' and 'Apologia' from *Collected Poems* (1987).

Gomer Press for the extract from *A Mouse Ran Up My Nightie* by Edith Courtney (1974), and for the extracts from 'Gwalia Deserta' and for 'Capel Calvin', 'Capel Hebron' and 'Morning Comes Again' from *Collected Poems of Idris Davies* (1972), and for 'In Welsh Uplands' from *Collected Poems of A. G. Prys-Jones* (1988).

Patrick Hannan and Gomer Press for the extract from *Wales on the Wireless* (1988).

Dr John Harris on behalf of the estate of Caradoc Evans for the extract from 'The Glory That Was Sion's' from *My People* (1915), and for the extract from 'Horse Hysbys and Oldest Brother' from *The Earth Gives All and Takes All* (1946).

David Higham Associates Ltd and J. M. Dent & Sons Ltd for 'Hold Hard, These Ancient Minutes in the Cuckoo's Month' by Dylan Thomas from *The Poems* (1952).

Jeremy Hooker and Carcanet Press Ltd for 'The Mason's Law' from *Englishman's Road* (1980).

Emyr Humphreys and Black Raven Press for the extract from *The Taliesin Tradition* (1983); and Poetry Wales Press for the extract from 'Arnold in Wonderland' from *Miscellany Two* (1981).

J. Geraint Jenkins and the National Museum of Wales for the extracts from *Cockles and Mussels: Aspects of Shellfish Gathering in Wales* (1984).

Bobi Jones and Gomer Press for the translation of 'An Invitation to Dyddgu' from *The Dragon's Pen* by Bobi Jones and Gwyn Thomas (1986).

Glyn Jones for the extract from an interview with Gwyn Thomas from *The Dragon Has Two Tongues* by Glyn Jones (1968), and Laurence Pollinger Ltd for the extract from 'The Boy in the Bucket' from *Selected Short Stories of Glyn Jones* (1971); and Oxford University Press for the translation of 'The Shearing' from *The Oxford Book of Welsh Verse in English*, ed. Gwyn Jones (1977).

Gwyn Jones for the extracts from *The Mabinogion*, transl. Thomas Jones (1974), revisions with Mair Jones, and for the extract from 'Mabinogi and Edda' from *Saga-Book XIII* (1946) and for the extract from 'The Brute Creation' from *Shepherd's Hey* (1953); and Oxford University Press for the extract from the Introduction to *The Oxford Book of Welsh Verse in English* (1977), and for 'The Sun of Llanfabon' from *Welsh Legends and Folk Tales* (1955).

Jonah Jones for the extract from an essay in *Artists in Wales*, vol. 2, ed. Meic Stephens (1973).

Madeleine Jones and Gomer Press for 'Head in the Clouds' by T. Harri Jones from *The Collected Poems of T. Harri Jones* (1977).

Mair Jones for the translations by Thomas Jones from *The Chronicle of the Princes*, and *The Mabinogion* (with Gwyn Jones).

Michael Joseph Ltd on behalf of the estate of Richard Llewelyn for the extract from *How Green Was My Valley* (© 1939 by the estate of Richard Llewelyn).

Lloyd Laing and Jennifer Laing and William Collins Sons & Co. Ltd for the extract from *Celtic Britain* (1981).

John de Lannoy on behalf of the estate of Emlyn Williams for the extract from *The Corn Is Green*, pub. Heinemann (1938).

Eiluned and Peter Lewis and Batsford Ltd for the extract from *The Land of Wales* (1937).

Alan Llwyd and Christopher Davies Ltd for 'Cymru'.

Roland Mathias and Gomer Press for the extract from 'Laus Deo' from *Burning Brambles* (1983).

Robert Minhinnick for an extract from his article 'Shadow of the Trees' in *Rural Wales* (summer 1988); and Poetry Wales Press for his poem 'The Strata: to Llewelyn Siôn' from *Native Ground* (1979).

Robert Morgan and Campbell Thomas & McLaughlin Ltd for the extract from 'Rainbow Valley' from *The Night's Prison* (1967).

Leslie Norris and Poetry Wales Press for the translation of 'The Spear' by Dafydd ap Gwilym from *Selected Poems* (1986).

John Ormond and Poetry Wales Press for the translation of 'The Hall of Cynddylan' from the Heledd Saga from *Selected Poems of John Ormond* (1987).

Trefor M. Owen and the National Museum of Wales for the extracts from *Welsh Folk Customs* (1959).

Oxford University Press for the translation 'I Am Taliesin' by Sir Ifor Williams from *The Oxford Book of Welsh Verse in English* (1977).

Iorwerth C. Peate and Brython Press for the extract from *The Welsh House* (1946); and Faber & Faber Ltd for the extract from *Tradition and Folk Life: A Welsh View* (1972).

John Peddie and Alan Sutton Publishing Ltd for the extract from *The Roman Invasion of Britain* (1987).

Penguin Books Ltd for the extracts from *The Journey Through Wales and The Description of Wales* by Gerald of Wales, transl. Lewis Thorpe (1978), and for 'The Laws of Hywel Dda' and 'The Black and White Sheep and the Blazing Tree' from A *Celtic Miscellany*, ed. Kenneth Hurlstone Jackson (1971), and for the extract from 'The Squire of Havilah' from *The Penguin Book of Welsh Short Stories*, ed. Alun Richards (1976), and for the extract from *Tacitus: The Agricola*, transl. H. Mattingly (1948).

The estate of John Cowper Powys and Laurence Pollinger Ltd for the extract from *Owen Glendower*, pub. John Lane (1941).

Ken Radford and Skilton (Publishers) for the extract from 'Lovers' Well' from *Tales of North Wales* (1982).

Alun Rees and Seren Books (Poetry Wales Press) for 'Cardiff Arms Park' from A *Cardiff Anthology*, sel. Meic Stephens (1987).

Alwyn D. Rees and University of Wales Press for the extract from *Life in a Welsh Countryside* (1975).

Lynette Roberts and Faber & Faber Ltd for 'Poem from Llanybri' from *Poems* (1944).

Tony Roberts and Aber Castle (Publishers) for 'The Water Horse of St Bride's Bay' from *Myths and Legends of Wales* (1987).

Michael Senior and Robert Hale Ltd for the extract from *Portrait of South Wales* (1974).

Meic Stephens for 'Ponies, Twynyrodyn' from *Exiles All*, pub. Triskele Press (1973); and Gomer Press for the extract from an essay by Jonah Jones from

Gwyn Williams and Faber & Faber Ltd for the extract from *The Land Remembers* (1977), and for the extract from the Introduction to *Welsh Poems, Sixth Century to 1600* (1973), and for the extract from the translation of 'The Death of Llewelyn ap Gruffud', and for the translation of 'The Lover's Shirt', and for the extract from the translation of 'Sycarth' by Iolo Goch; and Gomer Press for the extract from 'Foundation Stock' (1974).

Gwyn A. Williams and University of Wales Press for the extract from *The Merthyr Rising of 1831* (1988).

Herbert Williams and J. M. Dent & Sons Ltd for 'The Castle Choir' from *Welsh Voices*, ed. Bryn Griffiths (1967).

James Williams and Gomer Press for the extracts from *Give Me Yesterday* (1971).

John Stuart Williams and Gomer Press for the extract from 'Dic Penderyn' from *Dic Penderyn and Other Poems* (1979).

Kyffin Williams and Duckworth & Co. Ltd for the extracts from *Across the Straits* (1974).

Margaret Williams and Oxford University Press for the extract from 'Adjudication' by Islwyn Williams from *Twenty-five Welsh Short Stories* (1971).

Rhydwen Williams and Christopher Davies Ltd for 'Uncle Johnnie' from *Rhondda Poems* (1987).

Every effort has been made to contact the copyright owners of material included in this anthology. In the instances where this has not proved possible, we offer our apologies to those concerned.

# INDEX OF AUTHORS

# INDEX OF SUBJECTS